Corporate Governance in China

The nature of corporate governance is a key determinant of coporate performance, and thereby of a country's overall economic performance. A sound corporate governance system is particularly important for China's ongoing reforms and helps in achieving stable and sustainable growth of its economy. This book, based on extensive original economic analysis, examines key questions relating to corporate governance in China, including the relationship between ownership structure and corporate performance, the determinants of capital structure, and the nature of contemporary governance structures. It concludes – interestingly and controversially – amongst other things that corporate performance is positively related to ownership concentration, but negatively related to state ownership, and that contemporary corporate governance structures are heavily dependent on previous structures in the centrally-planned economy and on the path of transition to the market economy.

Jian Chen is currently a Senior Lecturer in Finance at Business School, the University of Greenwich. He is an active researcher in the issues of corporate governance, corporate finance and their applications in the Chinese economy. He received his PhD in Finance from King's College, the University of London. He is the President of the Chinese Economic Association in the UK (2003–2004).

RoutledgeCurzon studies on the Chinese economy
Series editors
Peter Nolan
University of Cambridge

Dong Fureng
Beijing University

The aim of this series is to publish original, high-quality, research-level work by both new and established scholars in the West and the East, on all aspects of the Chinese economy, including studies of business and economic history.

Corporate Governance in China

Jian Chen

RoutledgeCurzon
Taylor & Francis Group
LONDON AND NEW YORK

First published 2005
by RoutledgeCurzon
2 Park Square, Milton Park, Abingdon,
Oxon, OX14 4RN

Simultaneously published in the USA and Canada
by RoutledgeCurzon
270 Madison Avenue, New York, NY 10016

RoutledgeCurzon is an imprint of the Taylor & Francis Group

© 2005 Jian Chen

Typeset in Times New Roman by
Newgen Imaging Systems (P) Ltd, Chennai, India
Printed and bound in Great Britain by
Antony Rowe Ltd, Chippenham, Wiltshire

British Library Cataloguing in Publication Data
A catalogue record for this book is available
from the British Library

Library of Congress Cataloging in Publication Data
A catalog record for this book has been requested

ISBN 0–415–34513–8

I dedicate this book to my wife Min Zhao and daughter Aileen Cong Chen

Contents

8 General conclusions and future work   **146**

Figures

Tables

Preface

This book is a study of corporate governance in the context of the Chinese economy. The starting point is that the observed patterns of corporate control and capital structure cannot be fully explained if the world is characterised by comprehensive contracts that define all the future contingencies. Rather, contracts are incomplete, and economic agents are endowed with rights to specify actions in future contingencies that are not explicitly written in prior contracts. The combination of the incompleteness of contracts and the separation of ownership and control leads to agency problems because managers (agents) have their private interests that may conflict with those of the shareholders (principals). There is thus a need for a sound governance system to ensure that managers work effectively to maximise shareholders' wealth.

The book focuses on four issues in corporate governance: ownership structure and the underpricing of initial public offering; ownership structure as a corporate governance mechanism; the determinants of capital structure; and a governance perspective of corporate groups. Correspondingly, there are four main chapters. The first looks at why IPOs are underpriced, and we find that there is a negative relationship between the largest shareholding and the extent of the underpricing. The second is an empirical study of the relationship between ownership structure and corporate performance. We find that corporate performance, measured by Tobin's Q, is positively related to ownership concentration, but negatively related to State ownership. In the third chapter, the study is extended to debt finance, investigating the determinants of capital structure, and we find that the determinants of capital structure in China are similar with those in other economies and agency costs have an effect upon the debt ratio. The fourth provides a political economy perspective on the governance structures of Chinese corporate groups, and we argue that the contemporary governance structures are dependent both upon the impacts of the previous centrally-planned economy and the path of transition to the market economy.

The book offers original contributions both in its theoretical work on corporate governance, and in the empirical studies of governance in China for which there has so far been very little published analysis.

Acknowledgements

I am extremely grateful to Mr Roger Strange, and also to Dr Limin Wang for their unfailing support and friendship, which began before my PhD study. With their warm support, I fortunately won two scholarships, an Overseas Research Student Award from the UK Committee of Vice-Chancellors and Principals and a K.C. Wong Education Foundation Scholarship. Without them, I would not have had enough financial resources to enable me pursue my favourite research topics. Their support did not end there. During my studies, they provided precise guidance in my scientific investigations, and the freedom to choose my research topics. This was priceless, allowing me to fly in an unlimited space, but I fully understand the extra burden this freedom put upon them as they had to squeeze their valuable time to comment upon the topics I had selected. I have yet to meet persons so well read in science, who are then able to apply their knowledge with such precise expertise to all aspects of my study. It has been a real privilege and pleasure to work together over the past years. Dr Limin Wang left for a post in the United States in 1999, and her leaving was a pity, but Roger has continued his committed support alone.

I would also like to thank Dr Athar Hussain of the London School of Economics for his support, and guidance based upon his profound understanding of the Chinese economy and the institutional differences between it and the Western economies. He helped me choose my topics, formulate my arguments, and reach my conclusions.

I am grateful for the generous financial support from the Overseas Research Student Award Scheme and from the K.C. Wong Education Foundation.

Jian Chen

Abbreviations

ADR	American Depository Receipts
A-shares	Shares only issued to domestic institutions or individual investors
BSAM	Bureau of State Asset Management (China)
B-shares	Shares only issued to foreign investors and traded on the Shanghai Stock Exchange or the Shenzhen Stock Exchange
CAPM	Capital Asset Pricing Model
COEs	Collectively owned enterprises
CSRC	China Securities Regulatory Commission
EPS	earnings per share
GDP	Gross Domestic Product
H-shares	Shares traded on the Hong Kong Stock Exchange
IPO	Initial Public Offering
LBO	Leveraged buy-out
MBR	Market to book ratio
MOF	Ministry of Finance
NETS	National Electronic Trading System
N-Shares	ADRs of Chinese Companies listed on the New York Stock Exchange
NYSE	New York Stock Exchange
OECD	Organisation for Economic Co-operation and Development
OTC	Over-the-counter
P/E ratio	Price/earnings ratio
PRC	People's Republic of China
RMB	Ren Min Bi (Chinese Currency)
ROA	Return on Assets
ROE	Return on Equity
RPS	return per share
SEO	Seasonal Equity Offering
SERC	State Economic Reform Commission
SEZs	Special Economic Zones
SHSE	Shanghai Stock Exchange

SOEs	State owned enterprises
SPC	State Planning Commission
SSB	State Statistics Bureau, China
SZSE	Shenzhen Stock Exchange
T Bill	Treasury bill
T Bond	Treasury Bond
TICs	Trust and Investment Corporations
TVEs	Township and Village Enterprises

1 Introduction

What is corporate governance?

This is a study of corporate governance, with particular reference to listed companies in China. The theoretical framework underpinning the book is the incomplete contracts, or property rights, approach which recognises that issues related to firms' ownership structure, capital structure[1] and corporate control cannot be fully understood if one assumes a world of comprehensive contracts that can define all future contingencies. Rather, contracts are incomplete and economic agents are endowed with rights to specify actions in future contingencies not specified in prior contracts, that is they are endowed with property or ownership rights.

In applying this framework to modern corporations, we find that the combination of the separation of ownership and control, and the incompleteness of contracts, may lead to agency problems: that is, a situation where the management[2] of the corporations, who are the agents of the shareholders (the principals), may have private interests that conflict with those of some or all of the shareholders. There is thus a need for a sound corporate governance system through which management can be induced to ensure the maximisation of shareholders' wealth whilst protecting the interests of all parties involved, including the managers, large and small shareholders, and creditors.

Two decades ago, the term 'corporate governance' had not been coined (Kay and Silberston, 1995), yet the associated issues date back to the formation of joint stock companies and stock markets. Today, corporate governance is a central political and economic topic, not only in well-developed market economies but also in emerging economies. However, there is still considerable debate as to what corporate governance actually entails, as the following selection of definitions will testify:

- 'Corporate governance is an institutional arrangement by which suppliers of finance to corporations assure themselves of getting a proper return on their investment' (Shleifer and Vishny, 1997, p. 737).
- 'The purpose of corporate governance is to minimise the total cost in aligning managers' and shareholders' incentives, and in unavoidable self-interested managerial behaviours' (Jensen and Meckling, 1976).

- 'The phrase corporate governance is often applied narrowly to questions about the structure and function of boards of directors to the rights and prerogatives of shareholders in boardroom decision-making. Now this definition has been broadened to refer to the whole set of legal, cultural, and institutional arrangements that determine what publicly traded corporations can do, who controls them, how that control is exercised, and how the risks and returns from the activities they undertake are allocated' (Blair, 1995, p. 3).
- 'Corporate governance is the system or process by which companies are directed and controlled' (Cadbury, 1992, p. 2).
- 'Corporate governance is the system by which business corporations are directed and controlled. The corporate governance structure specifies the distribution of rights and responsibilities among different participants in the corporation, such as, the board, managers, shareholders and other stakeholders, and spells out the rules and procedures for making decisions on corporate affairs. By doing this, it also provides the structure through which the company objectives are set, and the means of attaining those objectives and monitoring performance' (OECD, 1999).
- Zingales (1998) defines corporate governance as including anything that affects the ex post bargaining power over the value created in the firm. This definition gives the broadest coverage of corporate governance. It recognises the potential conflicts between involved parties, including the large shareholders, the small shareholders and management, and the institutional arrangements which entitle specific parties with rights when disputes arise which are not foreseen prior to the establishment of contracts.

In drawing upon these definitions, we would like to make the following points:

- All definitions of corporate governance are concerned with the objectives of the corporation: whose interests should the corporation take care of and how? But there are heated debates about which stakeholders (including employees, input suppliers, and customers) should be taken into consideration (Blair, 1995), and the way of putting theory into practice is still unknown.
- In this study, we focus more narrowly on the institutions and mechanisms by which the suppliers of finance to corporations (i.e. the owners) exert control over the managers to ensure satisfactory returns on their investment.
- There is good corporate governance, as well as poor corporate governance. Good corporate governance can improve corporate performance by minimising the total cost of aligning managers' and shareholders' incentives, and of unavoidable self-interested managerial behaviour (Jensen and Meckling, 1976). Good corporate governance should provide proper incentives for the Board and management to pursue objectives that are in the interests of the company and its shareholders, and should facilitate effective monitoring thereby encouraging firms to use their resources more efficiently. In contrast, poor corporate governance can damage the interests of the parties involved,

either the managers or the shareholders, and may lead to poor performance and the collapse of the corporation.

- Corporate governance is only part of a larger economic context in which firms operate which includes, for example, macroeconomic policies and the degree of competition in product and factor markets. The corporate governance framework also depends on the legal, regulatory, and institutional environment (Roe, 2000). In addition, factors such as business ethics, and corporate awareness of the environmental and societal interests of the communities in which it operates, can also have an impact on the reputation and the long-term success of a company.

Research objectives

The overall aim of this book is to examine the effectiveness of the corporate governance system in China, and to suggest ways of improving it. We take the view that one of the objectives of the reform of Chinese State-owned enterprises (SOEs) is to seek an appropriate mechanism of corporate governance which (a) provides sufficient incentives for management to work hard, (b) prevents management from asset appropriation, and (c) replaces them when they are found to be incompetent. These issues are particularly relevant in the context of the reform of the SOEs and the establishment of a modern enterprise system in China, which are embedded in the whole process of transition from a centrally-planned economy to a market economy. Furthermore, these notions of modern corporations, the corporatisation of SOEs, and corporate governance are closely linked to a perception of superior corporate performance.

We focus on the case of Chinese listed companies using data from the two leading Stock Exchanges, namely, the Shanghai Stock Exchange (SHSE) and the Shenzhen Stock Exchange (SZSE). Both Exchanges have been established for 12 years, and list stocks for more than 1,100 corporations. We focus on listed companies for similar reasons to those discussed by Zingales (2000):

- The first is that this book is about corporate governance issues, hence we must consider corporations, and not other types of business organisation. Although there are many corporations that are not public companies, public companies are favourite subjects of theoretical studies (see, e.g. Grossman and Hart (1980) on the free-rider problem in takeovers, La Porta *et al.* (1998) on small investor protection issues). The investors are dispersed and unable to coordinate, and this is the perfect background within which theories related to corporate governance can be developed.
- The second is the ease of obtaining data, and the possibility of being able to use economic measures of performance such as the market to book ratio (MBR) or Tobin's Q, instead of having to rely on accounting measures[3] such as the return on equity (ROE) or the return on assets (ROA). The data for listed companies are also generally more accurate than for non-listed companies in

all economies throughout the world, making listed corporations natural research subjects.

- The third is the importance of listed companies in national economies, in terms of employment, Gross Domestic Product (GDP), technological innovation, tax revenues to the government etc. In the Chinese case, many of the listed companies are among the largest firms in their industries or among the first to have undergone corporatisation from the original SOEs, Township and Village Enterprises (TVEs) or foreign-owned firms. A comprehensive examination of their experience will increase our understanding of the effectiveness of the Chinese reforms.

This study embraces multiple facets of the issue of corporate governance in China, but focuses on four major issues:

- The underpricing of Initial Public Offerings (IPO) of equity – The IPO is the first stage when a company is going public. 'Traditional' theories see the IPO as a process for the company to finance its growth, and the value of the stock is simply the present value of all future cash flows. But new theory and empirical findings suggest that going public is a complex process with distinct markets for dispersed shares and controlling blocks, and that the underpricing of IPOs, which is common throughout the world, is influenced by the ownership structure at the time of the IPO.
- How corporate performance depends upon the ownership structure – On the one hand, the size distribution of shareholders may affect performance because small shareholders may not be able to, or have the incentive to, monitor management to the same degree as large shareholders. On the other hand, large shareholders may monitor management, but more often they may pursue their own interests which do not necessarily correspond to those of other, smaller, shareholders. Furthermore, the nature of the large shareholders (e.g. State, or domestic institutions) may also have an effect.
- How corporate governance may affect the capital structure of a company – Ever since the seminal work of Modigliani and Miller (1958), various explanations about why firms choose one financial instrument over the other have been offered, under different assumptions and in different economic systems. We look here at the effects upon the debt ratios of Chinese firms of a management shareholding and of a large major shareholder.
- The development of corporate governance in the wider context of the transition of the Chinese industrial structure and the move towards a market economy.

These four issues are addressed in four separate chapters, but share a common approach based on a combination of agency theory and the theory of incomplete contracts. The issues are also linked within the whole system of corporate governance. The first issue studies the relationship between the large, initial shareholders and the small, outside shareholders from the perspective of the private gain of corporate control. From a temporal point of view, the IPO is also the stage when a corporation forms or reestablishes its corporate governance mechanism. The second issue looks at how corporate performance is affected by the mechanism of corporate governance after the firms' IPO. We focus on the relationship between the large shareholders as principals, and the management as agents. The third issue emphasises the role of debt as an instrument to mitigate agency costs. The basic argument is that debt, which is a pre-emptive financial instrument, will trigger financial distress when the management does not work well and does not generate sufficient cash flows to meet the payments required by debt contract. Thus the controlling shareholders may use their influence in deciding the choice of capital structure. We apply theories of debt to explore the possible role of debt as a complementary mechanism of corporate governance. The fourth issue is a study of the Chinese corporate groups, with the perspective at the governance structure since the era of industrial restructuring. The main theme of this chapter is that the division of the government into territorial jurisdictions, and of the division of economic administration by industrial branches, imposes a two-way grid on economic decision-making that has had wide ramifications for the governance structure of large enterprises/corporate groups in China and their evolution. This grid is currently undergoing a radical change because of the abolition of many of the central industrial Ministries and also of industrial bureaux in territorial governments, that may in time have a profound influence on the organisational structure of corporate groups. But the territorial division of the government has been, and will continue to be, of special importance in China because of its geographical expanse and regional diversity.

This book is certainly the first systematic study of corporate governance in China, and the results will provide insights into how well the system is functioning and suggestions as to possible improvements. However, it should be pointed out that the system of corporate governance in China is still in the process of evolution, and it would be premature to recommend the 'best' model of corporate governance for China. Furthermore, the book stresses only the micro, particularly finance, aspects of corporate governance rather than the macro aspects, and does not attempt to identify best practices or suggest codes of conduct as in the Cadbury Report (1992) or OECD (1999).

The data and methodology

Data

The dataset used in Chapter 4 covers 467 IPO issues between 1995 and 1999. The other two empirical studies use cross-section data for 1997. 1997 data is used because of the lag in the publication of Annual Reports. Much of the 1997 data only became available in late 1998, or early 1999 for some companies. In 2000, when these studies were being undertaken, the most comprehensive dataset was that based upon 1997 data. But the findings should be fairly robust in that there have not been any fundamental institutional changes since.[4]

The following sources of data were used:

- 'A Guide for Investment in Shanghai and Shenzhen Securities Exchanges', published by *Securities Times*, based at Shenzhen. *Securities Times* is one of the major news agencies and publishers of financial and economic information in China. The 1996 volume provides information on the corporations listed on both Exchanges in the year 1995. The 1997, 1998, and 1999 volumes do likewise for the years 1996, 1997, and 1998.
- The CD-ROM of Chinese Listed Corporations' Annual Reports (1997) (Abstract). This CD-ROM contains abstracts of annual reports of all listed companies ending at 27 May 1998. *Securities Times* is the publisher of the CD-ROM.
- The data on stock prices were taken from the database on the central computer at the SZSE. Prices were available for all listed companies, beginning from the opening days of both Exchanges in December 1990 (SHSE) and July 1991 (SZSE), and ending on 29 March 1999. We extracted the share prices and trading volume of the first trading days of all stocks, which are used to study IPO underpricing in Chapter 4.
- The data for Chapter 7 were drawn mainly from various years of the China Statistical Yearbook.

The data for many variables were only available in hard copy, and had to be entered into a computer database manually. All the data input into the database were checked twice to ensure accuracy. Furthermore, all the data were cross-checked in different sources to ensure consistency. When inconsistencies were found, a third data source was consulted. However, the accuracy of the information reported by the listed companies and audited by auditing companies relies on the companies themselves, subject to the legal restraints. Like researchers throughout the world, we can only take an 'as it is' attitude. The establishment of the dataset was thus a lengthy and exhausting task. The major variables used in this study include ownership structure (names, characteristics and shareholdings of the largest ten shareholders), accounting indicators (sales, gross profits, after-tax profits, total assets, total liabilities (long-term as well as current), equity, tax, and earnings per share). Other information includes the industry of each company, the names and responsibilities of the Directors of the Board, major events in the company's history, and major decisions made.[5]

Methodologies

In deciding upon appropriate econometric methods, we considered the use of time series analysis and panel data analysis. However, there were several problems with the use of time series analysis. The first was the short histories of both SHSE and SZSE, established in 1990 and 1991 respectively, and the small numbers of listed companies during the early years (only fourteen by 1992). The second, and more important, problem was the leakage of insider information. This was a common practice, and the trading of shares between insiders and other interested parties before important announcements make it impossible to determine cause and effect. A third problem, as found by Shyam-Sunder and Myers (1999), is the difficulty in distinguishing statistically between different models of capital structure. As regards panel data analysis, the main problem is its inability to deal with variables, such as ownership structure, which are relatively stable over time (Zhou, 2001). Zhou shows that a combination of relatively stable ownership structure and more volatile corporate performance will give rise to misleading statistical conclusions.

Thus three different cross-sectional regression techniques are employed. The first is Ordinary Least Squares (OLS). One potential problem with the use of OLS in cross-section models is the possible presence of heteroscedasticity, with the result that the coefficient estimates are inefficient and the estimates of the standard errors are biased. Thus a second, robust, regression technique is also used.[6]

The first step is to estimate the model by OLS, then calculate Cook's D by

$$D_i = \frac{h_i e_i^2}{ks^2(1 - h_i)^2}$$

where h_i is the diagonal elements of the hat matrix: $h_i = \mathbf{x}_i(\mathbf{X'X})^{-1}\mathbf{x}_i'$; in which $\mathbf{x}_i$ the vector of the ith observation and $\mathbf{X}$ the data matrix; e_i the residual of the ith observation; k the number of independent variables including the intercept; and s^2 the mean square error of the regression.

Any observations with Cook's $D > 1$ are discarded. The procedure then reruns the regression, calculates Huber (1964) case weights based on absolute residuals, and regresses again using these weights.

The Huber case weights are computed by

$$w_i = \begin{cases} 1 & \text{if } |u_i| \le c_{\mathrm{H}} \\ \dfrac{c_{\mathrm{H}}}{|u_i|} & \text{otherwise} \end{cases}$$

where $c_{\mathrm{H}} = 1.345$ is the Huber tuning constant, defined by the STATA program; $u_i = e_i/s$, the ith scaled residual; $s = M/0.6745$ stands for the residual scale estimate; and $M = \mathrm{med}(|e_i - \mathrm{med}(e_i)|)$, the median absolute deviation from the median residual.

According to the Huber weighting, observations with small residuals receive weights of 1 and observations with absolute residuals larger than $(1.345/0.6745)M \cong 2M$ receive gradually smaller weights. This process repeats until convergence.

Then the third step is to give all observations with non-zero residuals some downweighting according to the smoothly decreasing biweight function:

$$w_i = \begin{cases} \left[1 - \left(\dfrac{u_i}{c_{\mathrm{b}}}\right)^2 \right]^2 & \text{if } |u_i| \le c_{\mathrm{b}} \\ 0 & \text{otherwise} \end{cases}$$

where $c_{\mathrm{b}} = 4.685 *$ biweight tuning constant/7.

This means that cases with absolute residuals of $(4.685/0.6745)M \cong 7M$ or more are given a weight of zero, and are thus effectively dropped.

Setting $c_H = 1.345$ and $c_b = 4.685$ enables the program to obtain about 95 per cent of the efficiency of OLS when applied to data with normally distributed errors. The reasons that both Huber weighting and biweighting are used are that Huber weighting has a problem dealing with severe outliers, and biweighting sometimes fails to converge or have multiple solutions. Therefore, I perform Huber weighting first to improve the behaviour of the biweight estimator. The whole process works iteratively until the convergence criteria of 0.05 for both Huber weights and biweights are met.

An additional method of correcting for heteroscedasticity, the White–Sandwich method, is used in Chapter 6 and is further discussed there.[7] We used this second method as the study on capital structure was the first empirical study in the book, and we wanted to check on the robustness of our results. We found little variation in the results using different correction methods so we thereafter only used the one method in other chapters, and generally reported the results obtained from both the OLS and robust regressions. It is relevant to point out that the use of multiple methods is common in the study of corporate governance.[8]

The structure of the book

This book is divided into eight chapters, including this chapter as an introduction. Chapter 2 outlines the various theoretical approaches to the study of corporate governance, and looks briefly at the distinctive features of the study on corporate governance system in China. The emergence and evolution of the joint stock system in China are detailed and analysed in Chapter 3. This includes a discussion of the history of financial system reform, and an investigation into the process of SOE reform and corporatisation. Those aspects of the corporate governance system which are pertinent to the decision to go public, ownership structure, and capital structure are highlighted. Chapters 4, 5, and 6 are the main empirical chapters characterised with data set collection and econometric analysis. Chapter 4 carries out a study on the underpricing of IPO, and hypothesises that ownership structure has an impact upon the degree of IPO underpricing. Chapter 5 follows up, and looks at the relationship between ownership structure and corporate performance, and argues that ownership structure matters. Chapter 6 investigates the determinants of capital structure. This chapter argues that debt finance is more than a source of capital, but is also a governance instrument with contingent control rights. Chapter 7 provides a political perspective on corporate groups in China during the era of economic transition, with emphasis on the governance structure of corporate groups. The insights of this chapter are helpful in that the corporate groups mainly control the headquarters of the listed companies. The last chapter, Chapter 8, summarises the conclusions, points out the implications, and suggests directions for future work.

Concluding remarks

A final word of caution is in order. Agency theory, incomplete contracts theory, the theory of capital structure and the theory of corporate control are all in their infancy, and much theoretical work still remains to be done. Much of the literature emanates from developed countries, though some studies do cover developing countries. But there has been no comparable work on China. The study of corporate governance in the Chinese context has been carried out in a normative manner, mainly arguing what the structure of corporate governance should be. On the one hand, this presents an opportunity for original positive research. On the other hand, there are legitimate concerns that capital markets in China are immature, that investors are not as rational as those in developed markets, and that legal systems are weak. Basic institutional differences exist, which may weaken the applicability of the theories, the arguments and conclusions of the study.

2 Theoretical approaches to corporate governance

Introduction

Corporate governance and the theory of the firm are two of the fastest growing topics in modern economic theory, after a long silence since the publication of the seminal works by Berle and Means (1932) and Coase (1937). Berle and Means argued that modern US corporations were so dependent upon professional managers that a managerial economy had emerged, characterised by the separation of ownership from control in corporations. The managers decided upon the running of the corporation whilst the shareholders, though they were the owners, were only entitled to receive cash flows. This leads to potential conflicts between the interests of the shareholders and those of the management.

Following these two pioneering works, significant contributions have since been made in the areas of property rights theory (Alchian and Demsetz, 1972; Grossman and Hart, 1986; and Hart and Moore, 1990), agency theory (Jensen and Meckling, 1976), the theory of incomplete contracts (Williamson, 1975, 1985; Grossman and Hart, 1986; Hart and Moore, 1990), and transactions cost theory (Williamson, 1975, 1985). All these theories contribute from different angles to an understanding of the issues of corporate governance, and fundamentally affect our thinking about what is a firm, and in whose interests the firm is governed.

It is interesting to note that recent studies of corporate governance, which is a topic within the increasingly broad area of corporate finance, have merged into the area of the theory of the firm. As Zingales (2000) notes

> The interaction between the nature of the firm and corporate finance issues has become so intimate that answering the fundamental questions in the theory of the firm has become a precondition for any further advancement in corporate finance.
>
> (p. 1624)

The link between theory of the firm and corporate governance is even more compelling, and I have already argued for it in Zingales (1998). The word governance implies the exercise of authority. But in a free-market economy, why do we need any form of authority? Isn't the market responsible for allocating all resources efficiently without the intervention of any authority? In fact, Coase (1937) taught us that using the market has its costs, and firms alleviate these costs by substituting the price mechanism with the exercise of authority. By and large, corporate governance is the study of how this authority is allocated and exercised. But in order to understand how this authority is allocated and exercised, we first need to know why it is needed in the first place. We need, thus, a theory of the firm.

(p. 1630)

The task of this chapter is to review and discuss the prevalent models and theories of corporate governance, both in the context of corporate finance and the theory of the firm, in both developed and developing economies. The objective is to provide a broad theoretical foundation for the more specific topics, which were identified in Chapter 1, and which will be considered in detail in subsequent chapters. More specific discussion of the literature on these particular topics will be provided in the respective chapters.

The rest of this chapter is arranged as follows. The next section provides a historical perspective on the theory of the firm. We introduce agency theory in addressing the issue of the separation of ownership and control in the section on 'Agency theory'; the theory of incomplete contracts in the section, 'The theory of incomplete contracts', Property rights theory in the section 'Property rights theory' and transaction costs economics in 'Transactions cost economics as an alterative approach'. In the section 'The theories compared' we briefly compare and contrast these theories. The section 'Stylised models of corporate governance' examines two stylised models of corporate governance systems. In the penultimate section we discuss the extant studies on corporate governance in China. The last section concludes.

The historical perspective

The study of corporate governance is about how authority originates in companies, and how it is allocated amongst the parties involved. It is thus natural to start this discussion with Coase (1937) who observed that some transactions were carried out through the market, whilst others were carried out within organisations called firms. He asked why a firm emerges at all in a specialised exchange economy – in a perfect market, all transactions can be carried out through the price mechanism. He wrote

But in view of the fact that it is usually argued that co-ordination will be done by the price mechanism, why is such organisation necessary? Why are there these islands of conscious power? Outside the firm, price movements direct production, which is co-ordinated through a series of exchange transactions on the market. Within a firm, these markets transactions are eliminated and in place of the complicated market structure with exchange transactions is substituted the entrepreneur – co-ordinator, who directs production. It is clear that these are alternative methods of co-ordinating production.

(p. 19)

He offered an initial explanation of the existence of the firm, which is that there are costs to using market mechanisms, which he defined as transactions costs.[1] As a result, the inputs, including labour, are organised into the firm. Meanwhile, there are also costs to using firm institutions, which he called management costs though he didn't explicitly define them. These two costs, according to his theory, are balanced to define the size of the firm[2] – when the costs of using the market are too high, this leads to larger firms. But greater size makes management less efficient, which constrains the firm from becoming too big. The optimal size of the firm is determined by the trade-off between the costs of inefficient markets and of managerial inefficiency. This analysis has been criticised,[3] because it does not answer the questions of when and why the costs of supervising the execution of instruction by central authorities, and the frictions internal to the firm, result in lower costs than bargaining over contracts in the markets. These criticisms of Coase (1937) have been fruitful, leading to the birth of the modern theory of the firm.

Berle and Means (1932) investigated 'modern corporations': that is, production organisations with multiple owners and multiple agents – see Figure 2.1. An important difference between the modern corporation and other forms of production organisation was the dispersion of ownership, and the resultant separation of ownership and control. As Berle and Means pointed out, 65 per cent of the 200

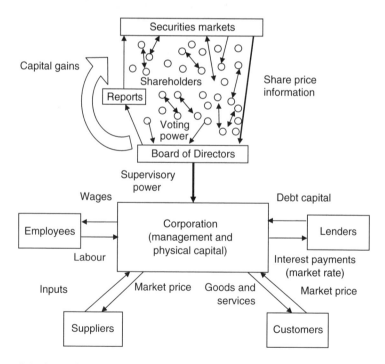

Figure 2.1 The Berle and Means model of the modern corporation.

Source: Blair (1995), p. 31.

largest American non-financial corporations were controlled by management, who held only a small ownership stake. The governance structure of a typical corporation was that the shareholders each held only an insignificant proportion of the outstanding shares, which effectively excluded them from exercising power over strategic decisions. The share certificate simply provided proof of a claim to dividends. Thus Berle and Means defined the ownership of the firm in terms of the residual claim rights, and shareholders as the residual claimants.

Berle and Means' classic analysis is now seen as having less relevance in a world in which widely-dispersed share ownership is the exception rather than the norm, and in which it is no longer apparent that widely-dispersed share owner-ship will necessarily lead to inferior monitoring of management by the share-holders (Blair, 1995). Recent studies suggest that the Berle and Means model of widely-dispersed corporate ownership is not common, even in developed coun-tries. Rather, large shareholders control a significant number of firms in many countries, including developed ones. In Italy, 88 per cent of manufacturing com-panies (accounting for 91 per cent of the employed labour force) are controlled by one person or family (Barca *et al.*, 1994, cited in Pagano *et al.*, 1998), and shareholders own more than 50 per cent of the voting rights in the majority of publicly-listed companies (Zingales, 1994). In Germany, 85 per cent of public companies have a major shareholder, and in France the corresponding figure is 79 per cent. The comparable figure in the United Kingdom is 16 per cent (Franks and Mayer, 1994).[4] Even in the United States, where ownership structures are claimed to be more dispersed than other industrial countries, concentrated share-holdings are commonly seen (Demsetz, 1983; Shleifer and Vishny, 1986; Morck *et al.*, 1988; Shleifer and Vishny, 1997; Holderness *et al.*, 1999).

Studies by La Porta *et al.* (1999), with a sample of more than 3,000 firms across 49 countries, and Claessens *et al.* (2000), covering 2,980 firms in nine South East Asian countries,[5] all show that a significant fraction of shares rests in the hands of a small number of shareholders. All the evidence suggests that the distribution of shareholdings involves a mixture of large shareholders and small shareholders. The equity holdings of contemporary corporations are actually nei-ther totally controlled by one investor, nor fully dispersed. Thus, the structure of the contemporary 'modern corporation' may perhaps be more accurately illus-trated by Figure 2.2, which indicates the co-existence of a group of significant shareholders exercising their influence (not necessarily direct control rights) over the firms, and a large number of small investors effectively deprived of control rights except the rights of the 'Wall Street Walk'.

As Blair (1995, p. 32) points out, the separation of equity holders from man-agement through the financial markets raises four types of governance problems:

- For firms to operate efficiently, management must have enough leeway to take risks, make strategic decisions, and take advantage of investment opportunities as they arise. Management cannot submit every decision to a shareholder vote, and, even if it could, shareholders who are not close to the operations of the company probably would not be able to make informed

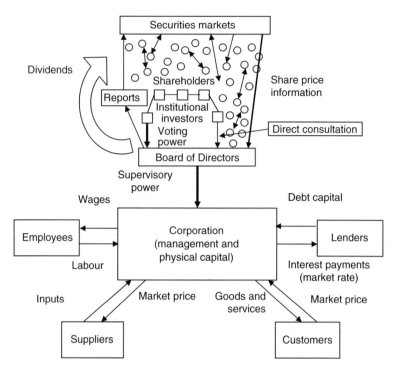

Figure 2.2 The modern corporation with concentrated ownership.
Source: Blair (1995), p. 47.

decisions. Nonetheless, management must be prevented from abusing its power and position by spending resources or undertaking investments that benefit management at the expense of the shareholders. Hence, shareholders need mechanisms for effectively monitoring and restraining management.

- A small, close-knit group of shareholders with a large total share of equity might be quite effective at monitoring management but, if they are given enhanced control rights, then their power must also be restrained to prevent them from taking unfair advantage of other shareholders.
- A major commitment of time and resources is necessary for investors (or any-one else) to act as effective monitors. But many investors prefer the advantages of liquidity and diversity in their portfolios – advantages that may not be consistent with the time and resource commitment involved in monitoring.
- Investors need reliable and accurate information, developed using consistent measuring and accounting procedures. But any measure of performance can provide misleading information or distorted incentives by encouraging management to focus attention on inappropriate or partial goals. Moreover, releasing certain kinds of information to the public can sometimes weaken a company's competitive position.

Thus, to achieve sustained economic growth, a sound micro-mechanism must provide incentives to ensure that both investors and other stakeholders benefit from their 'investments'.

Agency theory

Agency theory addresses the question of the separation of ownership and control, as identified by Berle and Means (1932). Alchian and Demsetz (1972) challenged Coase's explanation of the existence of the firm, arguing that there was no difference between market transactions by contracts, and operations in the firm characterised by authority. One vivid example was to contrast the manager in a firm, who has the authority to sack an employee (stop the employee from providing his/her service to the firm), with a customer who also has the right to 'sack' a grocer by ceasing to make purchases at the shop (Alchian and Demsetz, 1972, p. 778). Alchian and Demsetz maintain that the existence of the firm is due to the fact that production involves joint efforts by multiple workers. Since it is difficult to differentiate between the efforts of the individual workers, it becomes problematic to allocate *ex post* rewards for these efforts, and incentives in an organisation can be easily subdued. Consequently, a monitor needs to be introduced to supervise the teamwork to avoid opportunism.

Jensen and Meckling (1976) are credited with the systematic use of principal–agent relations to characterise the problem of governing the relationship between shareholders and managers. Jensen and Meckling define an agency relationship as a contract under which one or more persons (the principals) engage another person (the agent) to perform some service on their behalf which involves delegating some decision-making authority to the agent (p. 308). Since the interest of the agent is not always in line with that of the principal, the agent may act for himself even though his actions will harm the interests of the principal. To ensure the agent works properly for the principal, the principal has to incur extra costs (non-pecuniary as well as pecuniary) – these are called the agency costs. Jensen and Meckling (p. 308) listed the agency costs as the sum of '(1) the monitoring expenditures of the principal, (2) the bonding expenditures by the agent, and (3) the residual loss'. The residual loss is the reduction in the value of the firm that comes about when the entrepreneur dilutes his ownership. The shift out of profits and into managerial discretion induced by the dilution of ownership is responsible for this loss. For example, in a large firm (e.g. a corporation) the manager usually owns only a fraction of the shares due to wealth constraints and/or risk aversion. When the manager owns, say, only 10 per cent of the company, he pays for a dollar of perquisites with only 10 cents of his own forgone profits, and hence will overconsume perquisites. Of course, there may be mechanisms for keeping down the consumption of perquisites, such as oversight by boards of directors, the managerial labour market, takeovers, and so on. But the basic problem remains namely that, as long as there are outside investors, managers will have a tendency to consume more when they have smaller shareholdings in the companies.

According to Williamson (1988), the residual loss is the key feature, since the other two costs are incurred only to the degree to which they yield cost-effective reductions in the residual loss. That is, agency costs include the costs of structuring, monitoring, and bonding a set of contracts among agents with conflicting interests. Agency costs also include the value of output lost because the costs of full enforcement of contracts exceed the benefits (Jensen and Meckling, 1976). Monitoring expenditures and bonding expenditures can help to restore performance toward pre-dilution levels. The irreducible agency cost is the minimum of the sum of these three factors.

There are two broad approaches to remedying agency problems. The first one is through an incentive scheme to tackle the unobservable managerial effort and the moral hazard problem arising from it. According to Holmstrom (1979) and Shavell (1979), managers may slack off when shareholders do not know how hard they work. To elicit higher effort, shareholders should provide managers with incentives to work hard, in part through share ownership. If managers are risk-neutral, then in general it is optimal for them to own 100 per cent of equity in the companies they run. However, if managers are risk-averse, then the optimal management ownership is below 100 per cent and, in general, a fully-efficient effort cannot be extracted. In moral hazard models, excessive risk-bearing by managers is one of the costs of a high management ownership of shares. Risk-aversion reduces the optimal ownership to below 100 per cent, but in the process also reduces the effort that managers supply. While an incentive scheme may work well in motivating managers to exert effort, it is likely to be less effective in getting managers to cut back on empire-building or to relinquish control. The reason is that, if managers have strong interest in power, empire, and perks, a very large bribe may be required to persuade managers to give up these things.

Thus a second approach (Hart, 1995b) is that it may be better for investors to force managers to curb their empire-building tendencies. Placing debt in the capital structure is one way to do this. Moreover, debt is more flexible than an incentive scheme in that it makes the set of choices available to the manager sensitive to the market's assessment of company prospects (Hart, 1995b, p. 128).

Hence, the control of agency problems in the decision process is important when the managers who initiate and implement important decisions are not the major residual claimants, and therefore do not bear a major share of the wealth effects of their decisions. Without effective control procedures, such managers are more likely to take actions that deviate from the interests of the residual claimants. An effective system for decision control implies, almost by definition, that the control (ratification and monitoring) of decisions is to some extent separate from the management (initiation and implementation) of decisions.

The implication of both agency models is that, when management ownership is high, managers will take actions that are closer to maximising shareholder wealth than when management ownership is low. These actions include working hard, forgoing the consumption of perquisites, making positive rather than negative net present value investment decisions (such as diversification), and so forth. They also include quitting and agreeing to be replaced by another manager when the current manager is no longer the best person for the job. When incentives are strong enough, managers will be prepared to do what is best for the shareholders even to the extent that inferior managers will be willing to yield their positions to superior managers.

The theory of incomplete contracts

In the theory of incomplete contracts,[6] the firm is a vehicle for residual control, which gives one party or parties *ex post* control rights when there are events that are not explicitly covered in the incomplete contract[7] (Grossman and Hart, 1986; Hart, 1995a). According to this branch of the literature, a contract can be interpreted very broadly as any document regulating a quid pro quo: that is, one thing in return for something else (Hart and Holmstrom, 1987). The importance of the contract in the theory of the firm and corporate governance was recognised explicitly by Alchian and Demsetz (1972), who characterised the relationship between employers and employees as a contractual relation. Jensen and Meckling (1976, p. 312) went one step further by putting forward the view of the firm as a 'nexus of contracts', and arguing that the firm 'is just a legal fiction which serves as a focus for the complex process in which the conflicting objectives of individuals...are brought in equilibrium within a framework of a contractual relationship.' Contracts are particularly important in long-term relationships, when time elapses between the initial contracting and the actual performance, and between actions and payoffs (Berglof, 1990).

In contrast with both the Alchian and Demsetz version of employer–employee contracts, and the Jensen and Meckling version of a nexus of contracts, the theory of incomplete contracts argues that every economic transaction is mediated by a contract, whether explicit or implicit. Whilst agency theory acknowledges that the separation between ownership and control will lead to agency problems, it assumes that it is feasible to identify the complete set of possible contingencies and to write contracts that are sensitive to even the most minute details of the events arising in the course of the transaction. Thus, the agency problem can be eliminated by a complete contract, which can forecast all future events and specify the actions that should be taken. In a world of complete contracts, there are actually no agency costs (Hart, 1995a).

In contrast, the theory of incomplete contracts suggests that it is the impossibility of specifying complete contracts which provides the basis for the existence of firms. There are three reasons why it is not possible to have a complete contract.[8] First, it is hard for people to think very far ahead in a complex and highly unpredictable world, and to plan for all the various contingencies that may arise. Second, even if individual plans can be made, it is hard for the contracting parties to negotiate about these plans, not least because they have to find a common language to describe states of the world and actions with respect to which prior experience may not provide much of a guide. Third, even if the parties can plan and negotiate about the future, it may be very difficult for them to write their plans down in such a way that, in the event of a dispute, an outside authority – a court, say – can establish what these plans mean and enforce them (i.e. there are enforcement costs). In other words, the parties must be able to communicate not only with each other, but also with outsiders who may have little knowledge about the environment in which the contracting parties operate (Hart, 1995b, p. 23). It may be extremely costly to write a contract that specifies unambiguously the payments and actions of all parties in every observable state of nature (Grossman and Hart, 1986). Thus it is optimal for a contract to be incomplete, and *ex post* renegotiations are non-avoidable.

A simple model is useful for illustrating the basic ideas of incomplete contract theory – see Figure 2.3. Let x be a measure of the completeness of a contract, and

- $C_A(x)$ is the agency cost function, which is continuously decreasing in x. $C_A'(x) < 0$ and $C_A''(x) < 0$;
- $C_C(x)$ is the cost function associated with writing a contract. $C_C'(x) > 0$ and $C_C''(x) \geq 0$;
- $B(x)$ is the total cost function $B(x) = C_A(x) + C_C(x) \geq 0$.

There will be a contract, with a level of completeness (x^*), that minimises the total costs as shown by Figure 2.3.

Hence, according to incomplete contract theory, there are substantial costs associated with specifying a comprehensive contract. A more general contract, which only specifies trades and decisions for some events and which allocates the rights to make decisions for all other events in a summary way, will be more efficient than attempting to formulate a comprehensive one. In a world of incomplete contracts, it is optimal (though not first-best) to leave room for future renegotiations on what actions should be taken, and who has the authority to approve them.

The implications of incomplete contracts theory are rich and profound for corporate governance. First, the theory explains the origins of authority in firms,

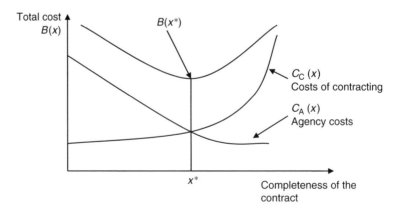

Figure 2.3 The optimal contract with the lowest combined agency and contracting costs.

which lie in the hands of the capital-providers. The bond-holders have the rights to future financial claims that are clearly stated in the debt contracts, regardless of the financial health of the firm. They can sue the firm if it fails to pay the coupons required in the contract, and any default will trigger the possible takeover of the assets of the firm. The equity-holders accept the residual risks by providing equity capital. Second and consequently, the burden of monitoring the managers falls on the shareholders. But, if it is optimal for contracts to be incomplete and for the allocation of some control rights to be deferred to the future, then who should assume these residual control rights and why? We will attempt to answer this question in the next section.

Property rights theory

The objective of property rights theory is to identify the boundary of the firm, since the boundary of the firm draws a line within which all transactions are carried out through authority from the management, and outside which all transactions are carried out through market mechanisms (i.e. contracts). Here we refer again to Alchian and Demsetz (1972) who argued that, because of the potential for opportunism, a monitor was required to ensure that team members could be properly supervised and rewarded. The problem then becomes one of who will be assigned the authority to monitor and judge the team. This monitoring function can only be fulfilled within the firm, and not by the market. They effectively argued that the firm manager has the authority because he has property rights, which include the rights to determine how assets are used (control rights) and the rights to the cash flows generated by these assets (return rights), as well as the rights to sell these rights. But where do the property rights come from, and who ultimately should be entitled to them?

Grossman and Hart (1986) categorised control into two components: 'contractual' control, which has been explicitly written in the (incomplete) contract, and 'residual' control, which is the right to decide what and when to do when an unexpected event take place. They defined property rights as the rights to return streams, and the rights to make strategic decisions in contingencies not explicitly contracted upon. A firm may thus be defined by its physical assets, and by the allocation of the property rights to these assets (Hart, 1988).

But a further question is who is entitled to possess the residual control rights: the capital provider, or the labour provider? Grossman and Hart suggest that the capital owner should possess these rights, since the capital provider can refuse labour access to the non-human assets,[9] and can walk away with all the non-human assets. In other words, control over the non-human assets leads to control over the human assets (Hart, 1995b). In a Nash equilibrium, it is optimal for both parties to agree to allocate the rights to the capital owners. This is a very important development in the theory of the firm and corporate governance since it defines property rights within a framework of the theory of incomplete contracts, instead of the 'traditional' property rights approach developed by Alchian and Demsetz (1972), whose view of the firm as a nexus of contracts ignores the problems of writing and enforcing complete contracts. Some researchers (e.g. Berglof, 1990) refer to this line of research as the 'new' property rights theory.

Transactions cost economics as an alternative approach

The key question addressed by the property rights approach to the theory of the firm is what defines the boundaries of the firm? Transactions cost economics provides another perspective on the issue of corporate governance. Basically, transactions cost economics regards the firm as a governance structure (Williamson, 1988), and its contributions may be summarised in three points.

First, it contributes to our understanding of the nature of contracts, particularly the costs of contracting. As pointed out by Hart and Moore (1999), the incomplete contracts literature can be seen as a development of the transactions cost literature.

Second, transactions cost economics recognises the importance of asset specificity in explaining why there is the firm. Williamson (1975) identified relationship-specific investments as the main obstacle to the use of market. Suppose that a productive opportunity comes up which requires that at least one of the parties undertakes investments which are specific to this particular relationship (e.g. specific tools or machinery, or the location of a plant). This investment generates a significantly higher surplus in the relationship than outside. Joskow (1985) used the example of a coal-burning electricity generating plant situated next to a coal mine. The plant generates a higher economic value only if it is supplied by the particular mine next to which it is situated, because the boilers of the plant are particularly designed for the type of coal produced by the coal mine. Even though markets may be competitive so that there are many alternative parties (many different coal mines) with which to contract, there is only one party left after specific investments are sunk (after the electricity plant is built, only one mine supplies coal useable economically to the plant). Then the party which has not undertaken the investment has a lot of hold-up power and thereby the possibility of extracting some of the surplus generated by the investment. This leads to underinvestment, since some of the returns generated by relationship-specific investments are skimmed off in *ex post* bargaining. In these situations it is advantageous to use 'hierarchies' instead of the market and place the parties to the contract into the same firm. Thus, transactions cost theory explains the firm by viewing it as a mechanism for dealing with hold-up problems. This is important to strengthen incomplete contracts theory in that, if there is no specific investment by either side of the transaction, and when there are irresolvable disputes among the parties, one or both of the parties can stop doing business with each other and economically seek a third party to provide the business they need.

Third, the application of transactions cost economics to corporate finance leads to the finding that the financing instruments (i.e. debt and equity) are more than financial alternatives, but also alternative governance structures (Williamson, 1988). More specifically, the theory argues that the choice between debt and equity depends on asset-specificity and the investment attributes of projects, and the governance structure features of debt and equity need to be aligned in a discriminating way. If a new project involves a highly redeployable asset (e.g. a general purpose factory), it should be financed by debt at the 'going rate' for real estate using a mortgage as security. As asset-specificity becomes greater, however, the pre-emptive claims of the bondholders against the investment afford limited protection because the assets in question have limited redeployability. In this case, the preferred financial instrument for projects should be equity finance, which offers more intrusive oversight and involvement through the board of directors.

Notwithstanding these contributions to the theory of the firm, transactions cost economics is not central to our understanding of corporate governance, as will be discussed in the next section.

The theories compared

The different branches of the modern theories of the firm and corporate governance display the firm from different perspectives, yet have been developed interactively (Hart, 1988; Williamson, 1988; Holmstrom and Tirole, 1989; Hart and Moore, 1999). It is helpful to think of these theories as complementary, rather than contradictory and mutually exclusive. Certainly, any attempt to differentiate and disentangle them fully will cause confusion instead of clarification. Thus, as stated in Chapter 1, we stress that this is a study with an agency theory perspective within the framework of the theory of incomplete contracts. Agency problems cannot be properly understood in a world in which comprehensive contracts can be formulated.

The property rights theory provides the fundamental instrument of analysis for this study. Property rights theory and agency theory differ, as Bolton and Scharfstein (1998) point out, in that Berle and Means stressed the separation of ownership and control, and implicitly defined ownership as claims on the residual cash flows – what is available after paying other stakeholders. In contrast, Grossman and Hart defined ownership as the residual control rights – the right to make decisions about contingencies that are not specified in the contract. Thus the Grossman–Hart–Moore line of thought calls the shareholders 'owners' because they have the voting power to determine how assets are deployed, whereas Berle and Means think of the shareholders as 'owners' because they get the residual cash flows.

A potential shortcoming of property rights theory is the identification of control with ownership. As Kay and Silberston (1995, p. 86) puts it very effectively: 'if we asked a visitor from another planet to guess who were the owners of a firm [on the basis of this definition] by observing behaviour rather than by reading text books in law or economics, there can be little doubt that he would point to the company's senior managers.' Not surprisingly, this line of research has found it extremely difficult to deal with the separation between ownership and control, because it equates the two concepts, and this has also impinged on its ability to deliver implications for corporate governance. Thus, property rights theory may be most applicable to small or privately-owned firms where the owners are also the managers, and there

Table 2.1 A comparison between transactions cost economics and agency theory

	Transactions cost economics	Agency theory
Origination	Market structure	Corporate finance
What is the Firm?	A governance structure	Nexus of contracts
Focal dimension	Asset specification	Not specified
Minimum unit of analysis	Transaction	Individual agent
Focal cost concern	Maladaptation	Residual loss
Contractual focus	*Ex post* governance	*Ex ante* alignment

Source: Adapted from Williamson (1988).

is no delegation of management to professionals who are not significant share-holders. But, when ownership and control are separated as is usually the case in large listed companies, we need to broaden our perspective to agency theory.

Although the transaction costs economics approach is regarded as a major step forward, the explanation of the existence of firms as a governance structure to solely protect relationship-specific investments has been criticised because it lacks a criterion for the boundaries of the firm (Hart, 1995b). If there are potential benefits to integrating different firms because their assets are relationship-specific, but no countervailing costs, it is not clear why it is not efficient to concentrate all economic activities in one large firm. As Holmstrom and Roberts (1998, p. 75) point out, firms have to deal with a much richer variety of problems than simply the provision of investment incentives and the resolution of hold-ups. Ownership patterns are not determined solely by the need to provide investment incentives, and incentives for investment are provided by a variety of means, of which ownership is but one. Table 2.1 provides a brief comparison of the essential features of transactions cost economics and agency theory.

The main conclusion to emerge from this discussion is that corporate governance issues arise due to agency problems, caused by the combination of the separation of ownership and control, and the incompleteness of contracts. Furthermore,

- property rights theory explains the sources of authority;
- agency theory emphasises the separation of ownership and control, and points out that, in modern corporations, authority resides in the hands of management;
- incomplete contracts theory argues that the issue of corporate governance cannot be understood in a world in which comprehensive contracts are infeasible, as agency problems can be easily resolved with complete contracts.

Stylised models of corporate governance

It is accepted that there are two basic models of corporate governance, as defined in developed economies, but mostly applicable to the developing or transitional economies, though with a certain degree of variety. One is the Anglo-Saxon model, which is prevalent in the United States, the United Kingdom and other developed English-speaking countries such as Canada and Australia. And the

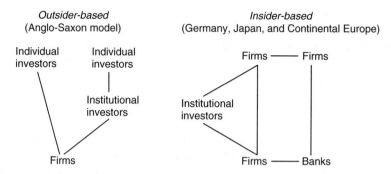

Figure 2.4 Insider-based and outsider-based systems of ownership and control.
Source: Mayer (1994).

other is the German-Japanese model, which is favoured in many Continental European countries and Japan. The former is also commonly referred to as an 'outsider system', whilst the latter is an 'insider system' – see Figure 2.4.

The Anglo-Saxon model is characterised by dispersed shareholding, shareholder sovereignty, and the alignment of shareholders' and managers' interests. This model also stresses the importance of the enhancement of monitoring, information disclosure, and accountability mechanisms such as a competitive market for corporate control (i.e. takeovers, mergers, and acquisitions). The largest shareholders play a passive role in the management of the corporation, and do not intervene directly in the day-to-day business. They protect their interests by voting with their feet: that is, they sell their shares when they are not happy with the management. The protection of small (minority) shareholders is well-established by law and regulations. Another important characteristic of the system is the existence of an active market for corporate control, where shareholders exercise control over management discretion through exit, and this establishes the threat of hostile takeover (Jensen and Ruback, 1983). From this follows the Kay and Silberston (1995) assertions that the threat of hostile takeover has led to the increased importance of shareholder interests in the Anglo-American system through the 1980s, and that corporate control was seen as one of the principal goals of company law.

The insider system of corporate governance is characterised by cross-shareholdings, cross-representation of directors, large investor involvement in corporate decision-making, and the concentration of share ownership. Much is made of the potential that this establishes for inter-firm co-operation and relationship-specific investments among companies and their employees, suppliers, purchasers, investors and consumer groups. There are virtually no markets for corporate control because only a small proportion of shares are circulated on the markets, and it is impossible to acquire sufficient shares to oust existing management teams. The safeguards for the interests of labour (through, e.g. the German system of co-determination, and the Japanese system of lifetime employment) have received much attention from stakeholder-oriented commentaries. Long-term relationships between the larger shareholders and the corporations are common practice. The mutual monitoring and selective interventions by large equity-owners are seen as a highly effective means of controlling the problems of corporate governance, provided that there is product market competition. Notwithstanding the many common points, the corporate governance structures in Germany and Japan still have some remarkable differences – see Table 2.2.

Theoretically, the pros and cons of each type of governance structure are as follows. Corporate governance through large controlling blocs more or less guarantees the effective control of management, but reduces the liquidity of the firm's shares in the secondary market and also reduces managerial incentives in decision-making (Burkart *et al.*, 1997). Alternatively corporate governance through takeover, which is assumed to be a mechanism that improves the allocation of resources, minimises the liquidity costs of larger stakes, but introduces some uncertainty as to whether takeovers succeed whenever they are needed.

Table 2.2 The importance of different corporate control mechanisms in large non-financial firms in four economies[10]

Mechanism	United States	United Kingdom	Japan	Germany
Board independence/ power over management	Little	Little	Little formally, more influence informally via President's Club meetings	Greatest
Importance of pay/performance relationship in top management compensation package	Small	Unknown, probably small	Less	Important for those firms that are owner-managed
Monitoring by financial institution stakeholders	Little	Little	Substantial	Some
Monitoring by non-financial firm stakeholders	Little	Little	Some	Substantial
Monitoring by individual stakeholders	Little	Little	Little	Important for those firms that are owner-managed
Frequency of hostile takeovers	Frequent	Frequent	Virtually non-existent	Virtually non-existent

Source: Prowse (1994), p. 52.

Empirically, there is considerable dispute about the effectiveness of the different corporate governance systems. Easterbrook and Fischel (1991), among many other researchers, make very optimistic assessments of the United States corporate governance system, whereas Jensen (1989, 1993) believes that it is deeply flawed and that a major move from the current corporate form to a much more highly-leveraged organisation – similar to the Leveraged buy-out (LBO) – is in order. There is also constant talk of replacing the Anglo-Saxon corporate governance systems with those patterned after Germany and Japan (see, e.g. Roe, 1993 and Charkham, 1994).

But a common feature of the corporate governance systems in the United States, Germany, Japan and the United Kingdom is that they work reasonably well. In contrast, Barca (1994, as cited in Pagano *et al.*, 1998) and Pagano *et al.* (1998) both maintain that Italian corporate governance mechanisms are so undeveloped as to substantially retard the flow of external capital to firms.[11] In less developed countries, including some transition economies, corporate governance mechanisms are practically non-existent. In Russia the weakness of the corporate governance mechanisms has led to the substantial diversion of assets by managers of many privatised firms, and the virtual non-existence of external capital supply to firms (Boycko *et al.*, 1995).

As a result, theorists, practitioners, and government policy-makers are all now exploring how to establish or improve the system of corporate governance. In the United Kingdom, there was the Cadbury Report (1992) and the Greenbury Report (1995). At the international level, there was the OECD (1999) 'Report on Corporate Governance'. All these reports suggest some remedies, or recommend codes of behaviours for Board directors and CEOs. But none of them provides any empirical evidence about which system is most effective and should be adopted. The task of establishing the most efficient corporate governance system requires empirical studies on a country-by-country basis.

Current studies on corporate governance in China

Studies of Chinese corporate governance issues are quite new, and very few have been published in English. But attention to these issues is increasing with SOE reform and corporatisation. It is commonly accepted that one of the main goals of China's market-oriented reforms has been to establish a corporate governance system that could provide incentives for investment, adequately restrain and monitor management, and promote the optimal use of resources for wealth creation. For example, in China, a prominent Chinese economist, Wu Jinglian introduced and promoted the concepts and importance of corporate governance in 1994 (Tam, 1999). Wu's definition of corporate governance is

Because a company does not have its own mind and consciousness, only through an organisational system – namely managerial staff directed by its corporate governance – it can be governed. Corporate governance means the organisational structure consisting of owner, board of directors and senior managers. A check and balance relationship is formed within that structure, through which the owner entrusts its capital to the board of directors. The board of directors is the highest level of decision making of the company and has the power to appoint, reward and penalise, and dismiss senior managers.

(Wu, 1994, p. 185, as cited by Tam, 1999, p. 19)

As we can see from the definition, it mostly echoes those found in other economies but with more emphasis on the role of the board of directors.

Two broad approaches may be identified to achieve the required system of corporate governance in transitional economies – the privatisation approach, and an approach based upon the assertion that effective corporate governance may be best achieved under government control. The privatisation approach argues that a sound corporate governance system in China can be achieved only through the privatisation of the SOEs, and if the government relinquishes all control (Lin, 2000). An efficient corporate governance system cannot be established without the exclusion of government ownership from, at least the majority of, SOEs as the Government has its own agenda which may or may not coincide with the public interest. For example, the government's first priority is maintaining political and social stability. And the Government is also interested in increasing the amount of revenue under its disposal (Shleifer and Vishny, 1994; Shleifer, 1998).

The second approach has been advocated by Qian (1995, 2001) and Che and Qian (1998). They argue that a corporate governance system without private ownership may be the second-best solution, and that the circumstances do not allow the achievement of the first-best outcome. They assert that contracting is more likely to be incomplete in developing and transition economies because of imperfect States and market institutions. For example, in the absence of the rule of law and an independent judicial system, the enforcer of a contract (i.e. the Government) may be corrupt or be a party to the contract. It is therefore more likely that contracts may become unenforceable in developing and transitional economies (Che and Qian, 1998), and incomplete contracting is a more natural assumption (Schmidt, 1996). They modelled a situation in which the interests of local governments did not align with those of central government. The local governments wanted to promote economic efficiency rather than pursue other political goals. Thus the SOEs owned by local governments could report outstanding performance, since the local governments act as a buffer between the SOEs and the Central Government, and could hide information from the Central Government. Obviously, this is not the first-best outcome, and it is tempting to conclude that Che and Qian (1998) were trying to justify the economic performance of China since economic reform without the large-scale implementation of privatisation.

In summary, even though there is an increasing literature on corporate governance (Xu and Wang, 1997; Tam, 1999; Tenev and Zhang, 2002), these provide little insight into China's predicament for four main reasons:

- The transition from a socialist to a market economy has demonstrated the old lesson that social transformation is driven by both economics and politics. The persistent influence of the State and its administration, of cultural values, and of social and political institutions influences the set of feasible evolutions of every transitional State.[12] The corporatisation of SOEs is an explicit goal of the micro-reconstruction of China's economy. But the objectives associated with establishing a corporate system are ambiguous and sometimes contradictory. For example, one stated objective for corporatisation is to improve the efficiency of the SOEs, which implies that the more efficient firms should be allocated more capital. But another objective is to keep alive poorly performing firms in order to avoid social instability. These contradictory objectives make it more difficult both for policy-makers and for theorists to work out a clear, long-term strategy for more sound corporate governance (Tam, 1999).

- History shows that the design of reform schemes varies according to political conditions across countries. China will need to find its own unique path of transition from a centrally planned to a market economy. In China, the stock markets, large shareholders and small shareholders co-exist. The large shareholders, such as the State-owned agents and institutional investors, control the corporations, whilst the small shareholders are dispersed and are mainly engaged in obtaining short-term capital gains.
- As noted by Schiavo-Campo and Pannier (1996), 'internal' improvements in corporate governance are an essential part of the public enterprise reform process and an adjunct to the 'external' reform measures. In their opinion, the principal dimensions of corporate governance reform are the process of corporatisation, the selection of agents to represent the State, management improvements, the role of the Board of Directors, and performance and management contracts.
- The development of the financial sector is an external factor for fostering the formation of a sound corporate governance system, but this is a complex and multifaceted process. It involves the balanced development of three essential elements (La Porta *et al.*, 1998) which are missing or incomplete in China: institutions, instruments, and markets. This gives rise to a situation in which a well-functioning financial market and its constituent participants (including the listed companies) are mutually dependent on each other. A problem or imperfection in one element causes problems for the others. This can be commonly seen around the world – the prevalence of bad corporate governance practices typically accompanying poorly-functioning financial markets (La Porta *et al.*, 2000).

There are also a number of particular features of the Chinese system that are relevant in the context of corporate governance reform:

- First, the institutional and cultural setting in China is quite different to that in the West and in the countries of the former Soviet bloc. China has not, as was the case in the former Soviet-bloc countries, undergone a rapid transition from a planned economy to a market economy. Market-based reforms and the adoption of the corporate form for enterprises were adopted in China as a pragmatic solution to poor economic performance under State planning. They were grafted onto an ideological position that remained essentially collectivist and socialist in its outlook.

- In setting up its joint stock system, China is forming a system with its own characteristics. One interesting feature of China's listed companies is that, for historical reasons (which will be discussed further below), much of the companies' total capital is made up of three types of shares: State-owned shares, legal person-owned shares,[13] and tradable shares. Neither the State-owned shares nor the legal person-owned shares can be traded on the stock markets.

- The State-owned shares may be held by the Central Government, by local government, or by wholly government-owned enterprises. It has been decreed that the ultimate owner of State-owned shares is the State Council of China. State shares may not be traded on the two main Exchanges, but are transferable to domestic institutions subject to the approval of the China Securities Regulatory Commission. The State is the largest shareholder in many of the publicly traded corporations.

- The legal person-owned shares are those owned by the domestic institutions, and are much more complex and various. The domestic institutions include stock companies, non-bank financial institutions, and SOEs that have at least one non-State owner.

- The tradable shares may be divided into four types: tradable A-shares, B-shares, H-shares, and N-shares. The tradable A-shares are held mostly by individuals and some domestic institutions, and can be freely traded on the domestic stock markets. B-shares are designed for foreign investors, and may be traded only on SHSE and SZSE. H-shares are listed on the Hong Kong Stock Exchange. N-shares, actually American Depository Receipts (ADRs), are listed on the New York Stock Exchange.

- In aggregate terms, the State-owned shares and the legal person-owned shares account for most of the capital, and therefore determine control of the firms. Takeover, as a mechanism of monitoring management, is meaningless in this situation because the bidder cannot gather enough shares to take over the control of the company. But not all the listed companies' stocks are dominated by State-owned and legal person-owned shares. The shares of about one-third of the listed companies can be traded on the stock markets, and these companies provide the opportunity to study the relationship between governance structure and corporate performance.

- In the West, creditors who supply loan capital are entitled to initiate a process (either in a Bankruptcy Court or through an out-of-Court settlement) to restructure and reorganise the firm. In China in contrast, the role of debt as an incentive mechanism is either absent or weak.

Concluding remarks

In the earlier sections, we have discussed theoretical approaches to the issue of corporate governance. Agency theory argues that the issue of corporate governance arises because of the separation of ownership and control, and points to possible conflicts between shareholders, bondholders and managers. But the theory of incomplete contracts points out that, in a world in which comprehensive contracts may be drawn, there are no agency problems since all agency problems can be anticipated, written in the contracts, and enforced by a third party (usually a court). The application of the theory of incomplete contracts to the firm leads to so-called new property rights theory, which argues that the firm is a vehicle to resolve the issue of residual control. Property rights are the residual rights that cannot be explicitly written in the initial contract, and it is optimal for the parties to leave a contract incomplete and renegotiate later when future contingencies arise. The contribution of transactions costs theory is that the incompleteness of contracts is due to transactions costs. It treats the firm as a governance structure, with emphasis of the role of debt/equity in the corporate governance.

Economists have used those ideas to model financial instruments not in terms of their cash flows, but in terms of the rights they allocate to their holders. In this framework, investors get cash only because they have power. This can be the power to change directors, to force dividend payments, to stop a project or a scheme that benefits the insiders at the expense of outside investors, to sue directors and get compensation, or to liquidate the firm and receive the proceeds.

The Chinese corporate governance system and related theories are under development. In transition economies such as China, contracts are more likely to be incomplete, due to the immature legal framework, the uncertain future, and the weak enforcement of the law. Agency problems are likely to be more serious – particularly in the public sector – and it is reasonable to assume that the theories reviewed are pertinent in the Chinese case.

The following chapters now utilise this general framework to examine the issues of the underpricing of IPOs, the ownership structure, and the capital structure in Chinese listed companies. As Zingales (2000) points out, these issues are inextricably linked to each other. These empirical studies will help our understanding of the mechanisms of corporate governance in China, and provide a fresh perspective on how these mechanisms impact upon the performance of corporations.

Appendix

The characteristics of the main corporate governance systems around the world

System of corporate governance	Market-oriented	Network-oriented		
	Anglo-Saxon	Germany	Latin	Japan
Countries (1995 GDP US\$ bn; 1995 GDP per capita US\$ at current prices and exchange rates)	US (7,246; 25,512) UK (1,107; 17,468) Canada (569; 18,598) Australia (349; 18,072)	Germany (2,259; 25,133) The Netherlands (396; 21,733) Switzerland (287; 36,790) Sweden (246; 22,389) Austria (233; 24,670) Denmark (175; 28,181) Norway (127; 28,434) Finland (126; 19,106)	France (1,567; 22,944) Italy (1,119; 17,796) Spain (574; 12,321) Belgium (264; 22,515)	Japan (4,961; 36,732)
Concept of the firm	Instrumental, shareholder-oriented	Institutional	Institutional	Institutional
Board system	One-tier (executive and non-executive board)	Two-tier (executive and supervisory board)	Optional (France), in general one-tier	Board of directors; office of representative directors; office of auditors; de facto one-tier
Salient stakeholder(s)	Shareholders	Industrial banks (Germany), employees, in general oligarchic group	Financial holdings, the government, families, in general oligarchic group	City banks, other financial institutions, employees, in general oligarchic group
Importance of stock market in the national economy	High	Moderate/high	Moderate	High
Active external market for corporate control	Yes	No	No	No
Ownership concentration	Low	Moderate/high	High	Low/moderate
Performance-dependent executive compensation	High	Low	Moderate	Low
Time horizon of economic relationship	Short-term	Long-term	Long-term	Long-term

Source: Weimer and Pape (1999).

Note
The market-oriented corporate governance system is also called an 'outsider system', and the network-oriented systems are termed 'insider systems'.

3 The evolution of corporate governance in China

Introduction

In 1990, China became the first communist nation in the world to have a Stock Exchange with the formal establishment of the SHSE. Five Chinese companies became the first batch of firms listed on the official Exchange. This was a result of China's determination to establish a market-oriented economic system through economic reform and openness to the world, though doing so in a gradual evolutionary manner. The general principle guiding this gradualist approach to reform in China is that every new institutional change should be first implemented in one geographical area or industry sector, before being later put into wider application when the paramount leaders believe it is good for the rest of the economy. This top-down approach has been criticised by many but, at least until now, the Chinese economy appears to be performing well in comparison to other transitional economies, many of which have experienced serious difficulties and which look likely to experience further difficulties in the future.

As part of the overall programme of Chinese economic reform, the reform of the financial system had four main objectives:

1   To provide additional finance channels through which the Government might raise capital for investment projects.
2   To address the bad loans/banking problem inherited from the central planning era.
3   To address the issues of control and ownership as the Chinese authorities hoped to establish a 'modern enterprise system', which 'clarified property rights, designated authorities and responsibilities, separated government and enterprise functions, and established scientific management' (State Economic Reform Commission, 1994). The authorities believed that the introduction of a joint stock system, and more specifically the corporatisation of the SOEs, was the main vehicle to achieve this objective.
4   To build an institution that can undertake the role of financial intermediation, which is essential to a market economy.

In this chapter, we detail and analyse the emergence and evolution of the joint stock system in China. This involves a consideration both of the development of capital markets at the macro-level, and of the corporatisation of firms at the micro-level, with an emphasis on the formation of corporate governance mechanisms. The general reform experience of China will not be reviewed in any detail, as this has been already done by many other researchers. Instead, our objectives in this Chapter are two-fold. First, we argue that the emergence and evolution of the joint stock system is the result of fundamental economic forces. As long as a system has the potential for generating an improved economic performance, it will sooner or later replace an older, less efficient system (North, 1992). Second, we give a snapshot of current corporate governance in China, and thus provide a general background for the rest of the book.

The chapter is organised as follows. In the next section, we discuss the history of Chinese financial system reform. The following section 'SOE reform and corporatisation' goes deeper into the micro-level, to investigate the process of SOE reform and corporatisation. The formation of a new corporate governance structure is then considered in terms of the decision to go public and the IPO in the section 'Going public and the IPO', the relationship between ownership structure and corporate performance in the section 'The post-issue ownership structure', and capital structure the section with the same name. In 'Other governance mechanisms' we discuss other corporate governance mechanisms. The final section concludes.

Financial reform and the establishment of capital markets

Fiscal constraints and financial reform

The revitalisation and evolution of the financial markets in China can be regarded as a microcosm of the overall picture of economic reform in China. With the introduction of economic reform, the planners of the Chinese economy felt that the fostering and development of competitive commodity markets were constrained by the fact that economic resources were limited due to the lack of capital markets. All resources were allocated by the planners through a State investment mechanism. To satisfy the new demands for goods and services, the State had to finance new investment projects either through administratively-guided bank loans, or through funds directly from the public reserves. But the State found that it was increasingly difficult to do the latter as fiscal revenues were declining as a result of decentralisation. New sources of capital needed to be found to finance the capital-thirsty sectors, as was common in many developing economies.

Table 3.1 presents data on government fiscal revenues, fiscal deficits, and household savings, from 1978, on the eve of reform, to 1999. It is evident from the table that Central Government's fiscal revenues declined steadily as a proportion of GDP through the 22-year period. Meanwhile, the net fiscal revenues decreased from a surplus of RMB1.0 bn in 1978, to a huge deficit of RMB174.4 bn in 1999. As a result, the Government's role in investment became steadily weaker, and new capital expenditure had to be concentrated on major infrastructure

Table 3.1 Central government fiscal revenues and fiscal deficits, and household savings 1978–99

Year	Central government fiscal revenues		Fiscal deficit		Household savings	
	RMB bn	*As % of GDP*	*RMB bn*	*As % of GDP*	*RMB bn*	*As % of GDP*
1978	113.2	31.2	1.0	0.28	21	5.8
1980	116.0	25.7	−6.9	−1.53	40	8.9
1985	200.5	22.4	0.1	0.01	162.3	18.1
1990	293.7	15.8	−14.6	−0.79	712.0	38.4
1995	624.2	10.7	−58.2	−0.99	2,966.0	50.7
1996	740.8	10.9	−53.0	−0.78	3,852.0	56.7
1997	865.1	11.6	−58.2	−0.78	4,628.0	62.2
1998	987.6	12.6	−92.2	−1.18	5,340.8	68.2
1999	1,144.4	14.0	−174.4	−2.13	5,962.2	72.8

Source: *China Statistical Yearbook* (2000).

Note
The figures are in nominal terms.

projects rather than being spread through every sector of the economy. The Government thus relinquished control over investment in many industries, some of which had previously been closed to private investment.

One feasible alternative source of finance is household savings. A tendency for high savings is a common phenomenon in South East Asia, and has been cited as one of the factors that enabled these economies to grow so fast (Schmidt-Hebbel *et al.*, 1992; Miller, 1997, 1998). Household savings increased dramatically between 1978 and 1999, both in absolute quantity and as a proportion of GDP (Table 3.1). In 1999, savings amounted to 72.8 per cent of GDP. But a high savings rate means that the banks are the main channels through which individuals invest. The banks thus bear all the investment risks, and they have to pay the individual savers interest. This causes two problems. The first problem is the size of the interest payments, which were estimated to be at least RMB300 bn in 1995, or almost half of the Government's annual fiscal revenue (SSB, 1995). The second and more severe problem is that, because direct stock shareholdings are forbidden by commercial banks according to the Chinese law, all savings in the banks have to be channelled to enterprises in the form of bank loans. As there are only limited sources of equity capital, the capital structure of enterprises, and particularly the SOEs, is thus predominantly made up of debt. As a consequence, a debt chain is formed between enterprises, banks, and individual savers. The creditors of this debt have no means to monitor the performance of the enterprises, unless the enterprises are in financial distress. This leads to the equity-owners, whose investment only accounts for a small proportion of total assets, tending to abuse their rights by overinvestment (Jensen and Meckling,

1976). A consequence is that default of debt becomes inevitable when business is bad, and may lead to national financial crises, as happened in the 1997 Asian Financial Crisis and in Japan's ailing economy (Miller, 1998).

When fiscal revenue decreases, the Government finds that it is infeasible to provide all the capital needed by the rapidly growing economy from the State budget. The establishment of a joint-stock system requires not only the transformation of the SOEs at the firm level, but also a capital market where investment may be financed from non-State financial resources and where the risks and returns of firm projects may be efficiently priced. In a survey of 59 countries around the world, Jones *et al.* (1999) report that the resolution of fiscal problems is the principal motivation for the implementation of privatisation schemes.

The establishment and development of stock markets

Demirguc-Kunt and Levine (1996) suggest that, although economic growth in developing countries initially relies on banking finance, stock markets play a more and more important role in corporate finance as the economies grow. Stock Exchanges did exist in China before the establishment of the People's Republic in 1949, though on a very small scale. The emergence of a joint-stock system and Stock Exchanges in 'Old China' was in part due to the introduction of Western management technology, and in part due to the natural need for broad financial channels. Capitalists favour the pooling of capital so that a larger scale of production can be financed. But soon after the establishment of the People's Republic, the Stock Exchange in Shanghai, and others in smaller cities, were abolished on the grounds that the joint-stock system was intrinsically contradictory to socialist ideas. Thereafter, anyone advocating the idea of a Stock Exchange was liable to serious punishment.

With the advent of greater freedom in decision-making since reform, some pioneering non-State firms, such as the collectively-owned firms, began to seek equity from 'private' investors, usually the firm's employees. Beijing Tiaoqiao Department Store was the first one in China to issue 'equity' to its employees. The motivation for this was to finance business expansion, and to link the performance of the firm with that of its employees (World Bank, 1995). But the 'shares' may be better understood as a bond-type security – the firm promised a guaranteed rate of return over five years and redemption of the initial investment at the five-year 'maturity' date. The shares were also not transferable before the maturity date. More importantly, there was no voting right associated with each share, and the firm did not set up a Board of Directors. Notwithstanding the simplicity of the 'shares', and their variation from the accepted definition, the issue was still significant in that it was an attempt to raise capital from private sources in the name of 'shares' and to introduce an incentive scheme other than the then prevalent bonus scheme. A more standard share issue was made by Shanghai Feile Co. Though not transferable, the Feile shares had all the other usual features of shares – residual claim rights, infinite maturity, and voting rights. The importance of these two pioneering firms was that they made people tolerate, then accept, the concepts of the shareholding system. The policy-makers silently watched everything without significant obstruction.

Increasingly other firms followed suit to issue equity or bond-type securities. But the lack of transferability increased the liquidity risk, thus higher returns were required by the investors, with consequently higher capital costs to the issuing firms. To tackle the problem, some local non-banking financial institutions in Shanghai set up a trading room to facilitate the trading of shares. This was the embryo of the SHSE.

The SHSE was formally organised on 19 December 1990. There were just simple rules to guide the transactions of shares issued by the five companies listed initially, a number which rose to eight by the end of the year. All the transactions were dealt with by manual bookkeeping. On July 3 of the following year, SZSE was established, initially for the trading of the stocks of only two companies.

The operations of the two Stock Exchanges are now carried out independently and separately – listing and trading of shares are exclusively for shares listed on each exchange. Once a company has chosen to list and trade its shares on one Exchange, it must stay listed on that Exchange and no cross-listing and trading are allowed: a different practice from that in many major Stock Exchanges around the world. Up until 1998, the two Exchanges belonged to their respective municipalities (i.e. Shanghai and Shenzhen), though they were national Stock Exchanges in that they provided listing and trading services to companies from all over the country. However, in 1997, the State Council, under Premier Zhou Rongji, decided to take control over the two Exchanges from the municipalities, and placed them directly under the control of the China Securities Regulatory Commission (CSRC), making them truly national exchanges. The official explanation for the takeover was that it would make the Exchanges serve better the needs of the nation (CSRC, 1997), but it was rumoured that the real reason was the perceived collusion between the Exchanges and some institutions (including listed companies and investment houses) which, with the connivance of the municipal authorities, violated official regulations by manipulating shares prices. Currently, the two Exchanges trade not only shares, but also Treasury bills (T bills) or bonds, corporate bonds and funds. All transactions are carried out by a continuous auction mechanism, and information regarding all the deals is scriptless and stored in central computers in the Exchanges. In term of the efficiency of making transactions, they are as modern as any other major Exchange around the world, though there is much room for improvement in the observation of regulations by the market participants. Advanced financial products, such as stock options and stock market index options, are not yet allowed to be traded.

Table 3.2 gives a summary of the development of the Chinese stock markets in terms of the number of listed companies, and the total capital raised.

From 1990 to 2000, the number of Chinese listed companies increased from 10 to 1,121: that is, an annual rate of growth of 53.2 per cent. Total capital raised from the various investors summed to RMB749.91 bn by the end of August 2001.[1] The largest (IPO) was that of China Petroleum Chemical Corporation (Sinopec), which raised US$6 bn from international capital markets. The market

Table 3.2 The development of the Chinese stock markets

Year	National				Shanghai SE		Shenzhen SE	
	No. of listed companies	Total market value (RMB bn)	As % of GDP	Capital raised (RMB bn)	No. of listed companies	Total market value (RMB bn)	No. of listed companies	Total market value (RMB bn)
1990	10	3.1	0.18	0.43	8	1.2	2	1.9
1991	14	10.9	0.54	0.50	8	2.9	6	8.0
1992	54	104.8	3.93	9.41	30	55.8	24	49.0
1993	183	353.1	10.20	37.55	106	220.6	77	133.5
1994	291	369.1	7.92	32.68	171	260.0	120	109.1
1995	323	347.4	5.96	15.03	188	252.6	135	94.9
1996	530	984.2	14.52	42.51	293	547.8	237	436.5
1997	745	1,752.9	23.54	129.38	383	921.8	362	831.1
1998	851	1,950.6	24.90	84.15	438	1,062.6	413	888.0
1999	972	2,647.1	32.32	94.46	495	1,458.0	477	1,189.1
2000	1,121	4,809.0	55.28	207.10	606	2,693.0	515	2,116.0

Source: *China Securities Statistical Yearbook* (2000).

Notes
1 Listed companies including those with A, B, and H shares.
2 Total market value = total outstanding shares × share price.

capitalisation of the listed companies amounted to 55 per cent of China's GDP at the end of 2000. Currently, there are 45 mn investors in the stock markets. All the above figures show that the establishment of the modern corporation system and capital market has evolved from an experiment to an essential part of China's path towards a 'socialist market economy', and that the process has become non-reversible.

Foreign investment in the Chinese stock markets

China has been among the largest recipient countries of foreign investment since the implementation of its open-door policy. But nearly all the investments have been in the form of FDI (SSB, 2000). There has been comparatively little indirect investment via the stock markets, yet this provides greater liquidity for potential investors. B-shares fulfil two needs: they enable firms to raise foreign capital, and they allow foreign investors to make alternative investments with higher liquidity. To facilitate the inflow of foreign capital in the stock market, an issuer of B-shares must, besides satisfying the requirements stated in the securities regulations, meet the following conditions:

- It must have obtained approval from the relevant authorities for its use of foreign investment, or for its conversion into a foreign-funded enterprise.

- It must have a stable source of adequate foreign exchange income, and the total amount of its annual foreign exchange income must be sufficient to pay the annual dividends.
- The proportion of B-shares to the total number of shares must not exceed the ceiling determined by the relevant authority. The aggregate amount of shares to be issued is fixed in each year, and the total number of firms allowed to issue foreign shares is also limited.

Currently, there are 102 companies with B-shares listed on SHSE and SZSE, which have raised total capital amounting to US$4.93 bn (RMB41.16 bn, or 5.5 per cent of the total equity capital raised since the establishment of stock markets) by September 2001. The capitalisation and turnover of the B-share markets are only 2.2 and 3.2 per cent respectively of the corresponding figures for the stock markets in aggregate. The B-share markets thus play an insignificant role in capital-raising compared with the more important A share markets,[2] and the intended liquidity benefits are limited by the fact that trading can only take place on the B-share markets, and is limited to foreign investors.[3]

Remarks

Notwithstanding the fast speed of development of the Chinese stock markets since their establishment in terms of the number of listed companies, the markets, similar to those in other immature economies, still have a long way to go in terms of sophistication. The main focus of this book is corporate governance, so here we merely highlight some macroeconomic issues which are relevant to the reform of the Chinese financial system reform:

- The function of the Chinese stock markets is mainly to raise capital, either through an IPO or a subsequent Seasoned Equity Offering (SEO). Other possible functions such as the efficient allocation of resources, or the pricing of risk and returns, are carried out by the markets in mature economies, but have not yet been fully developed in China. This issue was pointed out by the World Bank in 1995, but is still pertinent 10 years after the formal establishment of both the major Exchanges.
- Whilst the Chinese Government has enthusiastically boosted the equity-raising function of the capital markets, additional sources of finance should also be pursued. For instance, the underdevelopment of the corporate bond market has restrained the flexibility of choice of finance by firms. The only source of debt capital is from the banks. Bank debt can involve additional monitoring over the firm, and an over-reliance on bank lending will reduce the efficiency of debt capital pricing (Yafeh and Yosha, 1995; Houston and James, 1996). As Miller (1998, p. 14) points out, relying on bank loans instead of public debt markets is a disaster-prone strategy requiring enormous amounts of direct government supervision to reduce the frequency of crises.

- More fundamentally, during the process of establishment of a market economy, the Chinese policy-makers have been seeking a mechanism that improves the corporate governance from the external market, but they appear to be constrained by the limitations of the Anglo-American and German–Japanese models. On the one hand, dominant State shareholdings have to be retained so as to ensure control over the firm by the State, thus giving rise to an insider-based governance structure as stylised in the German–Japanese model. On the other hand, the over-dispersed outside shareholdings and the active markets for shares resemble the Anglo-American model, but with the lack of a market for corporate control to correct for the failure of corporate governance in poorly-performing firms. Certainly it takes time to develop a good market mechanism, and the final Chinese model will inevitably have its own distinctive features, but the potential costs in the meanwhile are massive and careful planning is essential.

SOE reform and corporatisation

A more important motivation for the authorities to implement financial reform was to resolve the problem of a lack of incentives in manufacturing production. This had been easily resolved in the agricultural sector, by simply allocating farmland to individual households, though this policy did entail some costs particularly linked to the loss of scale economies. But it did ease, in just a couple of years, the problem of food shortages that had troubled China for decades. Such a solution was not feasible in the industrial sectors, as dividing the means of production was not a sensible way of linking the output to individual workers. This is a problem which has taxed practitioners and theorists not only in centrally-planned economies, but also in the West (Alchian and Demsetz, 1972). The problem is understandably more severe in centrally-planned economies, in that there are no clearly-defined ultimate owners who can monitor the performance of the firms, nor are there competitive capital and commodity markets to punish poorly-performed firms through bankruptcy or takeover.

The economic performance of the SOEs was improved during early 1980s by the introduction of the bonus system (Xu and Zhuang, 1996). This was based on the belief by the authorities that the poor performance was caused by the lack of an appropriate incentive mechanism to individual employees, including top management. But soon the authorities found that the bonus system produced a ratchet effect – all decisions to increase the bonus were welcomed, but to punish firms or individual workers for poor performance by reducing or removing bonuses was simply not politically possible.

Contract responsibility systems were introduced in most large and medium-sized State industrial enterprises during 1986–97. The system was officially intended to place (governmental) ownership at arm's length to enterprise management, so allowing more decision-making space to the latter (Child, 1994). In the contract, the firm hands over an agreed amount of annual profit and tax for which they have contracted. It was permitted to retain a proportion of any surplus it achieved above the contracted level. Also, the firm guaranteed to invest to increase asset values and to develop technology by an agreed amount, using retained profits during the period of the contract. But substantial collusion soon emerged between the Directors of the companies, and the Heads of the supervising government departments, leading to widespread corruption (Hay *et al.*, 1994). The Directors found that it was easier and quicker to reward themselves by simply transferring the firms' assets to their own firms. The lesson was that it is not feasible for the authorities simply to relinquish control to the firms' managers in an attempt to improve performance. Rather a new relationship between the State, as owner, and the firm needed to be developed. Consequently, in 1993, the National People's Congress passed a resolution to establish a Modern Enterprise System, indicating a commitment to long-lasting progress towards a market economy.

It was evident that the policy-makers in China clearly understood that a clear-cut system of property rights was required as a prerequisite for widening the finance channels and permitting the introduction of non-State capital into the SOEs. This, in turn, required the new institutional arrangement of a joint-stock system.

With the endorsement by the Fourteenth National Congress of the Chinese Communist Party in 1993, the corporatisation of the SOEs and their listing on the Stock Markets was carried out very quickly (see Table 3.2), only three years after small-scale experiments had been carried out on collectively owned enterprises (COEs) and selected SOEs. The key features of this initiative were the approval of diversified forms of ownership by State, private and foreign investors, which would compete on equal terms in the marketplace, and the introduction of a framework for the modern corporate governance of State-owned firms. The resolution was broadened and accelerated after the Fifteenth National Congress in the autumn of 1997, when it was announced that smaller State-owned enterprises would be effectively privatised by converting them into various forms of non-State and non-collective ownership, especially stock co-operative companies owned by their employees.

For the large and medium-sized SOEs, the favoured organisational structure was the corporation (Hussain and Chen, 1999). 'Corporatisation' involves the setting up of an independent legal entity, with the State as owner. Corporatisation usually involves commercialisation of activities so that public enterprise operations are governed by commercial law like private enterprises. The original capital must be audited and registered, and the owners of the capital must be identified. In cases where all the assets belong to different State agencies, the assets still need to be attributed accordingly. For example, if the assets of a firm are invested jointly by the Provincial Government and the Municipal Government, then the assets must be so recorded, and representatives must be assigned from the respective owners, even though both are State agencies. A typical process of corporatisation may be summarised as follows:

- Asset assessment and verification. This work is carried out by chartered accounting firms.
- Identification of owners and allocation of ownership. For historical reasons, firms may have received finance from different State investors, through different channels, and for different objectives. There may be disputes about the

classification of some capital. For example, some debt capital previously issued by State banks might be classified more properly as equity capital.[4]

- Choice of company form. According to the 1994 Company Law, the enterprise may choose to be either a limited liability company, or a joint stock company.
- Establishment of the Board of Directors. If the enterprise does choose to become a joint stock company, then the first general shareholder meeting will be required to approve the company charter and the appointment of the Directors.
- Appointment of Senior Managers. The Board of Directors appoints the Chief Executive Office (CEO),[5] and approves the CEO's nominations for deputy CEO and other senior managers.
- The new company begins business.

The corporatisation of firms which had previously been solely-owned leads to a new corporate structure, as well as to the formation of a new financing vehicle as many firms choose to get listed and raise new capital from the stock market. Further, the corporatisation of SOEs and other firms introduces a governance structure within which multiple owners jointly share finance and control, a phenomenon never seen before in China's planned economy. Each owner needs to both co-operate and compete with the other owners to ensure both the protection of their investment, and a good financial return. The separation of ownership and control renders the situation more complex, especially in the case of an economy in continuous transition, where old practices and laws are being abolished and new ones established. Experience shows that constructing a workable system of ownership rights is a complex problem, even in mature and developed markets, and has been the subject of heated debate in many countries.

Going public and the IPO

The primary aim of corporatisation for a firm is to raise funds for their business by going public (World Bank, 1995). In China, the policy-makers have an additional objective, namely the transformation of the governance structure of the firm by introducing monitoring by the capital markets. Furthermore, an implicit motive of the policy-makers is to privatise at least some of the previous SOEs.

This section will consider the development and current conditions of equity issue in China, by focusing on the various changes in the system for the approval of equity issues, in the issue procedures and methods, and in the rules for setting offer prices. Finally, a brief analysis is provided of the implications for corporate governance of going public.

The approval system for an equity issue

The system of approval for equity issue in China shows traces of its origins in a planned economic system, but has also been marked by the continual adjustment of regulations and the adoption of new laws. The approval of a share issue to the public involves a two-stage quota system. At the first stage, the aggregate amount of new shares to be issued each year is determined by a quota set by the State Planning Committee, the Central Bank and the CSRC. The quotas are then distributed to individual Provinces or Ministries that own key SOEs. In the years 1993–97, the quotas were RMB5, 5.5, 15, and 30 bn shares respectively. At the second stage, each Province or Ministry chooses the firms in the light of certain stated criteria. These criteria reflect the central Security Regulatory Authorities' perceived regional development needs, and provincial differences in production structure and industrial base. Within each regional quota, the local Security Regulatory Authorities invite enterprises to request a listing, and make a selection based on criteria which combine good performance as well as sector development objectives. Infrastructure enterprises, especially those specialising in electricity and water supply, have often been given priority for approval (Su and Fleisher, 1999). The local Securities Regulatory body then forwards the applications of the chosen firms to the CSRC for final approval, though this is usually a routine matter.

To ensure the quality of the firms to be listed, the CSRC introduced a series of new directives in 1995, which put forth several additional requirements that firms would need to meet before a formal listing, even though their applications might already have been approved.

- The first directive required that all issuing firms operate for one year before formally issuing shares to the public, so that their performance might be monitored during this 'probationary period'.
- The second was that, during this period, all directors, senior managers and supervisors needed to pass examinations organised by the CSRC in order to test their capability and knowledge of management, and their understanding of relevant laws, regulations and policies.
- The third was that the issuing firms should provide their supervising department with profitability forecasts for all the projects which were to be financed by the capital raised.
- The fourth was that the underwriters should coach the issuing firms for one year on the matter of issue procedure, to ensure a successful issue.[6]

The approval system has been widely criticised for the intrinsic drawbacks in the selection and application process of issuing firms. First, the requirement that IPO reports be verified by local governments is likely to promote interventions from governments, and to blur the relationship between the administration and the enterprises. Second, the whole process of approval takes a long time to conclude. As a result, firms that have obtained approval usually hurried to a formal listing regardless of market conditions. Finally and most seriously, the exclusive and non-transparent policy implemented by the CSRC and its associated administrative organisations was the source of widespread corruption as firms pursued approval to raise much-needed capital. The firms were either forced to offer bribes to secure the success of their applications, or to construct fraudulent profitability figures, or both. The system was also biased toward the SOEs, and good firms with other ownership structures found it difficult to compete on an equal basis. This undermined one of the basic functions of capital markets as a means of resource allocation.

In March 1999, the issue quota system was abolished, though any unfulfilled quotas set earlier remained valid until they were used up. A new approval procedure was introduced which was based on a 'verification system'. According to the new regulations, any firm that is able to achieve certain pre-determined standards can apply for listing on the Stock Exchanges. These standards relate to the applying firm's business line, its financial strength, quality and prospects, the minimum number of shares to be issued, and the offer price. Listing is authorised by a scrutiny committee consisting of professionals and experts. The transition from an administrative approval system with annual quotas, to a verification system reflects progress towards a market economy system. However, there is still a strong element of administrative intervention, and much still needs to be done before the system is similar to that in the West, where the financial authorities only ensure that the disclosed information is genuine and the offer price is set by the firm itself according to market conditions.

The procedure and methods for an equity issue

On the more technical aspects of issue, there are a number of steps a firm must take after it has been selected for an Initial Public Offering, but before market trading begins. Some typical steps include

- the setting of offer prices by the lead underwriter, according to the regulations of the CSRC;
- the publication of a prospectus in newspapers, and the selection of underwriters;
- the purchase of application forms by prospective investors;
- the choice of application method. The firm needs to choose one of three major application methods, as will be discussed in more detail later;
- the delivery of shares to the lottery winners, after payment has been made.

The choice of application method is central, in that it affects the chances of success of individual investors and hence the eventual distribution of share ownership. All three methods involve a lottery mechanism as the primary means of share allocation, but the mechanism has undergone several substantial changes over the years.

Before October 1992, the Security Regulatory Authorities designed a lottery system based on a pre-announced fixed number of application forms. Each retail investor was allowed to purchase a limited number of lottery forms from the Central Bank or its subsidiaries. The lottery winners were entitled to a certain number of shares per winning form. With the number of lottery forms pre-determined, the odds of winning the lottery was known to investors. But the frantic demand for shares by investors made the forms the passport to an instant gain, and this led, not surprisingly, to the corruption of people who had easy access to the forms. In recognition of the problem, the CSRC introduced, in December 1992 and August 1993, two new lottery mechanisms to replace the old one. One mechanism was based on an unlimited number of application forms. The issue agency sold as many lottery forms at a low cost as investors were willing to buy. The other lottery mechanism was based on savings deposit certificates. Investors were required to deposit a certain quantity of funds into a special saving account when submitting an application for shares, and these funds could not be withdrawn until the lottery was completed. Deposits in these special savings accounts earned relatively low interest. Both new methods imposed a cost on speculative applications by investors. Under all the lottery mechanisms, the IPO price is determined before the publication of the prospectus.

In April 1994, two new auction mechanisms were introduced. Under the first auction mechanism, an issuer set an initial price and investors were required to bid for the price and quantity. The final offer price was set at the level where the accumulated quantities demanded by investors equalled the total number of new shares available. But soon the authorities found the new methods problematic. The former method, when oversubscribed, would give rise to a high offer price and subsequently to a negative return during the first trading days. Resentful investors put pressure on the authorities to abolish the methods after the IPOs of a mere three firms. Under the second auction mechanism, the IPO price was fixed and investors were invited to bid for the quantity of shares. In case of oversubscription, all investors were guaranteed a certain amount of shares and the remaining shares were distributed in proportion to investors' bids. The latter method led to a widely-dispersed distribution of shareholdings – in several cases, investors were offered only tens of shares. This increased transaction costs for the small investors – they had to pay a minimum commission for the transfer of a mere 10 shares.

Since then, and based on past experience, the CSRC has introduced three new methods, all with pre-determined and announced offer prices. All three methods require investors to set aside full deposits according to the number of shares for which they are bidding, and the offer price. Each investor is then given a series number, and waits for the results of the lottery. The winners receive their shares, whilst the unsuccessful investors are refunded their money within eight days of the lottery. The proceeds raised in the IPO are then transferred to the account of the issuing firm. Each investor can bid for a maximum of 1 per cent of the total number of shares.

The differences between the three methods mainly concern the agency through which the bidding takes place. In the first method, the bidding is effected through the national securities trading network. This is very sophisticated, even in comparison with developed markets, and this method has become increasingly popular as it is highly efficient in both cost and security terms. The second method is carried out through local issue agencies, which take both the deposit and issue certificates with series numbers to investors. The lottery is carried out in a local public place, with official notaries as witnesses. The agencies keep the deposits, and distribute the share certificates to the successful shareholders. The advantage of the second method is that it can attract new local investors to join share-trading activities. The third method is similar to the second one in that the IPO is effected though local agencies but the difference is that, after the lottery, the unsuccessful bidders have to leave their funds in the banks for 3–6 months.

In this and the following chapters, we categorise for simplicity the issue methods as either bidding through the national trading network, or bidding through a local issue agency – see Figure 3.1.

The pricing of the IPO

The pricing of an IPO is a critical step as it directly affects both the wealth distribution between the initial and the outside owners, and also the success of the equity issue. Thus IPO pricing is a matter which not only involves the issuing firm and the underwriters, but also regulatory bodies around the world. Prior to the establishment of the Chinese stock markets, most equity was issued at face value. From the early 1990s to March 1999, the offer price was set under the strict regulation of the CSRC. If the price was set too low, then the State-owned assets were depleted. If too high, then there was a crash of the post-issue stock markets. The benchmark for pricing was the price–earnings (P/E) ratio, though with some adjustment and variation.

In the early 1990s, the CSRC required that all offer prices should be determined solely by a P/E ratio of 13 (SHSE, 2001). But earnings could be calculated arbitrarily by the issuing firms, hence they could justify a range of offer prices using the set P/E ratio. From 1994 onwards, the CSRC maintained the P/E ratio as a benchmark, but insisted that earnings per share should be calculated on the basis of past accounting profit figures together with a prediction of future profitability. And the CSRC permitted a range of P/E ratios between 15 and 20. This rigid offer pricing thus ignored other important aspects of asset pricing, such as industrial characteristics, firm size, and the potential for future growth. We leave this issue and its implications to be discussed in more detail in the next chapter.

In March 1999, the CSRC amended the regulations on IPO pricing to a more market-oriented approach.[7] Thereafter, the issuing company and the underwriter had to submit an IPO pricing report to the CSRC, and the offer price had to be agreed by the CSRC. But the firm was allowed to consider factors other than the P/E ratio in setting the offer price. The pricing reports of new IPOs should thus include industry analysis, company analysis, and an analysis of current market conditions such as the share prices of comparable companies. The offer price should reflect these factors, and be agreed initially by the issuing firm and the lead underwriter. After reviewing the report, the CSRC sets a narrow price range within which the issuing firm can make adjustments according to market conditions. The effect of the new rules is that the average P/E ratio of companies listed

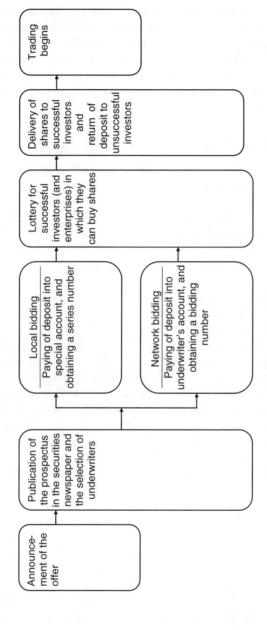

Figure 3.1 The procedure for an IPO on the Chinese stock markets.

after March 1999 has increased substantially, from the previous range of 15–20 to around 30.[8] Once an offer price has been set, it is announced in the prospectus, together with the numbers of shares available to the public, and cannot then be changed.

It is noteworthy to point out that an IPO price ceiling is not unique to China. In the United States, the SEC regulations specify that new offer prices should reflect a maximum P/E ratio of 200, and prices are usually filed two weeks in advance of the actual offering, although they can be adjusted in some cases. This point is important, as it will be argued in subsequent chapters that both the theories and empirical findings on IPO underpricing in developed economies are applicable to developing countries such as China.

The role of the underwriters and the costs of an equity issue

The underwriters play a key role in the success of an IPO (Rock, 1986). There are broadly two possible arrangements which can be made between the issuing company and the underwriters: one based on a 'firm commitment' and the other on 'best effort'. Under the former, the underwriter guarantees a minimum level of proceeds from the IPO, based on an agreed offer price and number of shares, and regardless of how many shares are sold. If not all the shares are sold, then the underwriter will take over the remaining shares at a price a little lower than the market price. But if demand is higher than anticipated, the underwriter can issue a further 15 per cent of shares and earn extra commission. The alternative is the 'best effort' arrangement, under which the underwriter helps the issuing firm to issue the shares, but does not guarantee a full sale. The issuing firms may then find that some shares cannot be sold to the public, and that the proceeds raised may be smaller than anticipated.[9] Clearly the 'firm commitment' arrangement is safer for the issuing firm, but riskier for the underwriter.

In China, there are a number of features related to the role of underwriters in the IPO process which should be stressed. First, all IPOs are made under a 'firm commitment' arrangement. This is not a problem for the underwriters, as almost all IPOs have been oversubscribed and the shares have performed well afterwards. But the underwriters are not permitted to issue additional shares, even when there is substantial demand. Second, there is little competition for underwriting business, unlike in the West, since all Provinces and major cities in China have set up their own securities companies, which are owned either by the Provincial or the Municipal Government and which undertake both IPOs and any subsequent SEO by local firms. As a consequence, the choice of underwriter in China is usually made according to the issuing firm's geographic location – the issuing firm will only employ the local securities company, either because of their relationship or because of pressure from the local government.

According to the CSRC, the underwriting costs include the commissions paid to the underwriters, to the accounting firms for auditing, asset assessment and verification, and profit forecasting, and to the lawyers for legal consultations. The costs of document preparation, printing, dissemination, prospectus publication, and advertisement are not listed as issue fees. The underwriting fees, which constitute the largest part of the total direct costs of IPOs, are strictly regulated by the CSRC. The standard charge is linked to the issuing method. For an IPO through the national trading network, the fee is

- 1.5–3 per cent of proceeds, when the proceeds are smaller than RMB200 mn;
- 1.5–2.5 per cent of proceeds, when the proceeds are between RMB200 and 300 mn;
- 1.5–2 per cent of proceeds, when the proceeds are between RMB300 and 400 mn; and
- a maximum fee of RMB9 mn for an IPO with proceeds of more than RMB400 mn.

For an issue through a local agency, the maximum commission per share is limited to 0.1 RMB, and the total commission to RMB5 mn (CSRC, 2000).

Interestingly, the underwriters in China also are responsible for some duties both during the IPO and after the issue, which are not common in the West. One of them is to provide a one-year training programme to the issuing firm prior to formal listing. This is to ensure, according to the CSRC, that the company to be listed is well prepared to meet the requirements of publicly listed companies (e.g. information disclosure, accounting standards, general meetings, and Boards of Directors). The effects of such an arrangement are uncertain, since there is not much for the underwriters to do when everything has already been arranged by the local government.

The implications for corporate governance of going public

The IPO and the process of going public are not merely means of raising finance, but also entail a change of governance structure and mechanism. In particular, management is exposed to new discipline from the market, as intended by the decision-makers, and listed companies are subject to regulations on information disclosure, to public criticism, and to fluctuations of stock prices.

A further implication, which will be explored in depth in Chapter 4, is the impact of the initial ownership structure upon the underpricing of the IPO. The underpricing of the IPO may be used to achieve multiple objectives. It may be used to signal the quality of the firm (Grinblatt and Hwang, 1989; Welch, 1989), to increase liquidity (Booth and Chua, 1996), or to maintain control over the firm as a dispersed outside shareholding makes takeover harder (Brennan and Frank, 1997).

Notwithstanding the requirement that the fraction of shares offered to the public during an IPO should be at least 25 per cent, the Chinese Government still maintains control over many previously State-owned firms. The Government has introduced a variety of share categories, so that ownership of the SOEs is dispersed between the Government itself, other SOEs, the firms' own employees, the domestic public and foreign investors (Table 3.3).

Table 3.3 The listing requirements on various stock exchanges

Exchange	Minimum number of shares in public float[a]	Minimum number of public shareholders
SHSE	10,000,000	1,000
SZSE	10,000,000	1,000
NYSE	1,100,000	2,000
AMEX and NASDAQ NMS	1,000,000	400
or	500,000	800[b]
NASDAQ (small cap market)	100,000	300

Sources: For flotation on the SHSE and the SZSE, see CSRC: *The Provisional Regulations on Stock Issuance* (1996); for floatation on the US market, see the *NYSE Fact Book 1988, AMEX Fact Book 1993*, and *NASDAQ Fact Book* 1989 as cited in Booth and Chua (1996).

Notes
a Exclusive of the holdings of officers, directors, controlling shareholders, and other concentrated or family holdings.
b If a firm has 500,000 shares and maintains a constant daily trading volume of 2,000 shares. The minimum number of public shareholders is 400.

   Whereas in the United States, the financial authorities impose Exchange listing requirements to increase liquidity (Booth and Chua, 1996), the regulations in China should be interpreted as an attempt to keep control. A scrutiny of the dataset used in the empirical chapters reveals that the initial ownership structures of the Chinese listed companies are dominated by State or institutional shareholders – see Table 4.6 in Chapter 4. Among the 467 firms, the Bureau of State Asset Management (BSAM) is the largest shareholder in about 5 per cent of the sample, and State-owned institutions control 40 per cent. Domestic institutions are the largest shareholder in only 7 per cent of the firms, and there are no individual shareholders among the top five positions. The three main groups dominated the control of the listed companies with 52 per cent of the total shares. We investigate the link between the ownership structure and IPO underpricing, an area of research which has been neglected in previous work, in Chapter 4.

The post-issue ownership structure

The ownership structure of a firm raises issues of corporate governance, in that it gives rise to a distinct structure of profit-risk sharing in the business, and to a distinct monitoring role for the shareholders over the management. An uneven distribution of shares leads to the existence of large shareholders, which may play a direct role in monitoring management. In contrast, a more evenly distributed ownership structure, with many small shareholders, implies a greater delegation of the policing role to the market, with the shareholders signalling their opinions by buying or selling their shares. Chapter 5 investigates the link between the ownership structure and corporate performance, to assess the effectiveness of the monitoring role of large shareholders.

The distribution of shareholdings

Three stylised models of the governance structure of listed companies after corporatisation and IPO are illustrated in Figure 3.2.

Model I is depicted in Figure 3.2(a) and is the most common in listed companies. It is characterised by the fact that the State-owned institutions and other institutions jointly hold the non-tradable shares, and thus have control over the firms. The State-owned institutions are in turn owned by the BSAM.

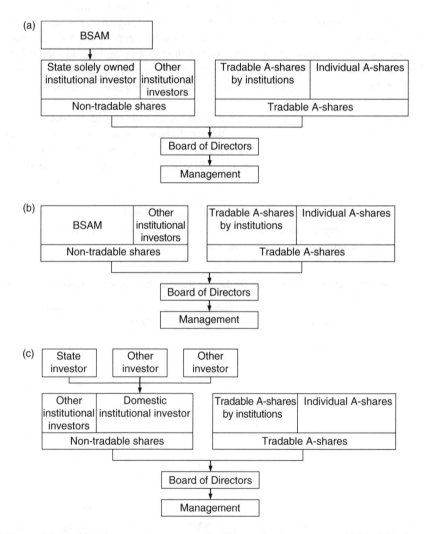

Figure 3.2 Models of governance structure in Chinese listed companies: (a) Model I: State dominating indirectly; (b) Model II: State dominating directly; (c) Model III: Domestic investors dominating directly.

Model II – see Figure 3.2(b) – involves the direct ownership of shares by the BSAM, at different administrative levels, and this can be regarded as direct State shareholding. Model III – see Figure 3.2(c) – has some domestic institutional shareholders. Domestic institutions are those with the greatest variety of shareholders: State agencies, private shareholders, COEs, or firms with foreign investors in non-financial industries. In all three models, there are both tradable shares and non-tradable shares. The non-tradable shares are more numerous.

Table 3.4 provides an analysis of the dominant shareholders in 372 companies listed on SHSE, and 347 companies listed on SZSE. For each exchange, the table provides data on the numbers of companies where the largest, the top five, and the top ten shareholders hold shareholdings in the designated ranges. On the SHSE, for instance, the single largest shareholder controls, on average, over 45 per cent of the outstanding shares, whilst the top five and the top ten shareholders control 59 and 62 per cent respectively. There are 156 firms (42 per cent of the total) where the largest single shareholder holds 50 per cent or more of the outstanding shares.

A careful study of the table reveals that the smaller shareholders hold substantially smaller shareholdings. Whereas the single largest shareholder accounts for 45 per cent of shares on average, the top five hold 59 per cent and the top ten only hold 62 per cent. These figures indicate clearly the dominant role of the single largest shareholder in many companies. The uneven distribution originates in the initial ownership structure after the IPO, and from the fact that the non-tradable shares cannot change hands on the open market (though they can be privately transferred between institutional entities, though this is quite difficult in practice). Nearly all the largest shareholders are institutional shareholders, which may be

Table 3.4 The shareholdings held by the largest shareholder in Chinese listed companies, 1997

% of shareholding	SHSE			SZSE		
	Top 1	Top 5	Top 10	Top 1	Top 5	Top 10
(0–10)	3	1	1	5	0	0
[10–20)	22	3	2	24	3	1
[20–30)	62	6	6	68	10	3
[30–40)	60	30	12	66	28	24
[40–50)	69	55	52	47	55	41
[50–60)	64	85	81	55	73	73
[60–70)	55	103	100	45	96	96
[70–80)	31	70	94	34	70	93
[80–90)	6	19	24	3	12	16
Total listed companies		372			347	
Means	45.54	59.11	62.07	43.91	58.41	61.56

Source: *A Guide for Investment in Shanghai and Shenzhen Securities Exchanges* (1997) (*Securities Times*, 1998).

controlled by the State. This may be important as domestic institutions may have economic objectives, but State-owned institutions need to take into account other social responsibilities such as employment generation and local development. The data for companies listed on SZSE reveal similar patterns.

The institutional shareholders

Many domestic institutions hold significant numbers of the shares traded on the Stock Exchanges. According to China Securities News,[10] the numbers of shares held by domestic institutional investors in China's two A-share markets had risen 26.5 per cent from 282,000 at the end of 1999 to 356,700 by the end of July 2001. Of this total, the shares owned by the institutional investors on SZSE grew from 107,200 to 129,100, an increase of 20.4 per cent. Those on the SHSE surged 30.2 per cent from 174,800 to 227,600. The increased number of institutional investors in China has been accompanied by a rise in shareholder activism.

In developed economies, institutional shareholdings predominate. In the United Kingdom, for example, institutional shareholdings increased steadily from less than one-third of the total in 1963, to two-thirds in 1993. It has been suggested that the active participation of institutional investors in the corporate governance mechanism can improve corporate performance, both due to the significant investment of funds and the input of professional knowledge (Cadbury, 1992). Whilst the appropriate role of institutional shareholders is still under debate in China, many regard institutional shareholdings as a way of establishing sound corporate governance. One role is to stabilise the highly volatile stock markets, as institutional investors are hoped to be strategic investors pursuing long-term returns rather than short-term profits, thus reducing short-term trading activities and mitigating substantial fluctuations in stock prices. A second role is that a large shareholding and the possession of investment expertise enable the institutions to play an active part in corporate governance.

But the role of institutional investors is questionable if they themselves are State-owned or State holding companies: by what mechanism can they monitor the managers of companies that they don't own? As Coffee (1991, p. 1331) pointed out,

> The problem of who will guard the guardian is a timeless one, but it is par-ticularly complicated when the proposed guardian is the institutional investor. Not only do the same problems of agency cost arise at the institu-tional investors level, but there are persuasive reasons for believing that some institutional investors are less accountable to their 'owners' than are corpo-rate managements to their shareholders. Put simply, the usual mechanisms of corporate accountability are either unavailable or largely compromised at the institutional level.

The question of which of the three models is best for corporate performance will be considered further in Chapter 5.

Capital structure

The traditional view of debt is that it serves as an alternative form of capital financing to equity. However, the development of debt theory sheds light on this understanding of debt. The first financial reforms of China involved the adjustment of firms' capital structure. Indeed, it can be argued that the path of economic reform in China can be viewed in terms of the adjustment of laws and policies with regard to debt and equity, both in the aggregate economy and in firms. On one hand, the pressure to make interest and principal repayments on debt forced the decision-makers to seek equity investment from non-State investors when facing fiscal constraints. On the other hand, the relinquishment of control over the firms to the non-State equity investors raised concerns about the socialist characteristics of the Chinese economy.

Concern about the debt burden was justifiable. As Miller (1998) has pointed out, the importance of capital structure can be observed directly from the South Korean and Japanese experience. Both economies are still struggling to solve the problems of debt accumulated from their over-dependence on debt during their periods of economic takeoff. The huge debts of the banks as a result of State policy towards the non-performing corporate groups constitute serious threats to their success. Given similar policy in China towards the market economy, it is natural to be concerned about the capital structure of listed companies in China.

Financial reform and the capital structure of Chinese firms

In a centrally planned economy, the distinction between debt and equity in a State-owned firm is not significant – since the State provides all the capital that the firm needs. At the macro level, the State borrows debt from households in the form of family savings, to complement other important sources of capital including fiscal revenue. The economy is organised like one huge company. The function of the firm is as a production unit, rather than as a self-sustained entity, and the cost of capital is not a matter of concern. Investment thirst and soft budget constraints are common (Kornai, 1980).

The dynamic of capital structure development in Chinese firms is illustrated schematically in Figure 3.3. In the pre-reform period, the capital structure of firms involved zero debt and 100 per cent State equity – point A in Figure 3.3. The State took all the profits (if any) earned by the firms, and compensated all the losses. The profits and losses were merely symbolic because of the lack of any measure of capital cost. Point B refers to the period from 1978 to 1980, when the SOE reforms only focused on giving a certain degree of autonomy to firms with regard to production quotas and bonuses. All working capital was still supplied by the State banks according loan credits.

Whilst providing SOEs with more autonomy, the State also introduced more constraints. In 1981, the provision of free working capital by the banks was replaced by loans with interest charges at rates determined by the Central Bank. The capital structure then shifted from point B to point C: all new capital was

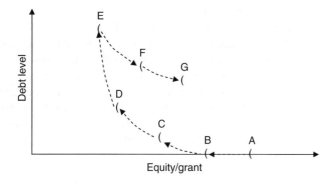

Figure 3.3 The experience of financial reform, debt level, and governance structure in China.

Source: Tam (1999), p. 42.

Notes
A = Pre-reform unified income and expenditure system;
B = 1978–80: enterprise autonomy was expanded;
C = 1981–83: experimentation with some forms of contract responsibility system;
D = 1984–85: introduction of li-gai-shui (tax substituting for profit remission);
E = 1987–91: nationwide adoption of contract responsibility systems;
F = 1986: local experiments with shareholding systems;
G = 1992–present: corporatisation of SOEs, shareholding regulations, proclamation of *Company Law*, national experiment in setting up modern corporations.

injected in the form of debt accumulating since point B. The objective was to curb excessive demand for working capital when it was free of charge. For the first time, firms felt the pressure of interest payments, though loan defaults did not necessary lead to bankruptcy. Since then, a series of financial reforms have been introduced and new capital, either working capital or fixed capital, must be sought from the banks within the national credit plan (Tam, 1999), except in the case of some key projects. From 1987, the contract responsibility system was adopted nationwide. One part of the contract requires that new capital should be raised either through retained profits or bank loans, and this gave rise to the highest national aggregate debt ratio – point E.

Before the introduction of shareholding, the 'equity' provided by the State should be more accurately described as a grant. Equity requires a return according to the risk it faces. In contrast, the State grants were used to achieve certain objectives required by the State, some economic but others social or political. The introduction of shareholding systems in some regions opened up new sources of capital, and effectively reduced the aggregate debt level to point F. Since 1992, the large-scale corporatisation of the SOEs has further reduced the debt level for two reasons. The first is that most of the new capital injected into SOEs has taken the form of equity, instead of debt or grants. The State is the provider of some of this new capital, but the ownership is clearly registered and traced.

The second reason is the participation of investors other than the State, including individuals, foreign investors, COEs, and TVEs.

These new investment sources have not only provided equity capital for the firms, but have also reduced the debt level. According to the SHSE Annual Report (2000), many firms repay a part of their previous debt with the proceeds raised during their IPO. Our data show that the debt level, measured by the ratio of total debt to total assets, of 711 listed companies in all industries was 43 per cent in 1997, compared to a figure of 62 per cent for all other firms (SSB, 2000). Although the two percentages are not strictly comparable due to the different numbers of firms in different industries and of different sizes, the magnitude of the difference is both striking and suggestive.

The monitoring role of banks

A stylised fact about the capital structure of Chinese firms is that the vast majority of corporate debt is privately placed debt in the form of bank loans. The total amount was RMB9,773 bn in 1999, and priority was given to State-owned or State-controlled firms who received over 70 per cent of total bank loans (SSB, 2000). Public corporate debt markets are not well developed in China. Publicly-placed debt, with merely twelve corporate bonds, only amounted to RMB17.9 bn with a market value of RMB15.3 bn. This accounts for just 6 per cent of the stock market in terms of total capital raised, and 0.6 per cent in terms of stock market capitalisation.[11]

The theory of corporate governance regards debt as a governance mechanism in that it provides additional monitoring over management. Furthermore, the placement structure of debt has implications for governance. Privately-placed debt, usually bank loans, enables the debt-holders (the banks) to monitor the corporations more directly and collectively than in the case of publicly-placed debt, where the scattered debt-holders do not have the same power over their loans (Lehn and Toft, 1996).

The Chinese Government has been trying to adopt the Anglo-American model of corporate governance, which is characterised by the protection of minority shareholders and the prohibition of shareholding by banks. Yet the Government also introduced a 'main bank system', based on the idealised Japanese model, in its financial reform package of 1996. This system is supposed to provide the participating main bank with a more comprehensive capability to monitor the performance of the enterprise. According to the *Interim Regulations for the Administration of the Main Bank*,[12] the firm is obliged to disclose information to the banks about the firm's major business and financial activities, and to accept monitoring from the main bank. The bank has the right to audit all the dealings between the firm and other banking institutions, and to punish the firm if there are any activities by the firm breaching the terms of establishment of main banking relations. For its part, the bank is supposed to give priority to the firm with regard to the provision of reasonable loans as well as other financial services. Officially, the idea was to promote a major monitoring role for the designated main banks to restrain the 'inside control' behaviour within large SOEs, and to develop a stable bank-centred financial environment for the enterprises to become modern corporations and to show better performance (Tam, 2000).

However, the realisation of the above objectives for the 'main bank system' was hampered by the fact that the choice of main bank is made by the firm's supervising Government department. The direct monitoring effect of the main bank is thus weakened by the intervention of the supervising department. It would be premature to conclude that the 'main bank system' will not function effectively in China, and there are obvious differences between the Chinese and Japanese realities. However, the Japanese model has been the subject of criticism on the grounds that banks have provided loans to their related firms for low-return projects, which this has led to a decade-long recession which shows no prospect of an end in near future (Miller, 1997).

Other governance mechanisms

A system of corporate governance exists in both an exogenous environment such as the political, legal and cultural framework, and an endogenous one defined by the Board of Directors, the incentive scheme for senior managers, and the structures of compensation, supervision and union membership. In the Chinese case, there is also the role of the Communist Party committee. Here we highlight some aspects of corporate governance that might form the basis for future research.

The role of the Board of Directors in listed companies

According to Williamson (1988), the Board of Directors should be regarded primarily as a safeguard between the firm and the owners of equity capital, and secondly as a way to safeguard the contractual relation between the firm and its management. In most listed companies, due to dispersed ownership, the directors only own a proportion of the total shares but, by law, they should act in the interests of all shareholders, not just themselves. According to the 1994 Company Law, the fiduciary duties of directors include the following (Tam, 1999).

- Implementing the resolutions adopted by the shareholders' general meeting;
- Making decisions on the business and investment plans of the company;
- Drawing up company budgets and profit allocation plans;
- Formulating corporate merger, division and dissolution plans;
- Appointing or dismissing the General Manager (i.e. the Chief Executive Officer) and appointing or dismissing the deputy general manager and financial controller on the nomination of the General Manager;
- Determining the basic management system of the company.

A comparison between these fiduciary duties of Boards of Directors in China, and those in Western countries (e.g. the United States and the United Kingdom), suggests that there are no significant differences. Indeed, the decision-makers in the Chinese Government have been introducing the UK/US version of Board structure. But a more careful scrutiny of the appointments and the roles of the directors does reveal some real differences.

The 1994 Company Law mandates that the number of directors on the Board should be between 5 and 19 persons. Table 3.5 provides data from a sample of 1,892 directors of listed companies.

Table 3.5 shows that, at the IPO stage, the average size of the Board was 10.3 directors, with 69 per cent of the directors representing shareholding institutions and 50 per cent appointed by the single largest shareholder. The implications of this are interesting. The average Board size is roughly in the middle of the range permitted by the Company Law. Does this suggest that there is an optimal size for the Boards of listed companies, which ensures an efficient monitoring and strategic decision structure? Some research in other economies (e.g. the United States) reveals that there is a link between the size of the Board and corporate performance, but no such

Table 3.5 The provenance of the directors of companies listed on the Shanghai Stock Exchange

Provenance of directors	IPO	1996	1997	1998	1999
From shareholding	7.07	6.6	6.49	6.81	6.92
institutions	(69%)	(65%)	(65%)	(69%)	(70%)
From the largest	5.1	4.51	4.66	4.97	5.33
shareholding institution	(50%)	(45%)	(47%)	(50%)	(54%)
From the second largest	1.5	1.37	1.38	1.42	1.56
shareholding institution	(15%)	(14%)	(14%)	(14%)	(16%)
From the third largest	1.02	0.96	0.94	0.95	0.99
shareholding institution	(10%)	(10%)	(9%)	(10%)	(10%)
From government	1.37	1.26	0.97	0.74	0.64
departments	(13%)	(12%)	(10%)	(7%)	(6%)
From banks	1.08	1.28	1.16	1.06	0.84
	(10%)	(13%)	(12%)	(11%)	(9%)
From non-banking	2.21	2.32	1.98	2.06	2.04
financial institutions	(21%)	(23%)	(20%)	(21%)	(21%)
From related institutions	4.45	3.78	4.38	4.59	4.81
	(43%)	(37%)	(44%)	(46%)	(49%)
From non-related	2.92	3.39	3.09	3.17	3.09
institutions	(28%)	(34%)	(31%)	(32%)	(31%)
From higher	0.85	0.67	0.77	0.81	0.70
administrative department	(8%)	(7%)	(8%)	(8%)	(7%)
Executive directors	6	6.4	5.9	5.48	5.31
(as % of the board)	(58.25)	(63.37)	(59.23)	(55.35)	(53.74)
Number of board member	10.3	10.1	9.96	9.9	9.88

Source: Shanghai Stock Exchange (2000), *Listed Companies*.

Notes
The data are based on a sample of 1,892 directors of companies which had IPOs in 1995. Some of the totals do not correspond to the sum of the individual headings because of inconsistencies in the data and overlap between the categories.

study has yet been undertaken for China. It is also noticeable that 50 per cent of the directors are from the largest shareholders, most of which are institutions. Given such a representation, it is doubtful whether the interests of the other shareholders can be effectively protected, and how balanced decision-making can be achieved. The survey also found that nearly half of the directors came from related organisations, including other shareholding institutions, business partners, and the debt-lending institutions. This raises the question of whether these directors play an active and independent role in corporate governance.

The table also reveals that executive directors have a dominant position on the Boards of many Chinese listed companies. The average proportion of executive directors is consistently above 50 per cent, both in the year of the IPO and over the period 1996–99.

Tam (1999) has analysed the administrative positions held by executive directors, and his results are summarised in Table 3.6. It is interesting to note the proportion of directors who combine the roles of Chairman and General Manager, and this raises an issue which is under debate both in China and in the West. In China, it has been argued that a high proportion of executive directors held the position even before the corporatisation of their firms, and that their professional expertise and knowledge of the business have a positive impact upon the firm's performance. But critics maintain that such insider control weakens the function of directors as monitors of the management, and harms the long-term interests of shareholders – as many scandals in the news media testify. They argue that Boards should be staffed by non-executive directors, at least in the long-term.

The Cadbury Report (1992) suggested a greater role for independent non-executive directors in the United Kingdom, as is the case in the United States and many other market economies. The objective of this recommendation is to avoid the insider control which, it was argued in the case of Japan (Aoki, 1995), had been harmful to sound corporate governance. There is substantial evidence (Mace, 1971) that, when directors have close ties with management, they are unlikely to be critical about inadequate performance. The independence of the directors should thus involve both incentives to exert supervisory effort, and safeguards against collusion with management and the diversion of funds for joint benefit. It thus appears that both the size and the composition of the Board of Directors may have an impact upon the performance of listed companies.

Table 3.6 The administrative positions held by executive directors in Chinese listed companies

None	General manager/ deputy general manager	Head of office of general manager	Chief accountant/ finance manager	Division manager/ managers of subsidiary companies	Communist party secretaries/ union chiefs
34	19	6	6	22	13

Source: Tam (1999), p. 73.

The decision-making behaviour of senior management

The same survey reported by *Listed Companies* (2000) also contained questions about the factors that constrained the decision-making behaviour of senior managers. Table 3.7 presents the analysis of the replies to the questionnaires received from 3,000 senior managers of listed companies during the survey. According to the survey, the most important internal constraint was considered to be the Board of Directors, with self-imposed restraint (i.e. the professional and fiduciary conscience of managers) cited as the second most important factor. Together these two factors were cited by 55 per cent of the respondents.

As regards the external constraints upon management, the nature of the product market dominates and was cited by almost four-fifths (79.1 per cent) of the respondents. Similar findings have been reported in the West (Harris and Raviv, 1988; Allen, 2001). Stock markets were considered to be the second most important factor, but were only mentioned in 4.8 per cent of the responses, suggesting that the managers were not particularly concerned about shareholders' interests as reflected in the stock prices. This may be because there is virtually no market for corporate control, due to the high concentration of non-tradable shareholdings. The managers thus do not have to worry about falling stock prices, and becoming a target for takeover, as is the case in the West. An alternative explanation might be that the managers believe that they can control stock prices. Although

Table 3.7 The internal and external constraints on the decision-making of managers in listed companies

Internal constraints		External constraints	
Factors	*Percentage*	*Factors*	*Percentage*
Board of Directors	29.2	Product markets	79.1
Self-restraint of managers	25.8	Stock markets	4.8
General meeting	19.9	Managerial job markets	4.4
Higher government departments	13.2	Labour markets	4.0
Local government	5.4	Consumers	3.2
Supervisory board	3.4	Banks	2.7
Company employees	1.7	Key suppliers	1.3
Party committee	1.3	News media	0.3
Trade union	0.1		
Total	100	Total	100

Source: Shanghai Stock Exchange (2000), *Listed Companies*.

Note
The figures in the table summarise the answers to 3,000 responses to a questionnaire survey undertaken in 2000.

this over-simplifies the situation, a casual scrutiny of the news reports in China reveals many instances of insider manipulations and collusion.

Legal aspects of corporate governance

The legal environment is the most important external influence over corporate governance, and provides the framework to the formation of companies, corporatisation, the IPO, and subsequently the raising of finance, investment, and information disclosure. These laws, and the quality of their enforcement by the regulators and courts, are essential elements of corporate governance and finance (La Porta *et al.*, 2002).

Currently, there are two major Laws passed by the National People's Congress of China, which set the legal framework in line with the needs of the socialist market economy. The first major law, the Company Law, was promulgated in 1994 and, together with later implementing rules, provides the foundation for the establishment of companies. The Law specifies two types of companies. The first is the limited liability company, which is established with the capital of a limited number of shareholders and where equity cannot be transferred. The second is the joint stock company, which is allowed to raise capital from the public and to be listed on the stock exchanges. The second major law, the Securities Law, was promulgated in July 1999, and its objective is to regulate the trading of securities in both primary and secondary financial markets.

The two major Laws are supplemented by various regulations and notices issued by the authorities. Those regulations cover issues such as accounting standards, information disclosure, State asset management in listed companies, and the conditions for SEOs. For instance, in 1997, the CSRC issued a regulation on 'Guidelines on Articles of Association for Listed Companies', whose purpose was to improve the accountability of management to the shareholders, and to ensure a fair, open, lawful relationship between the shareholders, the Board of Directors, and the company.

A comprehensive discussion of the legal system in so far as it relates to corporations and financial markets is beyond the scope of this study. However, it is useful to draw attention to two issues which influence the corporate governance mechanism. The first issue is that the laws and regulations are quite immature, and sometimes not in conformity with other relevant laws or regulations. For instance, there are inconsistencies between the 1999 Securities Law and the 1997 Criminal Law with regard to who is responsible for serious breaches of the fiduciary duties of large shareholders: the directors or the senior managers.

The second issue, and one which has generated widespread public concern in China, is the protection of small, outside shareholders. Too often, these shareholders have simply been sources of 'free cash'. The controlling shareholders either waste the capital raised from outside shareholders on inefficient projects, or simply transfer the funds to their own projects, or both. Financial reports are window-dressed to attract outside investors' funds during both the IPO and subsequent SEOs, and in many cases even compliant auditing offices have refused to verify the unrealistic figures. The listed companies thus become 'cash machines' for the large shareholders, until they become 'empty shells' without any capital. This is a serious problem when the major sources of finance are individual investors. The Chinese regulatory authorities have recently made attempts to protect minority shareholders in response to complaints of exploitation by the large shareholders.[13] However, a satisfactory level of protection for small shareholders still seems beyond reach in the foreseeable future.

A sound legal system is important for the healthy development and functioning of corporate governance and capital markets, yet it is not enough on its own. Effective legal protection involves both the content of the laws, and the quality of their enforcement. The willingness of all parties to observe laws is crucial for their successful implementation, and this requires a compatible, harmonised, social, cultural and broader legal system.[14] We finish this discussion on the legal aspects of corporate governance by citing La Porta *et al.* (2000, p. 6).

> One way to think about legal protection of outside investors is that it makes the expropriation technology less efficient. At the extreme of no investor protection, the insiders can steal a firm's profits perfectly efficiently. Without a strong reputation, no rational outsider would finance such a firm. As investor protection improves, the insiders must engage in more distorted and wasteful diversion practices such as setting up intermediary companies into which they channel profits. Yet these mechanisms are still efficient enough for the insiders to choose to divert extensively. When investor protection is very good, the most the insiders can do is overpay themselves, put relatives in management, and undertake some wasteful projects. After a point, it may be better just to pay dividends. As the diversion technology becomes less efficient, the insiders expropriate less, and their private benefits of control diminish. Firms then obtain outside finance on better terms. By shaping the expropriation technology, the law also shapes the opportunities for external finance.

Concluding remarks

This chapter has provided an introduction to the institutional framework of Chinese corporate governance. Various aspects, including the IPO, ownership structure, and capital structure, have been highlighted as they will be considered in detail in subsequent chapters. The main findings of this chapter may be summarised as follows

* Financial reform in China and the corporatisation of the SOEs has been motivated by the expansion of their economic activities, and their need for capital beyond the capacity of public fiscal revenues. As local government has taken a greater and greater share of fiscal income, Central Government has found it increasingly difficult to finance projects through the State budget. Given the high levels of personal savings in the State bank, the

Chinese Government first decided to reform the financing of the SOEs by funding new State projects, except some key projects, with debt instead of equity. The underlying motive was to make the project managers accountable for the repayment of debt, that is to make the capital invested by the government a 'hard constraint'.

- But the corporatisation of the SOEs is not just about the search for new sources of capital, and can only be properly understood in the context of the reallocation of resources. This is also true for the formation of the new governance structures, where there has been a shift from monopoly State control to shared control, even though control is still dominated by various State authorities.

- In choosing a model of corporate governance, the policymakers have favoured a stylised Anglo-American model in principle, but the reality has been a mixture of the Anglo-American and German–Japanese models. Furthermore, although the stated objective is an open, fair, multiple and competitive shareholding system, and the policy-makers have been trying to reduce over-concentrated State shareholdings, progress in moving from the current situation of insider-dominated shareholdings and a main bank system has been a gradual process and the end is not yet in sight.

Notwithstanding the fact that there is no perfect corporate governance mechanism, and that the development of an appropriate mechanism for China is a gradual and path-dependent process, there is still an imperative to move forward as quickly as possible in order to minimise the associated costs. However, the maturity of a sound corporate governance system that sustains longer-term development is inextricably linked to the success of economic, legal and cultural development in Chinese society as a whole.

4   The effect of ownership structure on the underpricing of Initial Public Offerings

Introduction

The IPO is an important step when a firm is in the process of going public, and is often the largest equity issue that a company ever makes. Furthermore, it is also an important event in the transformation of the governance structure. As new outside capital is taken into the company, the new owners obtain both residual claimant rights as well as residual control rights. During this process, the underpricing of the IPO of common stock has been a well-documented 'anomaly', and there exists a substantial body of empirical work documenting the underpricing phenomenon in many countries. In the United States, for example, Ibbotson and Ritter (1995) found that the amount of short-run IPO underpricing was 15.3 per cent over the 1960–92 period. Are the issuers of the stock deliberately underpricing the new stock offer to outsiders? Is it rational for secondary market investors to buy stocks at higher prices than the primary market investors?

The objective of this chapter is to extend existing theories and to investigate the impact of governance structure on the pricing of IPOs. It is argued that the IPO is not merely a process by which the firm finds new capital, but that it involves conflicts of interest between the different shareholders, especially between the large, controlling shareholder and small, outside shareholders. It will be argued that the pattern of corporate control plays an important role in the determination of the underpricing of IPOs, and that the initial owners of a firm going public are concerned about retaining control over the corporation because control brings private gains.

The basic argument is that corporate control brings private benefits for the controlling shareholders, and that the market recognises the potential transfer of wealth from the minority or outside shareholders and reduces the returns of the IPOs. We try to combine various theories based on the idea of asymmetric information with theories of corporate control. Whilst we agree that the theories of asymmetric information can explain why an IPO is commonly underpriced, they cannot explain the full extent of the underpricing and thus other theories are also needed. Therefore, our main objective is not to justify why the IPOs are underpriced, but to investigate the role of ownership structure in influencing the degree of IPO underpricing.

The rest of the chapter is organised as follows. The next section discusses the theories which attempt to explain the anomaly of IPO underpricing, and highlights the conditions under which the predictions of these theories hold. 'The data' section describes the data used in the analysis, and the section 'The regression model' outlines the variables and the model employed to calculate IPO returns. The extent of IPO underpricing in China is assessed in this section and contrasted with the results of analogous studies in other countries. The regression results are presented and discussed in 'Discussion of the empirical results'. The final section summarises the main conclusions, and suggests how the analysis could be usefully extended.

Literature review

All economic activities involve benefits and costs. In the decision to go public, the benefits include diversification, the possibility of equity financing beyond the limited wealth of the initial entrepreneur, less costly access to the capital market, increased liquidity of the company's shares, and some outside monitoring (Holmstrom and Tirole, 1993). Ritter (1987) classifies the total costs into 'direct costs' and 'indirect costs'. The direct costs include the registration and underwriting costs, which he estimated for the United States to account for, on average, 14 per cent of the funds raised. The indirect costs refer to those associated with the underpricing of IPOs, and were estimated for the United States to account for, on average, 15 per cent of the funds raised. Other researchers have argued that going public also involves annual disclosure costs, and the agency problems generated by the separation of ownership and control (Jensen and Meckling, 1976). Table 4.1, which is drawn from Pagano and Roell (1998), gives a partial summary of the benefits and costs of going public.

During the IPO process, the underpricing of IPOs is one of the major, and most studied, phenomena. Early studies by McDonald and Fisher (1972) and Logue (1973) noted the underpricing of IPOs, but their findings were based on casual observations and no explanations were offered. Ibbotson (1975) adopted a more sophisticated and systematic method. He formed portfolios of new issues with identical seasoning, then matched the returns of the portfolios with the month's market return, resulting in one pair of returns for a portfolio of two months seasoning. He then randomly selected one new issue for each of the 120 calendar months from the 2,650 new issues between 1960 and 1969. He concluded that the IPOs were systematically underpriced, and that the abnormal return was estimated to be 11.4 per cent after controlling for the risk and transactions costs and was statistically significant. He subsequently classified the IPO underpricing as a 'market anomaly', but did not offer any explanation.

Subsequent studies have shown that IPO underpricings may be observed not only during different time periods in one market, but also in different economies. Ibbotson *et al.* (1988) reported an average initial return of 16.4 per cent for IPOs during 1960–87 in the United States. Loughran *et al.* (1994) reviewed more than

Table 4.1 Empirical predictions of the main theories concerning the decision to go public

	Model	Empirical predictions	
		Effects on the probability of IPO	Consequences after IPO
Panel A: costs of going public			
Adverse selection and moral hazard	Leland and Pyle (1977), Chemmanur and Fulghieri (1995)	Smaller and younger companies less likely to go public	Negative relation between operation performance and ownership
Fixed costs	Ritter (1987)	Smaller companies less likely to go public	
Loss of confidentiality	Campbell (1979), Yosha (1995)	High-tech companies less likely to go public	
Panel B: benefit of going public			
Overcome borrowing constraints		IPO more likely for high-debt/ high-investment companies	Deleveraging/high investment
Diversification	Pagano (1993)	Riskier companies more likely to go public	Controlling shareholder decrease his stake
Liquidity	Market microstructure model	Smaller companies less likely to go public	Diffuse stock ownership
Stock market monitoring	Holmstrom and Tirole (1993), Pagano and Roell (1998)	High-investment companies more likely to go public	Large use of stock-based incentive contracts
Enlarge set of potential investors	Merton (1987)		Diffuse stock ownership
Increase bargaining power with banks	Rajan (1992)	IPO more likely for companies paying higher rates	Decrease in borrowing rates
Optimal way to transfer control	Zingales (1995)		Higher turnover of control
Exploit mispricing	Ritter (1991)	High market-to-book values in the relevant industry	Underperformance of IPOs; no increase in investment

Source: Pagano *et al.* (1998), p. 37.

thirty studies of IPOs in 25 countries (including the United States) and showed that IPOs provided, on average, large initial returns to investors who were able to buy shares at the offer price. The findings were robust throughout all 25 economies, though the average premium ranged from 4 per cent in the French study to 80 per cent in the Malaysian study – see Table 4.2.

The obvious 'windfall' to the outside investor over such a short period constitutes an anomaly both in financial theory, and for the financial industry. Many theories have been offered to explain the phenomenon, and these may be classified as either theories of information signalling or as theories of corporate control.

The key foundation for the information signalling theories is that there is an information asymmetry between the initial owners (issuers) and the outside investors. The issuers have more information about the firm going public, whilst the outside investors cannot tell the good firms from the bad ones. The issuers of shares in a good firm thus choose to underprice the shares at the IPO stage so as to ensure a successful IPO. And when the true information about the quality of firm is

Table 4.2 Evidence of IPO underpricing in selected developed and emerging markets[a]

Country	Average initial return (%)	Period studied	Sample size
Malaysia	80	1980–91	132
Brazil	79	1979–90	62
Korea	78	1980–90	347
Thailand	58	1983–87	62
Portugal	54	1986–87	62
Taiwan	45	1971–90	168
Sweden	39	1970–91	213
Switzerland	36	1983–89	42
Spain	35	1985–90	71
Mexico	33	1987–90	37
Japan	33	1970–91	472
New Zealand	29	1979–91	149
Italy	27	1985–91	75
Singapore	27	1973–87	66
Hong Kong	18	1980–90	80
Chile	16	1982–90	19
United States	15	1960–92	10,626
United Kingdom	12	1959–90	2,133
Australia	12	1976–89	266
Germany	11	1978–92	170
Belgium	10	1984–90	28
Finland	10	1984–92	85
The Netherlands	7	1982–91	72
Canada	5	1971–92	258
France	4	1983–92	187

Source: Loughran *et al.* (1994).

Note
a See Jones *et al.* (1999) for good accounts of the differences in IPO underpricing in different countries.

revealed after the IPO, the good firm can recover the costs of IPO underpricing. But the ways of recovering the costs of the IPO underpricing are conceived differently in different signalling theories.

The theories of corporate control take a different view of why IPOs are underpriced. They split the value of shares into two components: the rights to the residual cash flow and the rights to residual control. One section of the literature then studies the value premium of voting shares, when there are both voting shares and non-voting shares. A second, and more important in the Chinese context, section focuses on the ownership structure of the firms, and argues that concentrated shareholdings effectively provide large shareholders with control rights and deprive small, dispersed investors of voting rights.

Signalling theory, IPO underpricing and ownership structure

The basic argument of the signalling theories is that there exists an information asymmetry about the quality of issuing firms between the different parties involved. The relevant parties are usually the issuers (initial owners), the outside investors, and the underwriters. The signals that convey information of firm quality are either the underpricing of the IPOs, or the fraction of the equity retained by the initial owners. Leland and Pyle (1977) focus on the issue of why the initial owner might retain a certain fraction of equity when they decide to go public. They argue that the initial owners possess a better understanding of the likely future cash flows of the firm, but this information is not verifiable to the outside investor. However, the outside investors can find clues about the quality of the firm by observing the equity retention ratio. A higher ratio would indicate a higher quality firm, because the owners are reluctant to release a high proportion of the future cash flows to the outside investors. This is a single-stage model, which is based on the assumption that the initial owners have only one chance to sell their equity to outside investors. This assumption certainly limits its theoretical power and applicability to reality. More problematically, the model does not exclude the possibility that a bad firm might imitate a good firm by holding a large proportion of equity. Thus retained equity is a fallible signal of the quality of the firm, whilst IPO underpricing is not included in their model.

In 1989, two major papers on IPO underpricing, based on signalling theory, were published (Grinblatt and Hwang, 1989; Welch, 1989). Both models assume that there are both good firms and bad firms that want to issue equity to finance their projects. But only the issuer knows the quality of the firm, which is measured by the future cash flows and the variance associated with them. The information about the quality of the firm is not directly observable, nor is it verifiable by the outside investors. How then can the issuers of the shares in the good firm convey the message of quality to the outside investors?

Grinblatt and Hwang's model formalised the notion that the initial owner of high-quality firms might use both underpricing and retained shares as signals at an IPO in order to convey their private information about the firm value (in terms of future cash flows) to uninformed investors. The cost of the underpricing could then be recovered in the aftermarket by selling the shares retained at the IPO, or by issuing further shares through SEOs. The testable implication of their model was that there is a positive relationship between the IPO underpricing and the later SEO, as well as a positive relationship between the IPO underpricing and the divestment of the initial owners.

In Welch's model, the issuing firms are classified into high-quality firms and low-quality firms, and the quality of the firms can be distinguished after the IPOs by the market with a certain probability. The underpricing of IPOs is a cost for both types of firms, but high-quality firms can recover the cost at a later stage by SEOs with a higher price after the true value of the firm has been verified. However, it is too risky for the poor firm to pretend to be a good firm by underpricing the IPO. The cost of underpricing may never be recouped when the market obtains a better idea of the real quality of the firm, and is unenthusiastic about the firm's SEO.

The common conclusions from these two models were that bad firms could not afford to underprice their shares at the IPO stage, because they themselves doubted the chances of issuing new shares at a higher price when their true (bad) quality was revealed. Thus, in equilibrium, only good quality firms would under-price their shares at the IPO stage, in the expectation of being able later to recoup the IPO cost. In contrast, the bad firms could not afford to mimic the good firms and underprice at the IPO stage, because the true information would later be revealed and their share price would deteriorate, making it impossible subse-quently to issue new shares. A testable hypothesis is that underpriced IPOs should be followed by SEOs.

Rock (1986) divides the total investors' bidding for IPOs into two groups: the informed investors who know the true value of the firm, and the uninformed investors who have inferior information. The informed investors wisely choose not to bid for the IPO when it is overvalued, therefore the uninformed investors get all the shares of such projects. Rock argues that the bidding for the IPO by outside investors is risky because of this 'winner's curse'[1] and that, to avoid the situation, the IPOs must be underpriced to induce uninformed investors to join the bid. This explanation for IPO underpricing is problematic in that it has been typically applied to situations where there is no market consensus on the value of the project being auctioned (e.g. Barclay and Holderness, 1989 on oil or mineral rights for previously unexplored territories). Furthermore, the oversubscription of IPOs by informed investors is more common than undersubscription. The IPOs should thus be correctly priced according to the 'winner's curse' theory, yet this is not the case in reality.

Corporate control theory and IPO underpricing

The literature in the previous section focused on the information aspects of equity issues, whether it was the use of underpricing or retained equity as the signal to show the quality of the firm. But such theories have been subject to a number of criticisms. The first problem is that, supposing the issuer opts to underprice the IPO and then tries to recoup the loss of market value through SEOs, then clever outside investors may choose not to subscribe to the SEOs or simply to sell shares held prior to the SEOs. Indeed a powerful criticism of the signalling theories is that there are no empirical findings to support them. Michaely and Shaw (1994) used a sample of 947 firms to test the 'sweet mouth taste theory' and found that there were no substantial SEO issues following underpriced IPOs. The implication is that the initial owners lost out at the IPOs stage and either did not want to, or were not able to, make SEOs at a later stage. Signalling theories cannot explain why the initial owners were willing to give up SEOs which would help them recoup the losses incurred during the IPO.

The second and more fundamental problem is that the theories reviewed above all ignore the value of voting rights, and assume that the shares held by the controlling shareholder and by the other investors are identical. But the holding of a share not only gives the shareholder the right to a claim on the residual cash flow, but also the right to vote. The various signalling theories have not addressed the benefits of corporate control by addition of residual claim rights.

Since the early 1990s, the development of theories of corporate control has helped to increase our understanding of the valuation of stocks with, and of stocks without, voting powers. Control rights may be allocated either explicitly, through some de facto control mechanism. In the former case, the control rights might be guaranteed in the corporate charter.[2] Zingales (1995) suggests that the total value of the company can be divided into two parts: the public value (enjoyed by all shareholders) and the private value (enjoyed by the management team or controlling shareholders). It is clear that capital markets should value stock issued without voting rights lower than stock issues with voting rights. The voting rights are options that investors can exercise when they believe it is worthwhile to do so. And any option will be positively priced before it expires, and when there is a possibility that the stock price will go above the exercise price.

The second way to obtain a control right is by holding a sufficiently large proportion of the total outstanding shares, either by keeping the dominant holding at the IPO or by assembling such a holding through a series of small open-market purchases. A large enough shareholding, even if of the same class of stock and entitled to equal rights according to the law and to the charter of the company, effectively endows the large shareholder with control rights and deprives the minority shareholders of an effective voice (Zwiebel, 1995). Small shareholders have the same cash flow claims in proportion to their shareholdings as do larger or controlling shareholders, but the value of the controlling stake should theoretically be valued higher.

Empirically, Lease, McConnell and Mikkelson (1983, 1984) found for the United States that, when a firm has two classes of common stock outstanding with exactly the same terms except for voting rights, the shares with voting rights generally traded at a small premium (5.4 per cent) above their inferior non-voting counterparts. Zingales (1994) found that the premium on voting shares in Italy was as much as 80 per cent. Other studies, though not directly concerned with the private benefits of corporate control, have also found that voting shares have high premiums relative to non-voting shares in dual class companies. Bergstrom and Rydqvist (1992) found a premium of voting relative to non-voting shares of 6.5 per cent in Sweden; Levy (1983) found a premium of 45.5 per cent for Israel; Horner (1988) found a premium of 20 per cent for Switzerland; Megginson (1990) estimated a premium of 13.3 per cent for the United Kingdom; and Robinson and White (1990) calculated a figure of 23.3 per cent for Canada. These premiums can only be explained by the private benefits of control.

Empirical evidence on the private benefits of corporate control in firms with universal shares is much harder to collect, as unevenly distributed corporate control is less easy to detect and test, though it has been the subject of much theoretical study. Barclay and Holderness (1989) examined the pricing of 63 block trades and found them traded at substantial premiums to the exchange price. They attributed the premiums to the corporate benefits accrued by the blockholder – the private benefits from control. Slovin and Sushka (1993) found a two-day abnormal stock price reaction of 3.01 per cent when the deaths of insider blockholders were announced. This is consistent with the conjecture that some blockholders represent the interests of insiders rather than those of shareholders-at-large.[3]

Chandler (1990), among others, argues that founders and founding families may be more concerned with maintaining control of a business and its associated private income stream, than with maximising the value of the firm. Brennan and Franks (1997) suggest that initial owners underprice their IPOs to attract more applications for the primary shares. The resultant oversubscription means that the shares are rationed by the initial owners and they will discriminate between applicants so as to reduce the size of new shareholdings. The consequences will be a single founder (or several co-founders) dominating other small investors, thus suggesting that IPO underpricing, and the resultant dispersed ownership, may be used as a corporate control mechanism. They examined changes in ownership between the time of the IPO and seven years later, using data from a sample of 69 IPOs in the United Kingdom. They concluded that the insiders only reduced their ownership slowly over time, and interpreted this behaviour as being consistent with an attempt to retain control after the IPO.

The IPO as a means of privatisation around the world

A related literature addresses the issue of IPOs in privatisation schemes around the world, including in developed economies, emerging markets, and transitional economies.

Perotti (1995) presents a theoretical model of IPO underpricing and the privatisation of SOEs under government policy uncertainty. In the model, the government maximises the sum of expected revenues from IPOs and SEOs, plus the dividends on the retained shares during the privatisation process. Under policy uncertainty, the government may choose to retain a large stake in the SOEs, and to underprice a partial sale to signal its commitment to future pro-market privatisation policies. The model implies that IPO underpricing is positively related to the uncertainty of government policies, negatively related to the size of IPOs, and positively related to the size of government ownership and the length of time the government is expected to retain significant ownership.

Dewenter and Malatesta (1997) reported a much greater degree of IPO underpricing for government privatisations in emerging markets than in well-developed economies. In their survey of 109 government privatisation IPOs across eight countries, they estimated the following average IPO returns: Canada 2.5 per cent, France 11.4 per cent, Hungary 14.9 per cent, Japan 16 per cent, United Kingdom 18 per cent, Malaysia 52.2 per cent, Poland 50 per cent, and Thailand 46.6 per cent. Their explanation was that privatising governments may pursue objectives that are political, rather than maximising the firm's value in the privatisation process. For example, the government may allocate underpriced shares to the employees who might otherwise have misgivings about privatisation. Underpricing may thus be related to the size of the employee shares in an offering.

Jones *et al.* (1999) investigated a sample of 639 privatisations in 59 nations, including developed economies (United Kingdom, France, Canada) and developing or transitional economies (Hungary, Poland, China).[4] The evidence presented in all these studies indicated that IPOs of State-owned companies, like those of privately-owned companies, tended to be underpriced. Further, they found that *ceteris paribus* the privatisations of SOEs were more underpriced than private firm IPOs.

The Chinese joint stock system is under the control of various levels of government, with the aims being to establish a new enterprise management mechanism and to relieve the financing problems of the SOEs. This process leads to a de facto privatisation of the SOEs. Clearly shares are not retained as a signal for the quality of the firm as it is the authorities, not the firms, who decide how many shares can be issued to the public. Su and Fleisher (1999) investigated the underpricing of Chinese IPOs using data compiled for 308 'firm commitment' A-share IPOs and 57 B-share IPOs between 1988 and 1996. They found that the mean IPO initial return[5] was 948.59 per cent! In other words, the first-day market closing price was on average almost eleven times as high as the initial price offered to the domestic investors. They identified some of the causes of cross-sectional differences in the underpricing of Chinese IPOs, and their conclusions were threefold. First, the extraordinarily large IPO underpricing was at least partially due to a relatively small aggregate supply of shares. Second, the A-share underpricing was better explained by a signalling model that related IPO underpricing to SEOs, rather than by one linking government or employee ownership to equilibrium IPO underpricing. Issuers with larger IPO underpricing were more likely to raise larger amounts of capital through SEOs more quickly. Third, there was no evidence that lottery mechanisms had contributed to the high IPO underpricing in China. Their framework was based on signalling theory, whereas this study focuses more on fundamental factors (including corporate control) at the firm level.

Summary of the literature review

The main argument put forward in this review is that companies controlled by a majority shareholder have a significantly smaller IPO premium because the market correctly understands the value of control rights, and this information will be reflected in the market price. The underpricing becomes even smaller if the control of a company is not expected to change hands and there is no market for corporate control. This is exactly the case of Chinese stock markets where the fraction of shares held by the largest shareholder is pre-determined by the government, leading to a rigid ownership structure. Our argument is that a higher retained shareholding signals (more accurately, ensures) the private benefits of corporate control, and should thus be associated with smaller IPO returns. This is contrary to the prediction of signalling theory that IPO underpricing signals the quality of the firm, and that a higher retained fraction of ownership should be related to higher IPO returns.

The data

All the data used in this study were obtained from the database on the central computer of the SZSE, which provided stock prices and stock market indexes for both the SHSE and for the SZSE. The computers also provided summary information for each company, including their history, financial indicators, IPO terms, and ownership structure. A supplementary source was *An Essential Guide to Investment in the Chinese Capital Market* (1996, 1997, 1998, 1999, 2000).[6]

The data used in this study relate to all 539 companies listed on the SHSE and the SZSE between January 1995 and February 1999. Seventy two companies, whose IPOs were made before both Exchanges were officially established, were excluded. The shares in these companies were offered initially to the public through the over-the-counter (OTC) market and then, after many years' applications, were given formal approval to be listed on one of the two national and official Exchanges. These companies were excluded for two reasons. The first reason is that, at the time when the companies first offered shares to the public, there were no official stock exchanges and thus it was not possible to calculate market-adjusted returns. The second reason is the long time span between the companies first offering shares on the OTC market and formal listing on the stock markets: some companies had to wait for seven years to have a successful listing. The risk and time values were thus hard to value for these companies. The dates for the remaining 467 IPOs included in the dataset are shown in Table 4.3. The information collected for each IPO was the name of the firm, its industry classification, issue size (in 100 million yuan), the offer price, the first-day closing price, the first-day trading volume, the percentage of the issue offered at a fixed price, the percentage of the firm's capital in the offer, and the names, and type of organisation, of the largest (several) shareholders.

Stock price indexes

There are two stock price indexes on the SHSE. One is a composite index which includes all the stocks listed on the SHSE, and which is weighted according to the companies' market values. If a company's shares split or are suspended for

Table 4.3 The numbers of IPOs on SHSE and SZSE, January
1995–February 1999

Month	1995	1996	1997	1998	1999
January	2	6	16	4	2
February	0	3	4	6	1
March	0	5	15	6	
April	0	7	25	16	
May	0	15	38	15	
June	0	24	38	16	
July	0	16	11	1	
August	0	18	11	6	
September	0	20	8	8	
October	1	19	10	7	
November	1	20	9	8	
December	0	20	3	6	
	4	173	188	99	3
Sample size			467		

Source: CSRC (2000), *China Securities Market Yearbook 2000.*

a certain period due to a news announcement, the index is adjusted so that its
value is unaffected by the split or the change of the company. The other price
index is a component index which only includes the share prices of 30 large listed
companies. Similarly, there are also two share price indexes on the SZSE. One is
a composite index which includes all the listed companies on the Exchange,
weighted by market value. The other is a 30 leading company index similar to that
for Shanghai. According to the rules of the two Exchanges, the share prices from
the first day of the IPO to one month afterwards are not included in the price
indexes, so as to avoid any impacts from big gains or volatile share fluctuations
during the first trading months. The same-day Shanghai and Shenzhen Composite
daily closing indexes were used as benchmarks to obtain comparable returns for
individual stocks. For instance, suppose that a stock's offer day and the first trading day were on 1 April 1996 and 19 April 1996 respectively. We use the 1 April
1996 and 19 April 1996 daily closing composite share price indexes to obtain the
comparable return to the company's share return. The specific formulae used to
calculate the returns will be discussed below.

No inflation adjustments were made to the prices for two reasons. The first was
that inflation in China was not severe between 1995 and 1999. The second was that
it is hard to deflate the stock market indexes when we use market-adjusted returns.

The measurement of IPO returns

It is important to consider the measurement and distribution of IPO returns. Returns
may be expressed either as simple returns or as market-adjusted returns, and both
may also be expressed as natural logarithms. Different researchers have used

different measures. For example, both Jones *et al.* (1999) in their international study on share issue privatisations (SIP), and Su and Fleisher (1998) on the IPOs of Chinese listed companies, used simple returns as defined below:

$$\text{SR}_i = \frac{P_{i1} - P_{i0}}{P_{i0}} \tag{4.1}$$

where SR_i is the simple IPO return of the ith company; P_{i0}, the initial offer price for the ith company; P_{i1}, the closing price for the ith company on the first trading day.

The simple return for an individual stock is a measure of the stock's performance during the IPO, and may fluctuate in response to factors which affect either the particular stock or the general market. We require a measure of the market-adjusted return in order to separate the impact of those factors related to the stock from those affecting the general market. The market-adjusted returns are generally expressed in the form of the return on a particular stock minus the return on the general stock market as:

$$\text{MAR}_i = \frac{P_{i1} - P_{i0}}{P_{i0}} - \frac{I_{i1} - I_{i0}}{I_{i0}} \tag{4.2}$$

where, MAR_i is the market-adjusted return of the ith company; I_{i0}, the opening stock market index for the ith company on the date the offer price is set; I_{i1}, the closing stock market index for the ith company on the date the offer price is set.

Although the simple return (SR_i) and the market-adjusted return (MAR_i) are useful statistical measures for descriptive purposes, their use in regression analysis is problematic. A basic assumption underpinning the use of Ordinary Least Squares (OLS) and its hybrid regression methods is that the variables are normally distributed. However, the returns calculated above are not normally distributed, and we thus need to estimate the distribution of returns and their variances. One alternative is to assume that the natural logarithm of the single-period returns (r_{it}) are IID normal, which implies that the single-period gross raw returns are distributed as IID lognormal variates, since $r_{it} \equiv \ln(1 + R_{it})$. We may then express the lognormal model as:

$$r_{it} \sim N(\mu_i, \sigma_i^2) \tag{4.3}$$

Under the lognormal model, if the mean and variance of r_{it} are μ_i and σ_i^2 respectively, then the mean and variance of the simple returns are given by

$$E[R_{it}] = e^{\mu_i + (\sigma_i^2/2)} - 1 \tag{4.4}$$
$$\text{Var}[R_{it}] = e^{2\mu_i + \sigma_i^2}[e^{\sigma_i^2} - 1] \tag{4.5}$$

Alternatively, if we assume that the mean and variance of the simple returns (SR_{it}) are m_i and s_i^2 respectively, then under the lognormal model the mean and variance of r_{it} are given by

$$E[r_{it}] = \log \frac{m_i + 1}{\sqrt{1 + ((s_i / m_i) + 1)^2}} \tag{4.6}$$

$$\text{Var}[r_{it}] = \log \left[1 + \left(\frac{s_i}{m_i + 1} \right)^2 \right] \tag{4.7}$$

We thus use two further measures of return in our econometric work (Campbell *et al.*, 1997, p. 15) so as to generate more accurate results. The first measure is the natural logarithm of the simple return. The second measure is the natural logarithm of the market-adjusted return. Following Dewenter and Malatesta (1997), we define the natural logarithm of the simple return as below:

$$\ln SR_i = \ln \left(\frac{P_{i1}}{P_{i0}} \right) \tag{4.8}$$

where ln SR_i is natural logarithm of the *i*th company's simple return; and P_{i1} and P_{i0} are defined as earlier

The natural logarithm of the market-adjusted return is

$$\ln MAR_i = \ln \left(\frac{P_{i1}}{P_{i0}} \right) - \ln \left(\frac{I_{i1}}{I_{i0}} \right) = \left[\ln(P_{i1}) - \ln(P_{i0}) \right] - \left[\ln(I_{i1}) - \ln(I_{i0}) \right] \tag{4.9}$$

where, $\ln MAR_i$ is natural logarithm of the *i*th company's market-adjusted return; and P_{i1}, P_{i0}, I_{i1}, and I_{i0} are defined as earlier.

The applications of these various measures of return are summarised here.

Definition	Simple return	Market-adjusted return	Natural log of simple return	Natural log of market-adjusted return
Symbol	SR_i	MAR_i	$\ln SR_i$	$\ln MAR_i$
Application	Description underpricing of IPO		Regression of IPO underpricing	

The lognormal model has the added advantage of not violating limited liability, since limited liability yields a lower bound of zero on $(1+R_{it})$, which is satisfied by $(1+R_{it}) = e^{r_{it}}$ when r_{it} is assumed to be normally distributed.

Descriptive statistics on IPO underpricing

Table 4.4 reports the IPO returns of the 467 firms, both in terms of the simple return and in terms of the market-adjusted return. The mean simple return is

130.01 per cent, and the median simple return 115.58 per cent. The returns adjusted by the stock market indexes are roughly the same, with a mean return of 129.77 per cent and a median return of 115.58 per cent. The closeness of the simple returns and the market-adjusted returns implies that market movements cannot explain the abnormal returns on the IPOs. Other factors clearly contribute to the underpricing of the IPOs.

There are two firms with negative returns.[7] The largest simple return is 469.09 per cent. Over half the firms provide returns between 60 per cent and 160 per cent, but there are many firms with much smaller or much larger returns. The mean

Table 4.4 The returns on IPOs in China, January 1995–February 1999

Return (%)	Simple return			Market-adjusted return		
	Number	Frequency (%)	Cumulative frequency (%)	Number	Frequency (%)	Cumulative frequency (%)
(−40, 0]	2	0.43	0.43	2	0.43	0.43
(0, 20]	16	3.43	3.85	16	3.43	3.85
(20, 40]	21	4.50	8.35	23	4.93	8.78
(40, 60]	37	7.92	16.27	32	6.85	15.63
(60, 80]	45	9.64	25.91	51	10.92	26.55
(80, 100]	59	12.63	38.54	57	12.21	38.76
(100, 120]	67	14.35	52.89	67	14.35	53.10
(120, 140]	51	10.92	63.81	50	10.71	63.81
(140, 160]	40	8.57	72.38	41	8.78	72.59
(160, 180]	32	6.85	79.23	32	6.85	79.44
(180, 200]	28	6.00	85.22	27	5.78	85.22
(200, 220]	14	3.00	88.22	14	3.00	88.22
(220, 240]	13	2.78	91.01	9	1.93	90.15
(240, 260]	17	3.64	94.65	16	3.43	93.58
(260, 280]	4	0.86	95.50	7	1.50	95.07
(280, 300]	3	0.64	96.15	4	0.86	95.93
(300, 320]	3	0.64	96.79	1	0.21	96.15
(320, 340]	7	1.50	98.29	6	1.28	97.43
(340, 360]	3	0.64	98.93	6	1.28	98.72
(360, 380]	3	0.64	99.57	1	0.21	98.93
(380, 400]	0	0.00	99.57	3	0.64	99.57
(420, 430]	1	0.21	99.79	1	0.21	99.79
(460, 470]	1	0.21	100.00	1	0.21	100.00
Sample size	467			467		
Mean	130.01			129.77		
Median	115.58			115.58		
Standard deviation	78.35			78.12		
Min return	−15.31			−14.36		
Max return	469.09			468.28		

Notes
1 See the text for details of the calculation of the simple and market-adjusted returns.
2 The IPOs are grouped according to the size of the return: the ranges are specified from −40 to 470 per cent.

simple return of 130 per cent is markedly higher than those that have been reported in all the other country studies – see Table 4.2.

One point to which attention should be paid is whether the pattern of returns in emerging markets is the same as that in developed economies. This concern was addressed by Rouwenhorst (1999), who showed that cross-sectional differences in expected stock returns in emerging equity markets were qualitatively similar to those that have been documented for developed markets, namely: the stocks exhibited momentum, small stocks outperformed large stocks, and value stocks outperformed growth stocks.

Administered offer prices and IPO returns

One question that naturally arises is whether high IPO returns are caused by low offer pricing, or by closing prices on the first trading day. As discussed in Chapter 3, the setting of the initial offer price (P_{i0}) is not solely the result of bargaining between the issuing firms and the underwriting firms. The CSRC has a rule that the offer price for an IPO should be set around fifteen times the earnings per share prior to the IPO issue, regardless of the industry, the prospects of the firm, and other characteristics which have been shown to have an impact on IPO price-setting in other economies. Table 4.5 provides a detailed breakdown of the price–earnings (P/E) ratios for the 467 firms in our sample. The table shows that 147 IPOs out of the total sample of 467 (31.48 per cent) had P/E ratios between 14 per cent and 15 per cent; 97 IPOs (20.77 per cent) had P/E ratios between 15 and 16 per cent. Thus over 50 per cent of the sample had P/E ratios between 14 and 16 per cent. The

Table 4.5 The distribution of the P/E ratios of the firms in the sample

P/E ratio	Number of observations	Frequency (%)	Cumulative frequency (%)
<10	2	0.43	0.43
[10,11)	5	1.07	1.50
[11,12)	12	2.57	4.07
[12, 13)	26	5.57	9.64
[13,14)	69	14.78	24.41
[14,15)	147	31.48	55.89
[15,16)	97	20.77	76.66
[16,17)	41	8.78	85.44
[17,18)	27	5.78	91.22
[18,19)	15	3.21	94.43
[19,20)	11	2.36	96.79
[20+)	15	3.21	100.00
Sample size		467	
Mean		15.04	
Median		14.80	
Standard deviation		2.37	
Minimum		8.8	
Maximum		37	

mean P/E ratio was 15.04 per cent, whilst the standard deviation was a mere 2.37, so the coefficient of variation was only 15.8 per cent.

It is instructive to compare these figures with those obtained by Kim and Ritter (1999) in their sample of 190 IPOs in the United States. The mean P/E ratio for their sample was 33.5, with a minimum value of 3.3 and a maximum value of 200. More interestingly, the standard deviation of the P/E ratio in their sample was 26.9, and thus the coefficient of variation was 80.26 per cent. It is evident that, in China, the setting of the IPO offer price is more influenced by government agencies than in the United States. This rigid policy reveals the intention of the government agencies as the controlling shareholder to maximise their proceeds by setting offer prices as high as possible, regardless of the firm's prospects and industry features.[8] With this special regulatory requirement in mind, we can assume that the low IPO underpricing is either caused by the relative low closing price on the first trading day, or by the high offer prices set by the largest shareholder to accumulate larger proceeds, or both. The two assumptions are not necessary exclusive and are actually mutually supportive. Both indicate the private benefits of corporate control by the largest shareholders.

The regression model

The dependent variable in our model is the IPO premium (PREMIUM) as measured (a) by the logarithm of the simple return (lnSR), as in Ruud (1993) and Asquith *et al.* (1998); and (b) by the logarithm of the market-adjusted return (lnMAR), as in Booth and Chua (1996) and Dewenter and Malatesta (1997). The explanatory variables are as follows.

Two different bidding mechanisms for the IPO offers have been used to allocate A-shares in China: bidding on the nationwide stock trading network, and bidding for the offer at a local issuing agency operating on behalf of the IPO firm. Further details were provided in Chapter 3. A report from the World Bank (1995) argued that the choice of offering mechanism adopted for the new share issue affected the degree of underpricing. We include a dummy variable (Methods) in the model to capture this effect, with the variable taking a value of unity if the shares were allocated by network bidding and zero if by a local issuing agency. We wish to test which of the mechanisms is more informationally efficient, and no prediction is made about the sign of the coefficient.

The size of the firm is included in various types of financial studies as a control variable. The common findings are that the return on stock is negatively related to the size of the issuing firm (Fama and French, 1992). One explanation offered by Booth and Chua (1996) is that larger IPOs are generally easier to value. We use the gross amount of outside capital raised (PROCEEDS) as a proxy for firm size, as suggested by Ritter (1987) and by Michaely and Shaw (1994) in their studies of the US market.[9] We expect the IPO return to be negatively related to PROCEEDS.

The earnings per share (EPS) prior to the IPO issue is a measure of market value, as suggested by Kim and Ritter (1999). We expect a positive relationship between EPS and the IPO return.

Beatty and Ritter (1986) report that IPOs which are oversubscribed to a greater degree are associated with higher underpricing. Chemmanur (1993) confirms their empirical findings with an IPO underpricing model. We use the ratio of shares offered to those demanded (LOTTERY) as an indication of oversubscription to the IPO offer. A small value of LOTTERY signifies that the outside shares are more dispersed and are allocated more evenly. We include the natural logarithm of LOTTERY as an explanatory variable, and expect it to have a negative relationship with the degree of IPO underpricing.[10]

Chowdhry and Sherman (1996) show that IPO underpricing is positively related to the time period between the IPO date and the first day of trading. These are calendar day intervals, not trading days. Some literature uses the time period between the date for the close of applications and the first trading day (Koh and Walter, 1989); others (e.g. Booth and Chua, 1996) use the longer period between the first application date and the first trading day. We follow Booth and Chua (1996) and include the variable IPODAYS as the time elapsed between the IPO offer day and the first trading day, and expect a positive effect upon IPO underpricing.

Beatty and Ritter (1986), Mauer and Senbet (1992) and Dewenter and Malatesta (1997) all testify that IPO initial returns are a decreasing function of the offer value. In other words, the IPO return will be lower when the offer price is set higher. We therefore include the reciprocal of the offer price (RCIPIPO) as a control variable, and expect it to have a positive impact upon IPO underpricing.

One aspect of IPOs often highlighted by the financial press is the heavy first-day trading, which results in many IPO firms appearing on the list of the largest volume stocks for the day. These huge trading volumes are usually accompanied by considerable stock price volatility. This phenomenon has been verified in many studies in many financial markets, and is robust to various time intervals (hourly, daily, and weekly) and types of financial markets (equity, currency, and futures). Karpoff (1987) cites many studies that document a positive relationship between price volatility and trading volume. Recent evidence (Schwert, 1989; Gallant *et al.*, 1992; Daigler and Wiley, 1999; Chan and Fong, 2000) all confirms the volume-volatility relationship. We use the total number of shares traded on the first day as a percentage of the number of traded shares offered in the IPO (TURNOVER) to control for the effect of trading volume on price, and expect a positive relationship between TURNOVER and IPO underpricing.

Last, but most importantly, we consider the effects of ownership structure. As noted above, signalling theory suggests that high-quality firms tend to retain higher proportions of shares at the IPO and that there should thus be a positive relationship between the retained fraction of shares and the IPO return. We would argue, however, that the largest shareholder intends to maximise the proceeds by setting offer price high and the market will value the stocks of companies with dominant shareholders lower, as there is a higher private benefit of corporate control and thus a lower IPO return. We therefore include the fraction of shares held by the largest single shareholder (TOPOWNER) as an explanatory variable, and expect it to have a negative impact upon the IPO return.

Descriptive statistics for the dependent and explanatory variables are provided in Table 4.6. The average IPO proceeds are 274 million yuan (£28.33 million),

Table 4.6 Descriptive statistics for the sample of 467 Chinese IPOs

Variable	Definition	Mean	Standard deviation	Min	Max
	Dependent variables				
$lnSR_1$	Natural logarithm of simple return	0.7790	0.3275	−0.1661	1.7389
$lnMAR_i$	Natural logarithm of market-adjusted return	0.7664	0.3280	−0.1547	1.6893
	Independent variables				
Methods	Methods of bidding: network bidding = 0; local branch bidding = 1	0.2527	0.4350	0	1
Proceeds	Outside equity capital raised (in 100 million yuan)	2.7423	2.7715	0.31	25.90
EPS	earnings per share at the offer (yuan per share)	0.4127	0.1427	0.1361	1.1655
Lottery	The percentage of successful application for the offer (%)	2.3824	6.9540	0.13	95.00
IPODAYS	Number of IPO days elapsed between the announcement of an IPO and the first day of market trading	27.5717	20.8752	5	149
Price0	Offer price (yuan per share)	6.04	1.71	2.45	14.77
Price1	The closing price on the first day of trading	13.69	5.58	4.41	53.65
TURNOVER	The trading volume on the first day/outstanding shares	66.6024	18.2286	8.6328	249.4590
	Ownership variables				
TOPOWNER	Percentage of shares held by the largest single shareholders	51.8936	17.7043	9.9053	84.9850
STATETOP	Percentage of shares held by either the Bureau of State Asset Management or by a State solely-owned institution as the largest single shareholder	44.8950	24.6492	0.0000	84.9850
STFRA	Percentage of shares held by the Bureau of State Asset Management (BSAM) as the largest single shareholder	4.6632	13.8638	0.00	75.00
SIFRA	Percentage of shares held by the State solely-owned institution as the largest single shareholder	40.2318	28.1319	0.00	84.98
DIFRA	Percentage of shares held by a domestic institution as the largest single shareholder	6.9986	18.3197	0.00	75.00

with minimum proceeds of 31 million yuan (£2.58 million) and maximum proceeds of 2,590 million yuan (£215.83 million). The average earnings per share at the IPO are 0.41 yuan, with a range from 0.1361 to 1.1655. The mean value of Lottery is 2.38 per cent, implying that the IPOs in the sample were oversubscribed 41 times on average, and suggesting that informed investors would easily exhaust the supply of shares. The average time for an IPO to be listed on the stock exchanges is 27 business days, with a range from 5 days to 149 days. The table also reveals that, on average, the largest single shareholder possesses 51.89 per cent of the equity, with a minimum shareholding of 9.9 per cent and a maximum 84.98 per cent. All were non-tradable shares. This provides direct evidence of the non-existence of a market of corporate control.

The model to be estimated was thus:

$$
\begin{aligned}
\text{PREMIUM} = \alpha &+ \beta_1 \text{ METHODS} + \beta_2 \text{ PROCEEDS} + \beta_3 \text{ EPS} \\
&+ \beta_4 \ln \text{LOTTERY} + \beta_5 \text{ IPODAYS} + \beta_6 \text{ RCIPIPO} \\
&+ \beta_7 \text{ TURNOVER} + \beta_8 \text{ TOPOWNER} + \varepsilon_I
\end{aligned}
\tag{4.10}
$$

ε_I is random disturbance term with zero mean and variance σ^2.

We estimate equation 4.10 using both the logarithm of the simple returns, and the logarithm of the market-adjusted returns, as the measure of the dependent variable, PREMIUM. Furthermore, both regressions are estimated by OLS, and by a robust version which addresses the problem of potential heteroscedasticity. Table 4.7 thus presents the results of four regressions on the full sample of 467 IPOs.

In addition, we divide the sample into four sub-samples according to the nature of the largest shareholder. These sub-samples comprise those IPOs where the largest single shareholder was the BSAM (STFRA – 56 firms), a State solely-owned institution (SIFRA – 344 firms), a firm owned by private shareholders (DIFRA – 67 firms), or either BSAM or State-owned institutions (STATETOP – 400 firms). These regressions are reported in Tables 4.8–4.11, and help to explain the effects of ownership on IPO underpricing.

Discussion of the empirical results

We first consider the results of the regressions using the data on all 467 IPOs – see Table 4.7. Most importantly, these all show a significant[11] negative relationship between the IPO market return and the single largest shareholding. In other words, the greater the proportion of shares held by the largest shareholder, the lower will be the IPO return *ceteris paribus*. This finding is consistent with our prediction that the market will value the stocks of companies with more dominant shareholders lower, because the potential benefits will be acquired by the controlling shareholders at the IPO stage either by the setting of high offer prices to accumulate proceeds or by the accrual of other future benefits. One potential future benefit is that larger shareholders can 're-privatise' more easily: markets perceive this and consequently value the shares lower. A second possible private benefit is that a higher shareholding held by one shareholder makes it more

Table 4.7 The regression results explaining the IPO premium for the full sample of 467 IPOs in China

	Log simple return		Log market-adjusted return	
	OLS	*Robust*	*OLS*	*Robust*
Methods	0.2103[a]	0.2169[a]	0.2076[a]	0.2111[a]
	(6.14)	(6.12)	(5.92)	(5.81)
Proceeds	−0.0089[c]	−0.0069	−0.0065	−0.0051
	(−1.68)	(−1.27)	(−1.21)	(−0.91)
EPS	0.0741	0.0560	0.0109	0.0081
	(0.46)	(0.34)	(0.07)	(0.05)
lnLottery	−0.1175[a]	−0.1168[a]	−0.1257[a]	−0.1253[a]
	(−8.98)	(−8.63)	(−9.39)	(−9.04)
IPODAYS	−0.0026[a]	−0.0029[a]	−0.0017[b]	−0.0021[a]
	(−3.77)	(−4.12)	(−2.44)	(−2.88)
RCIPIPO	0.9422[b]	0.8445[c]	0.7155[d]	0.7261[d]
	(1.98)	(1.71)	(1.47)	(1.44)
Turnover	0.0050[a]	0.0057[a]	0.0043[a]	0.0044[a]
	(6.62)	(7.28)	(5.53)	(5.46)
TOPOWNER	−0.0012[d]	−0.0014[c]	−0.0014[c]	−0.0018[b]
	(−1.50)	(−1.81)	(−1.83)	(−2.19)
Constant	0.3665[b]	0.3577[b]	0.4509[a]	0.4603[a]
	(2.38)	(2.24)	(2.86)	(2.82)
Sample size	467	467	467	467
R^2	0.3021		0.2576	
Adjusted R^2	0.2893		0.2578	
F	24.77	25.02	21.24	20.36
$P > 0$	0.00	0.00	0.00	0.00

Notes
1 The dependent variable is the IPO return, measured either by the natural logarithm of the simple return or the natural logarithm of the market-adjusted return.
2 Two estimation methods are used: OLS and robust regression, as discussed in Chapter 1.
3 The figures in parentheses are *t*-values.
4 The levels of significance are as follows: 'a' denotes 1 per cent, 'b' denotes 5 per cent, 'c' denotes 10 per cent, and 'd' denotes 15 per cent significance.

difficult to launch a takeover war. This finding contradicts the predictions of Leland and Pyle (1977) and Grinblatt and Hwang (1989), who maintained that a higher retained shareholding signalled higher firm quality of the firm, and should be associated with greater IPO underpricing.

Corporate law in China requires that key decisions should be made with the agreement of no less than two-thirds of the shareholders, but a high concentration of share ownership may sometimes enable one single shareholder to take or reject important proposals. There is ample anecdotal evidence that the attendants at Annual General Meetings are usually the delegates of the largest shareholders, and documented cases where decisions on the appointment of chairmen and top management are made by less than ten shareholders even when the total number of shareholders in the listed companies exceeds 10,000.[12] Another example of the private benefits of control rights is provided by the case of Hengtong Co. Ltd. Hengtong Co. Ltd. was the largest shareholder in Lengguang Communications plc, listed on the SHSE, and used its controlling holding to require Lengguang to guarantee a bank loan to the total asset value of Lengguang. It is also very common for controlling State companies, as the largest shareholder, to 'borrow' capital from listed companies at very low cost.

The second interesting finding is that the bidding mechanism for the IPO offer has a highly significant effect upon IPO underpricing. The IPO return will be higher when firms issue shares through local issuing agencies. One explanation is that local investors are less knowledgeable in valuing the shares, and thus require higher returns. In addition, a national issuing network is likely to be more cost-effective and informationally efficient, thus reducing investors' requirements for higher IPO returns. This evidence is consistent with the presence of information asymmetries.

The LOTTERY variable is negatively related to the IPO return, and is highly significant. This finding means that investors' rewards are higher when the chances of share allocation are smaller, and is consistent with the results of Brennan and Franks (1997) and Booth and Chua (1996). It suggests that the initial owners use IPO underpricing to attract oversubscription, with the intention of promoting a dispersed outside ownership and of retaining control after the IPO.

The time between the offer day and the first trading day has a very significant negative effect on the IPO return, contrary to our prediction. A possible explanation is that, whilst (too) long a time gap imposes more risk and thus merits a higher IPO return, too short an interval gives investors no time to collect information for the valuation of the IPO. The relationship between the time and the IPO return would thus be non-linear, and the optimal interval is a potential topic for future study.

The regression results also show that IPO underpricing is negatively linked with firm size, though none of the coefficients were significant. This finding is consistent with the findings of the IPO studies by Booth and Chua (1996) and by Brennan and Franks (1997). The coefficients of the other control variables (RCIP-IPO, TURNOVER, EPS) were all significant, though at different levels, and consistent with our predictions. The RCIPIPO was significantly positively related to the IPO return, confirming that a higher offer price leads to lower IPO returns. The highly significant positive coefficient of trading volume, TURNOVER, supports the similar findings in other economies. EPS had the correct sign, but was not statistically significant. We thus only have weak and inconclusive evidence that better firms are priced higher.

The results of the regressions on the sub-samples provided very similar results to those obtained for the full sample, though there are some interesting differences with regard to the ownership variables. The coefficients for STATETOP (see Table 4.8) and for SIFRA (see Table 4.9), estimated for the different measures of IPO return and using the different regression techniques, were again significantly negative, though the levels of significance were slightly different. But the coefficients for STFRA (see Table 4.10) were not significant, though they were negative. A possible explanation for this is that State-owned institutions are able to exact private benefits whereas the Bureau of State Asset Management, being both an administrative agency and a controlling body ensuring the value and securities of State assets, has no incentive to pursue private benefits (through, e.g. setting up their own projects by transferring capital from the IPO proceeds) as it does not have the rights to the proceeds.

The impact of domestic institutional shareholders is interesting, though the coefficients of DIFRA are not significant (see Table 4.11). The IPO returns are higher for larger domestic institutional shareholders. We believe that the market reacts positively to the presence of larger domestic shareholders, suggesting that

Table 4.8 The regression results explaining the IPO premium for the sample of 400 IPOs in China where either the BSAM or State solely-owned institutions are the largest single shareholder

	Log simple return		Log market-adjusted return	
	OLS	*Robust*	*OLS*	*Robust*
Methods	0.1997[a]	0.2098[a]	0.1942[a]	0.2041[a]
	(5.44)	(5.48)	(5.20)	(5.22)
Proceeds	−0.0070	−0.0060	−0.0047	−0.0042
	(−1.29)	(−1.06)	(−0.85)	(−0.73)
EPS	0.0970	0.0917	0.0420	0.0615
	(0.54)	(0.49)	(0.23)	(0.32)
lnLottery	−0.1214[a]	−0.1224[a]	−0.1281[a]	−0.1289[a]
	(−8.79)	(−8.50)	(−9.13)	(−8.76)
IPODAYS	−0.0028[a]	−0.0029[a]	−0.0019[a]	−0.0019[a]
	(−3.93)	(−3.80)	(−2.59)	(−2.47)
RCIPIPO	0.7707[d]	0.7176	0.5042	0.5742
	(1.50)	(1.34)	(0.96)	(1.05)
Turnover	0.0055[a]	0.0061[a]	0.0048[a]	0.0048[a]
	(6.77)	(7.22)	(5.81)	(5.60)
STATETOP	−0.0014[d]	−0.0016[b]	−0.0018[b]	−0.0021[b]
	(−1.65)	(−1.84)	(−2.10)	(−2.33)
Constant	0.3687[b]	0.3423[b]	0.4601[a]	0.4425[a]
	(2.20)	(1.96)	(2.70)	(2.48)
Sample size	400	400	400	400
R^2	0.3277		0.2942	
Adjusted R^2	0.3139		0.2797	
F	23.82	23.68	20.37	19.20
$P > 0$	0.00	0.00	0.00	0.00

Notes
1 The dependent variable is the IPO return, measured either by the natural logarithm of the simple return or the natural logarithm of the market-adjusted return.
2 Two estimation methods are used: OLS and robust regression, as discussed in Chapter 1.
3 The figures in parentheses are *t*-values.
4 The levels of significance are as follows: 'a' denotes 1 per cent, 'b' denotes 5 per cent, 'c' denotes 10 per cent, and 'd' denotes 15 per cent significance.

Table 4.9 The regression results explaining the IPO premium for the sample of 344 IPOs in China where a State solely-owned institution is the largest single shareholder

	Log simple return		Log market-adjusted return	
	OLS	Robust	OLS	Robust
Methods	0.1639[a]	0.1757[a]	0.1520[a]	0.1655[a]
	(4.01)	(4.08)	(3.65)	(3.77)
Proceeds	−0.0097[c]	−0.0087[d]	−0.0082[d]	−0.0082
	(−1.75)	(−1.50)	(−1.45)	(−1.37)
EPS	−0.0223	0.0179	−0.0664	−0.0168
	(−0.11)	(0.08)	(−0.32)	(−0.08)
lnLottery	−0.1027[a]	−0.1043[a]	−0.1119[a]	−0.1131[a]
	(−6.24)	(−6.03)	(−6.69)	(−6.40)
IPODAYS	−0.0029[a]	−0.0027[a]	−0.0021[a]	−0.0018[b]
	(−3.73)	(−3.29)	(−2.66)	(−2.20)
RCIPIPO	0.4891	0.4683	0.1963	0.2699
	(0.85)	(0.78)	(0.34)	(0.44)
Turnover	0.0054[a]	0.0062[a]	0.0046[a]	0.0046[a]
	(6.40)	(6.88)	(5.31)	(5.08)
SIFRA	−0.0014[d]	−0.0016[c]	−0.0021[b]	−0.0024[b]
	(−1.52)	(−1.63)	(−2.25)	(−2.43)
Constant	0.4898[a]	0.4253[b]	0.6208[a]	0.5845[a]
	(2.58)	(2.13)	(3.22)	(2.87)
Sample size	344	344	344	344
R^2	0.31		0.2737	
Adjusted R^2	0.2935		0.2564	
F	18.81	18.42	16.78	14.49
$P > 0$	0.00	0.00	0.00	0.00

Notes
1 The dependent variable is the IPO return, measured either by the natural logarithm of the simple return or the natural logarithm of the market-adjusted return.
2 Two estimation methods are used: OLS and robust regression, as discussed in Chapter 1.
3 The figures in parentheses are *t*-values.
4 The levels of significance are as follows: 'a' denotes 1 per cent, 'b' denotes 5 per cent, 'c' denotes 10 per cent, and 'd' denotes 15 per cent significance.

outside investors on the secondary market have some confidence in the domestic institutions. This is an encouraging sign, which is consistent with the conclusions in Chapter 5 given later.

We tried to model the effects of different industries on IPO returns. Two industry classifications were available from the Exchanges. The first was a rough classification separately identifying manufacturing, commercial, utility, real estate, and conglomerates. The second was a more detailed classification with twenty industries. The model was estimated by both OLS and robust regression using dummy variables to capture the industry effects, but found few of them to be significant. Notwithstanding the vague definitions used by the Stock Exchanges,

Table 4.10 The regression results explaining the IPO premium for the sample of 56 IPOs in China where the BSAM is the largest single shareholder

	Log simple return		Log market-adjusted return	
	OLS	*Robust*	*OLS*	*Robust*
Methods	0.2929[a]	0.2396[b]	0.3378[a]	0.2647[a]
	(2.93)	(2.46)	(3.42)	(2.74)
Proceeds	0.0463[d]	0.0681[b]	0.0600[b]	0.0886[a]
	(1.54)	(2.31)	(2.01)	(3.02)
EPS	0.1097	0.0827	0.0213	−0.0816
	(0.25)	(0.20)	(0.05)	(−0.20)
lnLottery	−0.1690[a]	−0.1745[a]	−0.1600[a]	−0.1621[a]
	(−6.13)	(−6.54)	(−5.88)	(−6.11)
IPODAYS	−0.0015	−0.0080[a]	0.0005	−0.0062[b]
	(−0.74)	(−2.88)	(0.24)	(−2.26)
RCIPIPO	1.3090	1.6264	1.1452	1.5587
	(1.01)	(1.30)	(0.90)	(1.26)
Turnover	0.0060[b]	0.0059[b]	0.0061[b]	0.0054[b]
	(2.14)	(2.16)	(2.17)	(1.99)
STFRA	−0.0016	−0.0009	−0.0020	−0.0015
	(−0.69)	(−0.40)	(−0.86)	(−0.63)
Constant	0.1136	0.1591	0.0557	0.1619
	(0.30)	(0.43)	(0.15)	(0.44)
Sample size	56	55	56	55
R^2	0.5176		0.5238	
Adjusted R^2	0.4355		0.4428	
F	6.30	7.68	6.46	7.22
$P > 0$	0.00	0.00	0.00	0.00

Notes
1 The dependent variable is the IPO return, measured either by the natural logarithm of the simple return or the natural logarithm of the market-adjusted return.
2 Two estimation methods are used: OLS and robust regression, as discussed in Chapter 1.
3 The figures in parentheses are *t*-values.
4 The levels of significance are as follows: 'a' denotes 1 per cent, 'b' denotes 5 per cent, 'c' denotes 10 per cent, and 'd' denotes 15 per cent significance.

these results suggest that industry had no influence on IPO pricing. The regression results incorporating the dummy variables are thus not reported here.

Two other matters merit attention. First, the values of the intercept coefficients, which in the full sample regressions vary between 0.3665 and 0.4603, are always significantly different from zero. This may be the result of a mis-specification of the entire model, or of a failure by the proxy variables to capture the value of the control allocated to the outside shareholders. Second, we need to stress the small coefficients of determination. However, small values of R^2 are common in similar studies: Kim and Ritter (1999) report values of R^2 around 0.08, even though they include many accepted determinants in their models. Similar results can be

Table 4.11 The regression results explaining the IPO premium for the sample of 67 IPOs
in China where a domestic institution is the largest single shareholder

	Log simple return		Log market-adjusted return	
	OLS	Robust	OLS	Robust
Methods	0.1654[c]	0.2023[b]	0.1950[b]	0.2187[b]
	(1.77)	(2.09)	(1.98)	(2.18)
Proceeds	−0.0183	0.0431	−0.0159	0.0517
	(−0.53)	(1.06)	(−0.43)	(1.23)
EPS	0.1538	0.0358	0.1161	−0.0376
	(0.45)	(0.10)	(0.32)	(−0.10)
lnLottery	−0.0623[d]	−0.0831[c]	−0.0921[b]	−0.1057[b]
	(−1.53)	(−1.96)	(−2.15)	(−2.40)
IPODAYS	0.0008	−0.0060[d]	0.0010	−0.0070[b]
	(0.44)	(−1.82)	(0.49)	(−2.04)
RCIPIPO	3.6653[a]	3.2883[a]	4.0630[a]	3.5414[a]
	(2.93)	(2.55)	(3.09)	(2.65)
Turnover	−0.0003	−0.0003	−0.0009	−0.0014
	(−0.16)	(−0.15)	(−0.42)	(−0.64)
DIFRA	0.0018	0.0002	0.0025	0.0010
	(0.95)	(0.09)	(1.26)	(0.50)
Constant	0.0639	0.2716	−0.0228	0.2776
	(0.16)	(0.67)	(−0.06)	(0.66)
Sample size	67	66	67	66
R^2	0.3277		0.3719	
Adjusted R^2	0.2350		0.2853	
F	3.53	3.34	4.29	3.91
$P > 0$	0.00	0.00	0.00	0.00

Notes
1 The dependent variable is the IPO return, measured either by the natural logarithm of the simple
  return or the natural logarithm of the market-adjusted return.
2 Two estimation methods are used: OLS and robust regression, as discussed in Chapter1.
3 The figures in parentheses are *t*-values.
4 The levels of significance are as follows: 'a' denotes 1 per cent, 'b' denotes 5 per cent, 'c' denotes
  10 per cent, and 'd' denotes 15 per cent significance.

found in Brennan and Franks (1997) whilst, in the Chinese case, Mok and Hui
(1998) report values of R^2 with a range from 0.05 to 0.247.

As pointed out by Roll (1988, p. 41), 'even with hindsight, the ability to explain
stock price changes is modest... The average adjusted R^2 is only about 0.35 with
monthly data and 0.20 with daily data.'

Concluding remarks

The underpricing of IPOs is a mysterious phenomenon in both theoretical and
practical circles. This chapter has investigated the underpricing of IPOs in the context of corporate control and its private benefits, in the particular case of China.
We found evidence of high IPO premiums in a sample of 467 listed companies that

had publicly issued equity to outside investors. We then linked the IPO underpricing to the corporate control mechanism, and found that the underpricing was negatively related to the proportion of shares held by the largest single shareholder, after controlling for other well-known factors. This finding confirms our argument that, when the regulatory environment is poor, the controlling shareholders are able to pursue their private benefits more easily and without penalty. The outside investors perceive this, and take a more cautious strategy to IPOs, leading to lower IPO pricing.

This study further examined the impact of the ownership of the largest single shareholders on IPO underpricing. We found that the IPO returns of firms where the largest shareholders are State-owned are lower. On the contrary, the IPO returns for firms with larger domestic shareholdings are higher, which implies the potential for a good corporate governance mechanism.

Our findings support the predictions of the extant literature, but add to it by highlighting the importance of corporate control in providing private benefits. Whilst the asymmetric information theory provides a powerful explanation of why IPOs should be underpriced, the theory cannot explain why there are different returns across the IPOs. But this can be explained by a consideration of the corporate control mechanism.

Given China's determination to move towards a market economy and to effect the transformation of the SOEs, this study provides important insights into the construction of a good corporate governance system. It can be used to aid the design of an initial ownership structure which benefits not just the largest shareholders but all the shareholders. The analysis is the most comprehensive yet on the subject of IPOs in China, yet much further work remains to be done. In particular

- It would be sensible to consider more fully situations where the largest single shareholder is holding only a few more shares than the second largest shareholder. The current model ignores the second largest shareholder, yet it might be relatively easy for the second largest shareholder to become the largest by simply purchasing a small proportion of the outstanding shares. In short, a more comprehensive analysis should take account of the relative sizes of the large shareholders.
- There is a substantial literature which confirms that stock prices decline over the long-term after an IPO. How do stock prices perform in the Chinese situation? Why should the investors in the secondary markets be willing to pay the investors who were lucky enough to be allocated primary shares during the IPOs? What are the implications for corporate governance?

5 Ownership structure as a corporate governance mechanism[1]

Introduction

In Chapter 4, we studied the relationship between large, controlling shareholders and small, outside shareholders, based on the theory of corporate control rights and associated private benefits. A related corporate governance issue is the 'agency problem' arising from the conflict of interests between the firm's management, as the agent, and its shareholders as the principals. This is caused by the separation of ownership by the investors, and effective control by the management, in publicly listed corporations. Furthermore, the agency problem is exacerbated when ownership is widely dispersed, due to the inability and/or the unwillingness of relatively small shareholders to police the behaviour of the management. The monitoring of management is also weakened by the 'free-rider problem' – the monitoring shareholders have to pay 100 per cent of the monitoring costs, but only gain an increased return in proportion to their shareholdings. Other, usually small, shareholders enjoy the rest of the improved gain but without making any effort. A consequence is that the residual control rights fall into the hands of management, instead of the residual cash flow claimants.

There is an increasing body of research that shows that the structure of share ownership can be an important source of incentives for management, for Boards of Directors, and for outside shareholders (Milgrom and Roberts, 1992). The pattern and amount of stock ownership can influence managerial behaviour, corporate performance, and stockholder voting patterns in election contests (Grossman and Hart, 1988). However, the interrelationship between ownership structure, firm characteristics, and corporate performance requires further investigation, both in developed economies and particularly in transitional economies. In this chapter, we will investigate the relationship between firm performance and ownership structure, using a sample of 434 manufacturing firms listed on SHSE and SZSE. The study involves two tests: the first on the link between corporate performance and ownership concentration, and the second on the link between corporate performance and different types of shareholdings.

The structure of this chapter is as follows. The next section is 'Review of the literature'. The section 'The model' discusses the theories related to ownership and corporate performance. The section termed 'The data' introduces the data sample and the variables. Econometric methodologies and results are discussed in 'The empirical results', and the final section concludes.

Review of the literature

Two important characteristics of modern corporations are the separation of ownership and control, and the diffusion of equity among investors (Berle and Means, 1932). Jensen and Meckling (1976) define agency costs as the sum of '(1) the monitoring expenditures of the principal, (2) the bonding expenditures by the agent, and (3) the residual loss'. More specifically, agency costs may involve both the direct expropriation of assets and/or losses due to managerial indulgence or incompetence. According to Shleifer and Vishny (1997), management can expropriate assets in various ways, including directly stealing money from the firm's accounts, transferring the firm's wealth through 'favourable' pricing to their own firms, or selling expensive firm assets to their own firms at low prices. But management indulgence may be the worse form of the agency problem. Management may increase their consumption of luxuries at the firm's expense, or heighten their status by expanding the size of the firm (empire building) even if the expansion is not warranted on efficiency grounds. The direct expropriation of a firm's assets is common in many developing countries and transitional economies, where legal systems are weak or in an immature state. But, in economies with more sound legal systems where asset appropriation can incur severe penalties, management overconsumption and incompetence has become the focus of attention for both theoretical research and policy formulation (La Porta *et al.*, 1999).

To mitigate the agency problem, an obvious remedy is to increase the management shareholding, making the manager a significant residual claimant. Jensen and Meckling (1976) argue that managers perform better, the greater their ownership stake within the firm. They hold that managers want to consume or pursue projects that benefit them personally. When managers own 100 per cent of the company, they pay for a dollar of perquisite with a dollar of their own profits. But, when managers own only 10 per cent of the company, they pay for a dollar of perquisite with only 10 cents of their own profits, and hence will overconsume perquisites. The argument is that, with a higher fraction of shares in hand, the manager may work harder to improve the performance of the corporation, which leads to an increase in firm value and hence his private wealth. The agency problem does not exist when management owns 100 per cent of the equity. Empirically, Murphy (1985), Morck *et al.* (1988), Denis and Sarin (1999), and Ang *et al.* (1999) have found an inverse relationship between managers' shareholdings and agency costs.

While stressing the importance of a management shareholding in reducing the agency problem, other research has focused on the role of the large shareholders. In the past two decades, a number of studies have begun to question the empirical validity of the Berle and Means model which conceptualises company ownership as a large number of small, heterogeneous shareholders, and to shed light on the role of large shareholders in monitoring management. As discussed in Chapter 2, various studies have discovered significant concentrations of ownership around the world. Other research (e.g. Kang and Shivdasani, 1995; Yafeh and Yosha, 1995) reveals that these large shareholders are active in corporate governance, in contrast to the Berle and Means idea that managers are unaccountable. This research suggests that the existence of large shareholders may provide another mechanism of corporate governance.

At a theoretical level, Shleifer and Vishny (1986) argue that larger shareholders can play an important role in corporations. They begin with the assumption that the firm is owned by one large shareholder, who does not participate in management, and a variety of small ones. In their model, the large shareholder has a large enough stake that it pays him to do some monitoring of the incumbent management. They conclude that, due to the fact that small shareholders are usually individuals, they prefer their returns in the form of capital gains. Large shareholders usually have corporate tax attributes so they prefer dividends to capital gains. Thus, some degree of ownership concentration improves control management and increases firm value. The most direct way to align cash flow and control rights of outside investors is to concentrate shareholdings. This can mean that one or several investors in the firm have substantial minority stakes, such as 10 or 20 per cent. A substantial shareholding provides the large shareholder with the incentive to collect information and monitor management, thereby avoiding the 'free-rider problem' (Grossman and Hart, 1980). A large number of empirical studies have confirmed their predictions (see, e.g. Wruck, 1989; Hertzel and Smith, 1993; Franks and Mayer, 1995), both in Germany and in the United States. However, the problem with the model is that it fails to take into account risk sharing and the wealth constraint, both of which are basic features of the joint-stock company.

In contrast, Hart (1995b) draws attention to two disadvantages of holding large shareholdings in a company. The first is that an investor owning a large fraction of the shares will lose many of the gains from going public, as the risk-reduction benefits from portfolio diversification are lost. The second is that, even though large shareholdings can mitigate the agency problems, they cannot eliminate them.

All the above-mentioned literature treats corporate performance as dependent upon ownership structure. Some other research (Demsetz, 1983; Fama and Jensen, 1983; Demsetz and Lehn, 1985; Kole, 1994; Cho, 1998) argues that ownership structure is endogenously determined in equilibrium, and that investors may select the ownership structure together with the optimal market value of the corporation. Whilst acknowledging the explanatory power of these studies, their argument is not really applicable in China where institutional shares cannot be freely traded. Institutional investors cannot sell their shares when the performance of corporations is poor, or buy when it is good.

In addition to ownership structure, the capital structure is also an important influence on corporate performance through its effects on corporate governance (Jensen and Meckling, 1976). Grossman and Hart (1982) predict that, in addition to the tax-shield advantages of debt over equity, the debt/equity ratio matters. The theory is that the distinction between debt and equity is fundamental to the way corporate governance works. Debt claims in general provide the holders with a fixed repayment schedule, but little in the way of rights to control the company as long as the repayment schedule (and sometimes certain other terms) is met. However, creditors can have a strong influence over a company if it gets into financial distress and, even if a company is financially sound, creditors can influence whether it can obtain additional funding for proposed new projects. As leverage increases, so does the risk of default by the firm, and hence the incentive for the lender to monitor the firm (Grossman and Hart, 1982; Bolton and Scharfstein, 1990; Hart and Moore, 1995). While the primary purpose of this monitoring is to prevent risk shifting by shareholders to debt-holders, increased monitoring should also inhibit excessive perquisite consumption by managers.

A smaller but increasing amount of research has started to shed light on various corporate governance issues in transition economies, such as the role of banks in the corporate governance mechanism (Coffee, 1996; Dittus and Prowse, 1996). Xu and Wang (1997) investigate the relationship between ownership structure and corporate performance in China, and find a positive effect of domestic institutional investors and the negative effect of State shareholding. But their research is limited to the roles of three groups of large shareholders. The current research is more sophisticated in that

1   We classify the State-owned shares into two sub-categories: those held by State agencies through the BSAM, and those held by State-owned institutions. The aim is to test whether firms owned directly by the State Bureau perform better (or worse) than those owned by State-owned institutions.
2   We add management shareholding variables into the analysis. The argument is that a higher proportion of shares held by management can reduce the agency costs. Therefore better performance is expected to accompany a higher management shareholding.
3   There is virtually no market for corporate control in China, due to the fact that most shares are held by institutional investors, and there are restrictions on the floating of these shares. Nevertheless there are still 180 corporations (in the sample of 434 companies) where the tradable shares account for more than 30 per cent of the total outstanding shares, and twenty where the tradable shares account for more than 50 per cent. These corporations are under greater pressure than those with fewer tradable shares.

Research into the link between ownership structure and corporate performance will not be complete unless the above groups of shareholders are included explicitly into the analysis.

The model

Ownership structure affects the efficiency of corporate governance and thus the intrinsic value of the firm, leading to a different corporate performance (Stoughton and Zechner, 1998; La Porta *et al.*, 2002). The dependent variable in the model, corporate performance, is an amended form of Tobin's Q. Tobin's Q (Tobin and Brainard, 1968; Tobin, 1969) is the ratio of the market value of equity and debt, divided by the replacement cost of total assets.

$$\text{Tobin's } Q = \frac{\text{market value of outstanding shares } + \text{ market value of total liability}}{\text{replacement cost of total assets}}$$

(5.1)

The basic idea is that the replacement cost is a logical measure of the alternative-use values of the assets. Unless the assets used by the firm are able to create at least as much value as the cost of replacing them, the assets would be better employed elsewhere. Thus those firms displaying a Tobin's Q greater than unity may be judged as using their scarce resources effectively, whilst those with a value of Tobin's Q less than unity may be judged as using their resource poorly.

An alternative measure of corporate performance, the accounting profit rate, was used in the Demsetz and Lehn (1985) study, but all subsequent studies have used Tobin's Q. As Demsetz and Villalonga (2001, p. 213) point out, there are two important respects in which these measures differ. One is the time perspective: backward-looking for the accounting profit rate and forward-looking for Tobin's Q. In attempting to assess the effect of ownership structure on firm performance, it is more sensible to look at an estimate of what management has accomplished or at an estimate of what management will accomplish? The second difference relates to who is actually measuring performance. For the accounting profit rate, this is the accountant constrained by the standards set by his profession. For Tobin's Q, this is primarily the community of investors constrained by their acumen, optimism, or pessimism. Economists, most of whom have a better understanding of market constraints than of accounting constraints, tend to favour Tobin's Q. We adopt Tobin's Q as the measure of corporate performance, bearing particularly in mind the notable differences in accounting practices and accuracy between different countries.

In practice, few Chinese companies issue publicly placed debt, so it is almost impossible to estimate the market value of the companies' debt. Furthermore, the companies do not report the replacement cost of their assets. To resolve these problems, we follow the practice adopted in a recent cross-sectional study of 27 countries (La Porta *et al.*, 2002) and in previous studies for the United States (Chung and Pruitt, 1994; Demsetz and Villalonga, 2001). We use total book liabilities as an approximation of total debt, and the book value of total assets as an approximation of the replacement costs of total assets. These approximations might be questionable in studies using time-series data, where inflation might have a large influence on the estimates of replacement cost, but are less problematic when cross-section data are being used. The following amended version of Tobin's Q is thus calculated:

$$\text{Tobin's } Q = \frac{\text{market value of outstanding shares } + \text{ total liability}}{\text{book value of total assets}}$$

$$= \frac{\text{outstanding shares } \times \text{ year end share prices } + \text{ total liability}}{\text{book value of total assets}}$$

(5.2)

The explanatory variables in the model may be sub-divided into those that relate to the ownership structure of the companies, and a number of control variables that have been identified in the previous literature. As regards the 'ownership' variables, these relate both to ownership concentration and to the shareholdings of different groups of shareholders. There are two measures of concentration: the first (T1) is the fraction of shares held by the single largest shareholder, and the second (T10) is the fraction of shares held by the 10 largest shareholders. The expected impact of these variables upon corporate performance is unclear, and depends upon the relative strength of the effects suggested by Shleifer and Vishny (1986) and Hart (1995b).

There are five variables that reflect the shareholdings of different groups of shareholders. The first three relate to the holdings of three categories of large shareholders, namely, State agencies, State solely-owned institutions, and domestic institutions. Maug (1998) identifies two effects that may have an impact on the behaviour of large shareholders: the 'lock-in effect' and the 'liquidity effect'. The 'lock-in effect' refers to the fact that a large shareholder may find it is more profitable to own a large stake, and hence provides a greater incentive to intervene. But holding a larger fraction of the total shares also makes the market less liquid in these shares. The 'liquidity effect' thus reduces the large shareholder's expected returns from trading on private information. The size of institutions has several implications for activism (Coffee, 1991; Carleton *et al.*, 1998). Many institutional shareholders' positions have become so large that they are essentially illiquid, unless they are willing either to accept a relatively large drop in price or to spread share sales over a long period of time. Furthermore, firms may wish privately to place *restricted* shares with institutions: because such shares are harder to sell, cut-and-run behaviour is reduced, and intervention becomes more attractive (Kahn and Winton, 1998). In China, the CSRC regulations forbid the floating on the stock markets of the above categories of shares that may therefore be regarded as restricted. The five variables are

1 The fraction of shares that are directly owned by State agencies (FSOS), usually in the name of the BSAM.
2 The fraction of shares owned by State solely-owned institutions (FSOIS). These institutions are predominantly the parent holding corporations of the listed companies. All shares held either directly by State agencies, or by State solely-owned institutions, are State-owned but different interest groups effectively control them. State agencies represent the State, whilst the State solely owned institutions represent the controlling corporations of the listed companies.
3 The fraction of shares owned by domestic institutions (FDIS).
4 The fraction of shares that can be freely traded on the Stock Exchanges (FTS). The owners of tradable shares are various, ranging from individual investors, to non-banking financial institutions and other institutions that can buy and sell the shares on open markets.
5 The fraction of shares owned by the top management (FMOS), including the Directors of the Board, the CEO, the Deputy CEO, and the members of any supervisory committee. Following Brook *et al.* (2000), we classify the directors

as top management because the Board members are State agents and are appointed by the State administration authorities. We expect a positive relationship between performance and the management shareholding.

It is not clear at this stage whether the first four variables will have a positive or a negative impact upon corporate performance – this remains to be established empirically. But a positive relationship is expected between the fraction of shares owned by management (FMOS) and performance due to the motivation provided by this incentive.

In addition to the ownership variables, there are a number of other factors that have been shown in the extant literature to have an impact upon corporate performance:

1   Years of listing on the Stock Exchange – Ang *et al.* (1998) argue that older firms are likely to be more efficient than younger ones, due to the effects both the learning curve and survival bias. In contrast, various studies (e.g. Pagano *et al.*, 1998, on Italian corporations; Degeorge and Zeckhauser, 1993; Jain and Kini, 1994; Mikkelson *et al.*, 1997, on US corporations) have documented a reduction in profitability after corporations have been floated. Degeorge and Zeckhauser (1993) attribute this to 'window-dressing' by the corporations that are about to be listed. They massage the information in their accounts through practices such as early/late registration of accruals. Pagano *et al.* (1998) suggest two more fundamental explanations for the decline in performance, namely, adverse selection and moral hazard. They point out that declining performance can be attributed to adverse selection existing during the pre-listing stage, at which a 'bad' firm might be wrongly chosen for listing, whilst a 'good' firm might not receive approval. Moral hazard, in their study, is defined as the misbehaviour of management after listing, when monitoring and protection for the legal rights of all related parties are weak and the management makes self-interested decisions at the expense of others. We include the number of years that a firm has been listed (Age) as an explanatory variable in the model. A positive effect upon corporate performance might thus be interpreted as reflecting the fact that firms with longer histories perform better because they have more experience in a market-oriented environment. A negative effect would tend to confirm the validity of the moral hazard and adverse selection explanations.

2   Firm size – There is a rich literature that investigates the relationship between firm size and corporate performance. Banz (1981) and Reinganum (1981) found that small firms had higher returns than large firms, even after adjusting for risk via the Capital Asset Pricing Model (CAPM). Lang and Stulz (1994) report a significant negative relationship between firm size and Tobin's *Q*. Firm size may be measured in many different ways, but Gilson (1997) maintains that alternative measures do not materially affect the inferences. We use the natural logarithm of total assets (lnAssets) as a proxy for firm size, and expect size to have a negative impact upon performance.

3   Firm growth – In an efficient market, companies with good growth prospects should be valued higher. We measure firm growth (Growth) by the average annual growth of sales over the most recent three years, and expect this variable to have a positive impact upon corporate performance.

4   Stability of the business environment – Demsetz and Lehn (1985) argue that firms with more stable prices, stable technology, and stable market shares exercise less managerial discretion, and therefore management can be monitored at relatively low cost. Stability should thus be associated with better performance. We use the standard deviation of the firm's sales over the previous three years (Instability) as a proxy for the instability of the environment: a greater standard deviation implies less stability. It is expected that this variable will have a negative effect upon performance.

5   Profitability – A higher return on assets should be more positively valued by the markets, and give rise to a higher Tobin's Q. We use after-tax profits divided by the book value of total assets (ROA) as a measure of profitability, and expect this to have a positive impact upon Tobin's Q.

6   The debt–equity ratio – As the level of debt increases so too does the incentive for the lender to monitor the firm, which hopefully leads to better performance. There are several alternative measures available, but here we use total liabilities divided by the total book value of net assets (DAR) and expect this to have a positive impact upon Tobin's Q.

Table 5.1 summarises the explanatory variables in the model, and their expected impacts upon corporate performance. The expected signs for the ownership structure

Table 5.1 The explanatory variables and their expected impacts

Variables	Description	Expected sign[a]
T1	Shareholding of largest shareholder (%)	+/−
T10	Shareholding of 10 largest shareholders (%)	+/−
FSOS	Fraction of shares owned by BSAM (%)	+/−
FSOIS	Fraction of shares owned by State wholly owned institutions (%)	+/−
FDIS	Fraction of shares owned by domestic institutions (%)	+/−
FMOS	Fraction of shares owned by the top management (%)	+
FTS	Tradable shares as % of total shares	+/−
Age	Years listed on Stock Exchange	+/−
LnAssets	Natural log of total book assets (10,000 yuan)	−
Growth	Average sales growth over past three years (%)	+
Instability	Standard deviation of sales over the previous three years (%)	−
ROA	Return on assets (%)	+
DAR	Ratio of debt to total assets (%)	+

Note
a +/− stands for the sign can be either direction.

variables are not specified, and this reflects the fact that the effects of ownership structure can not be determined a priori – large shareholders may play a positive role in corporate governance in one economy, but may be harmful in another.

The data

The sample consists of 434 manufacturing firms listed either on SHSE or SZSE. The reason that we choose manufacturing firms is that, under current regulations issued by the Chinese authorities, this is the most clearly defined industry. Some firms, for which the industry classification was vague, were omitted from the analysis. The CSRC requires both the Exchanges and the listed companies to pub-lish Annual Reports, which should include data on capital structure, the 10 largest shareholders, turnover, profit or loss, total assets, net assets, liabilities (long-term and current), and other important information. The data on the firms' ownership structures, their financial figures, and the holdings and classifications of the 10 largest shareholders have been extracted from the CD-ROM containing the 1997 Annual Reports of all listed companies, published by *Securities Times (Zhengquan Shibao)*. The prices of both A-shares and B-shares are taken from *A Guide to Investors in Chinese Stock Markets 1998*, also published by *Securities Times*. The H-share prices are from the *Hong Kong Stock Exchange Annual Report*. All share prices refer to the end of 1997. The prices for both B-shares and H-shares are converted into Chinese currency at the year-end exchange rate.

Table 5.2 presents descriptive statistics for both the dependent and the explanatory variables.

Table 5.2 Descriptive statistics for the dependent and explanatory variables

Variables	Mean	Standard deviation	Minimum	Maximum
Q	2.90	1.49	1.00	11.84
T1	47.97	17.59	4.19	88.58
T10	63.98	12.85	8.54	94.67
FSOS	11.05	20.29	0	83.75
FSOIS	28.29	29.27	0	88.58
FDIS	21.73	24.33	0	75
FMOS	0.09	0.53	0	10.85
FTS	29.06	12.85	1.11	99.98
Age	1.9	1.94	0	7
LnAsset	11.29	0.88	9.38	14.53
Growth	28.63	101.68	−10.93	1,352.19
Instability	45.94	175.37	0.80	2,347.66
ROA	2.84	6.07	−26.1	31.68
DAR	43.19	17.24	4.43	88.97

Sources: Annual Reports of Listed Companies, 1997; Hong Kong Stock Exchange 1997 Report.

Note
The data relate to 434 manufacturing companies listed on SHSE and SZSE in 1997.

These data show that the Tobin's Q for all firms was well above unity, with the mean value of 2.9 and minimum of 1.0. The largest Tobin's Q was 11.84, reflecting a high market valuation of that firm. The values of the ownership concentration ratios (T1 and T10) reveal highly concentrated shareholdings in the sample. The largest single shareholders held, on average, nearly 48 per cent of the total shares. In one case, the single largest shareholder controlled 88.58 per cent of total shares, leaving no doubt about the non-existence of a market for corporate control. Nearly 64 per cent of the shares are held by the 10 largest shareholders: a relatively high concentration ratio.

The table also reports that State agencies[2] owned, on average, about 11 per cent of the total shares. The shareholders with the largest proportion of shares were the State solely-owned institutions, with an average stake of 28 per cent. Thus, the shares held by the State, either directly or indirectly, accounted for 39 per cent. Domestic institutions ranked as the second largest shareholders (22 per cent). Top management held only a tiny (0.1 per cent on average) proportion of the total shares, but with a substantial range. This suggests that, while stock incentive schemes are prevalent in Western economies and perhaps other economies as well,[3] managerial shareholdings have not been widely adopted as an incentive instrument in China. Generally the firms are quite young, with an average listing of 1.9 years. Growth was fast, with an annual growth rate of sales of 29 per cent.

The empirical results

As the sample consists of a cross-section sample of 434 firms with substantial differences in size, there is the possibility of heteroscedasticity. As is well-known, the presence of heteroscedasticity means that the OLS estimates of the regression parameters are unbiased but inefficient, whilst the estimated standard errors can be biased (Greene, 1993). Thus, in addition to OLS, we also apply the robust regression methods as discussed in the Data and Methodology section of Chapter 1.

Following Demsetz and Lehn (1985) and Ang *et al.* (1998), two sets of regressions were performed with corporate performance as the dependent variable. The first set included the ownership concentration variables (either T1 or T10) as explanatory variables, together with the control variables. The second set omitted the ownership concentration variables, but included the explanatory variables related to the shareholdings of the different types of owners (i.e. the State agencies, the State solely-owned institutions, the domestic institutions, the management, and the public). All regression models were estimated using both OLS and the robust Huber procedure.

The relationship between ownership concentration and corporate performance

The objective of the first set of regressions was to establish the effects of ownership concentration on corporate performance, as measured by Tobin's Q, but without distinguishing between the different types of shareholders. The model to be estimated was thus:

$$Q = \alpha + \beta_1 \text{OCR} + \beta_2 \text{Age} + \beta_3 \text{LnAsset} + \beta_4 \text{Growth}$$
$$+ \beta_5 \text{Instability} + \beta_6 \text{ROA} + \beta_7 \text{DAR} + \mu_i \tag{5.3}$$

where Q is the Tobin's Q; OCR, the ownership concentration ratio (either T1 or T10); α, the intercept term; $\beta_1, \dots, \beta_7$, the slope coefficients to be estimated; and μ_i, the error term.

The regression results are presented in Table 5.3, with T1 being included in the first pair of equations and T10 in the second pair. The results are encouraging in that the adjusted R^2 for both OLS regressions is 0.50, and all four regressions

Table 5.3 The relationship between ownership concentration and corporate performance

Explanatory variables	T1		T10	
	OLS	Robust Huber regression with biweights	OLS	Robust Huber regression with biweights
Ownership variables				
T1	−0.0067[b]	0.0012		
	(−1.985)	(0.543)		
T10			0.0097[b]	0.0110[a]
			(2.391)	(3.759)
Control variables				
Age	−0.0359	−0.0399[c]	−0.0035	−0.0203
	(−1.215)	(−1.834)	(−0.120)	(−0.972)
LnAsset	−0.4603[a]	−0.4144[a]	−0.5132[a]	−0.4449[a]
	(−7.332)	(−8.963)	(−8.254)	(−9.925)
Growth	0.0073[a]	0.008[a]	0.0081[a]	0.0089[a]
	(2.577)	(4.092)	(2.896)	(4.429)
Instability	−0.0035[b]	−0.0045[a]	−0.0041[b]	−0.0048[a]
	(−2.203)	(−3.801)	(−2.562)	(−4.178)
ROA	0.1170[a]	0.1003[a]	0.1154[a]	0.1073[a]
	(10.065)	(11.718)	(9.976)	(12.859)
DAR	−0.0067[c]	−0.0039[d]	−0.0057[d]	−0.0027
	(−1.890)	(−1.489)	(−1.607)	(0.282)
Constant	8.047[a]	6.9514[a]	7.6072[a]	6.5293[a]
	(11.911)	(13.970)	(10.936)	(13.020)
Adj. R^2	0.50		0.50	
F-statistic	63.67	91.72	63.68	103.82
P-value	0.00	0.00	0.00	0.00

Notes
1　The dependent variable is corporate performance, as measured by Tobin's Q.
2　Two estimation methods are used: OLS and robust regression, as discussed in Chapter 1.
3　The figures in parentheses are *t*-values.
4　The levels of significance are as follows: 'a' denotes 1 per cent, 'b' denotes 5 per cent, 'c' denotes 10 per cent, and 'd' denotes 15 per cent significance.

are highly significant according to the F-statistics. It is apparent that T10 has a positive, and highly significant, effect upon performance but that the effect of T1 is insignificant.

The significant impact of ownership concentration (as measured by T10) on Tobin's Q supports the Shleifer and Vishny (1986) hypothesis that large shareholders may help reduce the free-rider problem of small investors, and hence are value-increasing. But such an explanation merits a word of caution. The majority of the 10 largest shareholders in the listed companies are State agencies and institutions. For example, in the Shenzhen sample, only 42 out of the 300 companies have individuals amongst their largest five shareholders (Xu and Wang, 1997). There are obviously more individual investors amongst the 10 largest shareholders, but the numbers are fairly small. The figures are even more stark if we consider the percentage shareholdings: only 3.4 per cent on average of the total outstanding shares in the 300 companies are owned by individuals amongst the 10 largest shareholders. The variable T10 therefore essentially measures the degree of ownership by the State, and the results in Table 5.3 should be interpreted accordingly.

As regards the control variables, the regression results suggest there is a negative, though not significant relationship between the firms' history of listing and their performance. This result recalls the negative but significant findings of Pagano *et al.* (1998), who offered an explanation based on adverse selection and moral hazard arguments. If the adverse selection argument is correct, this means that the procedure for approving firms for flotation is defective. And if moral hazard leads to a deterioration of firm performance after being listed, the issue is even more serious. Is the transformation of the SOEs through the establishment of a joint-stock system a feasible way to improve the performance of firms? Lipton and Sachs (1990) and Shleifer and Boycko (1993) argue that corporatisation is a useful form of enterprise reform even without privatisation. They argue that the directors of corporations become responsible for the assets of the company, and hence have an incentive to prevent asset appropriation, increase information exchange, and separate the State from the enterprises. But this study, plus the findings of the research on firms in other economies, throws doubts on this optimism. The reality of reform in Eastern Europe and Russia also suggests that this argument is simplistic. The question is thus how effective is the Chinese approach to SOE reform? Can corporatisation without privatisation improve the deteriorating performance of SOEs? We will investigate these questions further, when more time-series data become available.

The regression results confirm the expected positive effects of both profitability and growth prospects on Tobin's Q, and also the expected negative effects of firm size and an unstable business environment. Larger firms and those operating in volatile business environments both tend to exhibit worse performance.

But the debt–equity ratio has a negative, though insignificant, effect upon performance. This suggests that debt does not curb the agency problem, contrary to the hypothesis of Grossman and Hart (1982) and Bolton and Scharfstein (1990). A premise of this hypothesis was that the debt constraint should be hard enough to put pressure on management. If the firm cannot repay the principal and interest on its debt, the risk of bankruptcy will be imminent, and management will be in danger of the sack. But such a corporate governance mechanism may not currently be significant in China.

In conclusion, the positive effect of ownership concentration on corporate performance suggests that an over-dispersed ownership structure may not be the best way to improve the economic efficiency of the public sector. But it would be premature to conclude that continuing State control would lead to an improvement. In the next section, we examine the effects of different groups of shareholders (i.e. State agencies, State solely-owned institutions or domestic institutional owners) on corporate performance.

The effects of different shareholders upon corporate performance

To investigate the impact of different shareholders upon corporate performance, we estimate the following model:

$$Q = \alpha + \beta_1 \, \text{DTS} + \beta_2 \, \text{Age} + \beta_3 \, \text{LnAsset} + \beta_4 \, \text{Growth}$$
$$+ \beta_5 \, \text{Stability} + \beta_6 \, \text{ROA} + \beta_7 \, \text{DAR} + \mu_i \tag{5.4}$$

where Q is the Tobin's Q; α, the intercept term; *DTS*, the shareholding of the selected group (i.e. FSOS, FSOIS, FDIS, FMOS, or FTS); $\beta_1, \ldots, \beta_7$, the slope coefficients to be estimated; μ_i, the error term.

The regression results are presented in Tables 5.4 and 5.5. All five pairs of regressions are statistically significant (see the F-statistics) and have high values of the adjusted R^2. Furthermore, the estimated coefficients for the control variables are stable across the different types of shareholders. In Table 5.4, the link between State shareholdings and corporate performance is explored. It appears as though there is an inverse relationship between the percentage shareholding held, either directly or indirectly, by the State and performance, though the results are not statistically significant. As Hart *et al.* (1997), cited by Shleifer (1998), have suggested, a healthy economy should engage in two types of investments: those to reduce costs, and those to improve quality or to innovate. When assets are publicly owned, management has little incentive to make either of these investments, because the manager is not the owner and hence gets only a fraction of the return. In contrast, private investors have much stronger incentives because, as owners, they get more of the returns on the investment.

In Table 5.5, the relationships between non-State shareholdings and corporate performance are investigated. First, there is a significant positive effect of a domestic institutional shareholding upon performance. Why is there such a link? The first explanation is that the domestic institutions mainly consist of profit-oriented organisations, such as Chinese Trust and Investment Corporations, securities companies, COEs, TVEs, Sino-foreign enterprises, and private enterprises. They have a greater incentive to pursue profits than do State agencies or State solely-owned institutions, who often have objectives other than pure economic ones.

Table 5.4 The relationship between State shareholdings and corporate performance

Explanatory variables	FSOS (the fraction of shares owned by BSAM) included as an explanatory variable		FSOIS (the fraction of shares owned by State solely-owned institutions) included as an explanatory variable	
	OLS	Robust Huber regression with biweights	OLS	Robust Huber regression with biweights
Ownership variables				
FSOS	−0.0038[b]	−0.0009		
	(−2.369)	(−0.471)		
FSOIS			−0.0030[a]	−0.0015
			(−1.640)	(−1.107)
Control variables				
Age	−0.0144	−0.0441[b]	−0.0293	−0.0488[b]
	(−0.500)	(−2.074)	(−1.000)	(−2.259)
LnAsset	−0.4954[a]	−0.4150[a]	−0.4584[a]	−0.3943[a]
	(−7.969)	(−9.065)	(−7.130)	(−8.325)
Growth	0.0077[a]	0.0084[a]	0.0080[a]	0.0079[a]
	(2.719)	(4.039)	(2.827)	(3.833)
Instability	−0.0061[c]	−0.0044[a]	−0.0039[b]	−0.0042[a]
	(−1.702)	(−3.749)	(−2.437)	(−3.546)
ROA	0.1152[a]	0.0964[a]	0.1132[a]	0.1007[a]
	(9.891)	(11.242)	(9.712)	(11.723)
DAR	−0.0061[c]	−0.0043[d]	−0.0072[b]	−0.0044[c]
	(−1.702)	(−1.624)	(−2.014)	(−1.682)
Constant	9.0897[a]	7.0796[a]	7.8194[a]	6.8708[a]
	(11.815)	(14.039)	(11.379)	(13.573)
Adj. R^2	0.50		0.50	
F-statistic	62.51	87.99	63.08	90.88
P-value	0.00	0.00	0.00	0.00

Notes
1 The dependent variable is corporate performance, as measured by Tobin's Q.
2 Two estimation methods are used: OLS and robust regression, as discussed in Chapter 1.
3 The figures in parentheses are *t*-values.
4 The levels of significance are as follows: 'a' denotes 1 per cent, 'b' denotes 5 per cent, 'c' denotes 10 per cent, and 'd' denotes 15 per cent significance.

The second explanation is that, in addition to the incentive to pursue profits, the domestic institutions possess the ability to monitor management, and will do so as long as the gains from the monitoring are larger than the costs. They thus have an advantage over small investors, whose only mechanism to protect themselves is to follow the 'Wall Street rule' – sell shares if they disapprove, but often with capital losses.

Second, there is a positive, but insignificant, effect of a top management shareholding upon performance. The lack of statistical significance probably reflects the very low level of management shareholding in the Chinese listed companies,

Table 5.5 The relationship between non-State shareholdings and corporate performance

Explanatory variables	FDIS (the fraction of shares owned by domestic institutions) included as an explanatory variable		FMOS (the fraction of shares owned by the top management) included as an explanatory variable		FTS (the fraction of shares that are tradable) included as an explanatory variable	
	OLS	Robust Huber regression	OLS	Robust Huber regression	OLS	Robust Huber regression
Ownership variables						
FDIS	0.0079^a	0.0063^a				
	(3.734)	(3.150)				
FMOS			0.0597	0.0731		
			(0.624)	(1.046)		
FTS					-0.0107^b	-0.0073^b
					(−2.491)	(−2.367)
Control variables						
Age	−0.0178	-0.0457^b	−0.0190	-0.0441^b	−0.0060	-0.0284^d
	(−0.634)	(−2.251)	(−0.666)	(−2.109)	(−0.210)	(−1.356)
LnAsset	-0.4277^a	-0.3694^a	-0.4869^a	-0.4060^a	-0.5484^a	-0.4527^a
	(−6.797)	(−8.140)	(−7.880)	(−8.982)	(−8.334)	(−9.446)
Growth	0.0080^a	0.0063^a	0.0077^a	0.0082^a	0.0082^a	0.0082^a
	(2.892)	(3.150)	(2.742)	(3.972)	(2.914)	(4.003)
Instability	-0.0040^b	-0.0036^a	-0.0038^b	-0.0043^a	-0.0057^d	-0.0045^a
	(−2.209)	(−3.142)	(−2.379)	(−3.675)	(−1.604)	(−3.820)
ROA	0.1121^a	0.0932^a	0.1154^a	0.1039^a	0.1168^a	0.1149^a
	(9.754)	(11.243)	(9.883)	(12.169)	(10.075)	(13.612)
DAR	-0.0078^b	-0.0053^b	-0.0062^c	-0.0035^d	-0.0057^d	−0.0024
	(−2.209)	(−2.089)	(−1.728)	(−1.345)	(−1.604)	(−0.929)
Constant	7.2245^a	6.4906^a	7.9758^a	6.8851^a	8.9293^a	7.4926^a
	(10.308)	(12.839)	(11.705)	(13.813)	(11.621)	(13.389)
Adj. R^2	0.51		0.50		0.50	
F-statistic	66.33	88.98	62.41	94.11	64.09	104.43
P-value	0.00	0.00	0.00	0.00	0.00	0.00

Notes
1 The dependent variable is corporate performance, as measured by Tobin's *Q*.
2 Two estimation methods are used: OLS and robust regression, as discussed in Chapter 1.
3 The figures in parentheses are *t*-values.
4 The levels of significance are as follows: 'a' denotes 1 per cent, 'b' denotes 5 per cent, 'c' denotes 10 per cent, and 'd' denotes 15 per cent significance.

yet it is interesting that there is nevertheless a weak positive effect. And third, there is a significant negative relationship between the proportion of shares traded on the market and corporate performance. This suggests that the interests of minority shareholders might not be well protected in China, where there is a weak and unsophisticated legal system, and where the courts are not well equipped to deal with corporate affairs.

Even though a larger shareholding by the domestic institutions helps improve firms' performance, restrictions on the tradability of shares may prevent the formation of the optimal ownership structure. Cole and Mehran (1998) found that firm performance improved significantly, and the fraction of the shares owned by the managers and the firm's employees increased, after conversion and the expiration of any restrictions on ownership structure. Changes in performance were positively associated with changes in ownership by managers, but negatively associated with changes in ownership under employee stock ownership schemes.

Concluding remarks

The findings of this study suggest that the influence of ownership structure upon corporate performance is considerably more complicated than had been previously understood. Not only does ownership concentration have an impact upon firms' performance, but the nature of the large shareholders is also an important determinant. A State shareholding, either through a State agency or through a State solely-owned institution, leads to inefficient capital allocation. In contrast, the presence of domestic shareholders can improve firm performance. A management shareholding, as a mechanism for providing top management with a proper incentive scheme, needs more attention, both in theory and in practice. A negative response of corporate performance to the proportion of tradable shares signals the absence or immaturity of markets for corporate control. The tradable shares, mainly held by the public, do not have a sufficient influence, either through vote or by the 'Wall Street rule', to monitor management. This raises a number of issues related to the legal aspects of corporate governance, which require urgent attention both in China and in other transition economies (e.g. Russia) and also some developed countries such as Italy.[4] This research also suggests that the stipulation that all shares held by institutional entities at the IPO should not be freely traded, retards the formation of an optimal ownership structure which maximises firm value.

It is important to recognise that the results of this study are suggestive rather than definitive, and to be aware of the limitations. First, Tobin's Q requires a perfect stock market, which can accurately reflect all the information related to the firm and its environment, if it is to be a useful measure of corporate performance. This would be a strong assumption, even in many well-developed economies, and is certainly an optimistic portrayal of China. Second, there is substantial anomalous behaviour by individual firms, though the systematic effects of this can be minimised by analysing a large sample of firms.

This study has discovered a positive relationship between ownership concentration and performance. Yet Bolton and von Thadden (1996) show that either a concentrated or a dispersed ownership structure may be optimal, depending upon the characteristics of the firm and the environment in which it operates. They argue that when the average liquidity demand of investors is higher, the costs of controlling management lower, the potential benefits from correcting managerial failures higher, and the transaction costs for secondary market trading higher, it is optimal to have a dispersed ownership structure.

The study of corporate governance is still at an early stage, and many more factors related to legal, institutional and cultural aspects have yet to be identified. For example, several authors have pointed out that legal and institutional factors can determine both the degree of ownership concentration and the corporate control mechanisms. Shleifer and Vishny (1997) and La Porta *et al.* (1998) analyse the costs and benefits of ownership concentration, and argue that the weak legal protection of minority shareholders' interests in many continental European countries helps to explain the high concentration of ownership. If the interests of small investors can be easily ignored, then the choice for investors is to sell or become large (Shleifer and Vishny, 1997). In contrast, when there are strong mechanisms for the protection of small investors such as in the United Kingdom and in the United States, a more dispersed ownership structure may be observed. This is a legal aspect of corporate governance, and beyond the scope of this study.

6   The determinants of capital structure[1]

Introduction

The idea that the general characteristics of a firm's capital structure can affect its performance has been receiving increasing attention from the financial profession. Modigliani and Miller's (MM) classic 1958 paper demonstrated that the value of a firm with given cash flows was not affected by its debt–equity ratio, in a perfect market where there are no friction costs, bankruptcy costs, and taxes. However, extensions to their analysis, incorporating variables such as taxes, bankruptcy costs, and agency costs indicate that the mix of financial claims affects the value of the firm because changes in the mix change the firm's total cash flows. With the increasing interest in corporate governance issues, the link between corporate governance and capital structure has been attracting considerable theoretical attention.[2]

This chapter investigates the determinants of capital structure in Chinese firms, and will contribute to our understanding of the corporate governance mechanism in China. Although there have been many studies of capital structure for developed and developing countries alike, this is the first such study for China. Furthermore, this study combines insights from various strands of finance theory, notably agency theory, signalling theory, and the theory of corporate control to establish a more comprehensive model of the determinants of capital structure.

This study will also contribute to the increasing number of empirical studies from around the world, and fills a gap in the case of Chinese listed companies. The prevailing view, as expressed by authors such as Mayer (1990) and Rajan and Zingales (1995), and as commented upon by Booth *et al.* (2001), seems to be that financial decisions in developing countries are made somewhat differently from that predicted by the standard theories derived from developed economies. Booth *et al.* (2001) carried out a detailed study of ten developing countries, and showed that the determinants of capital structure are largely consistent with those in developed countries. This study will test the stylised facts we have learned from both developed and developing economies, and add new evidence on the determinants of capital structure in transitional economies such as China in which factors such as the taxation, accounting, banking, and governance systems are rather different from the countries already studied.

The structure of the chapter is as follows. In the next section, we outline the theory of capital structure, beginning with the classic MM paper and then discussing various subsequent refinements and extensions. An econometric model to explain the debt ratio is developed in the following section, and we suggest the expected impacts of the various explanatory variables. The dataset is then identified, and the regression methods are described in the section 'The data'. The section titled 'The empirical results' presents and discusses the empirical results from the regression analysis. The final section summarises the main findings.

The theory of capital structure

The modern theory of capital structure originated with the paper by Modigliani and Miller (1958) who demonstrated that, if investors can borrow and save on the same terms as firms, and if firms' financing decisions do not affect their total cash flow, then the firms' choice between debt and equity has no effect on their total market value. In other words, capital structure cannot create value unless it affects the total returns. This conclusion was based upon the rather restrictive assumption that the capital market was perfect, and that there was no taxation. Furthermore, it is clear that in reality firms have very different capital structures. The MM model should thus be seen as a starting point for modelling more realistic scenarios which explain why debt might be used in preference to equity.

One early extension was to allow for the incidence of taxation and financial distress. Since the late 1970s, there have been new strands of research which originate more from the theory of the firm. First, agency theory has been used to demonstrate how debt might be used by entrepreneurs with limited resources who were faced with new investment opportunities and who did not want to dilute their position (Jensen and Meckling, 1976). Second, it has been argued that the financial structure is an important source of corporate control and of imposing discipline on managers. Debt serves as a bonding or commitment device in that it places limits on the potential inefficiency of management, at least so long as management wants to repay the debt (Grossman and Hart, 1982). Third, debt can be used as a signal of differential prospects (Ross, 1977). Finally, a further strand of research has focused on the maturity structure of debt.

The trade-off theory of tax-shield benefits and financial distress cost of debt

One of the crucial assumptions of the MM (1958) model was that there is no taxation. Later work by Modigliani and Miller (1963), and Miller (1977) add tax effects into the original framework. An implication of this newer work was that firms should finance their projects completely through debt in order to maximise corporate value. Clearly this contradicts reality in that debt constitutes only a fraction of firms' total capital. Subsequent theoretical work seeks an optimal capital structure which results from a trade-off between the benefits of tax shield of debt and the costs of financial distress of debt. According to this line of theory, the benefits of debt arise from its tax exemption, which implies that a higher debt ratio will increase the firm's value. But the benefits can be offset by costs of

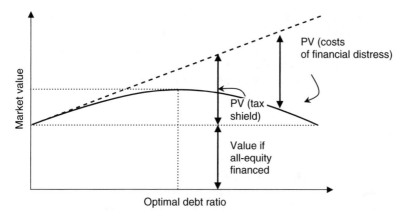

Figure 6.1 The optimal capital structure when debt is associated with tax-shield benefit and financial distress costs.

financial distress, which may destroy the value of the firm. Thus the optimal capital structure is determined by the trade-off between the tax-free benefits of debt and the distress costs of debt – see Figure 6.1. DeAngelo and Masulis (1980), Ross (1985) and Leland (1994) have shown that, in the presence of taxation, it is advantageous for a firm with safe, tangible assets and plenty of taxable income to take a high debt–equity ratio to avoid high tax payments. For a firm with poorer performance and more intangible assets, it is better to rely on equity financing.

One problem with the theories based on consideration of the tax-shield benefits is that they cannot explain why capital structures vary across firms that are subject to the same taxation rates. Empirical evidence from the United States (Copeland and Weston, 1992) shows that the capital structure of corporations did not change much after corporate income tax came into existence. In Australia, where there is no dual income taxation at all, capital structure is roughly the same as in other economies (Rajan and Zingales, 1995).

Signalling theory

Signalling theory was the most important theory of capital structure during the 1970s and 1980s. Ross (1977) was the first to address the function of debt as a signalling mechanism when there is information asymmetry between the firm's management and its investors. He argued that management has better knowledge of the firm than the investors, and that management will try to avoid debt when the firm is performing poorly for fear that any debt default due to poor cash flow will result in their job loss. The information asymmetry may also explain why existing investors may not favour new equity financing, as new investors may require higher returns to compensate for the risks of their investment thus diluting the returns to existing investors. Myers (1984) and Myers and Majluf (1984) developed their so-called 'pecking order' theory of financing: that is, that capital structure will be driven by firms' desire to finance new investments preferably through the use of internal funds, then with low-risk debt, and with new equity only as a last resort. However, Helwege and Liang (1996) found no empirical evidence for such a pecking order.

Agency theory

Even if markets are perfect and there is no tax impact, agency theory suggests that the appropriate mix of debt and equity is still an important matter for corporate governance. In general, debt claims provide the holders with a fixed repayment schedule but little in the way of rights to control the company, as long as the repayment schedule (and sometimes certain other terms) is met. However, creditors can have a strong influence over a company if it gets in financial distress but, even if a company is financially sound, creditors can influence whether it can obtain additional funding for proposed new projects. For example, a bank that has loaned a company the money for factory expansion can make it easy or hard for the company to borrow more money for a new office building.

Conversely, equity claims – in particular, common stock – give shareholders the right to vote for Boards of Directors as well as on other important corporate issues such as major mergers or plans that would dispose of substantial portions of the company's assets. Shareholders are also entitled to receive dividends or other distributions whenever the company pays them or, if the company is liquidated, to receive the net assets of the company after paying all debts and any securities, such as preferred stock, that rank ahead of common shares. These two features, the right to vote and the right to receive dividends and other distributions, are the defining characteristics of common shares.

Jensen and Meckling (1976) identify two potential sources of conflict. On the one hand, conflicts between debt-holders and equity-holders arise because the debt contract gives equity-holders an incentive to invest sub-optimally. More specifically the debt contract provides that, if an investment yields large returns well above the face value of the debt, equity-holders will capture most of the gain. If, however, the investment fails, debt-holders bear the consequences because of limited liability. As a result, equity-holders may benefit from 'going for broke'; that is, investing in very risky projects, even if they are value-decreasing. Such investments result in a decrease in the value of the debt. The loss in value of the equity from the poor investment can be more than offset by the gain in equity value captured at the expense of debt-holders. Equity-holders correctly anticipate equity-holders' future behaviour. In this case, the debt-holders receive less for the debt than they otherwise would. Thus, the cost of the incentive to invest in value-decreasing projects created by debt is borne by the equity-holders who issue the debt. This effect, generally called the asset substitution effect, is the *agency cost* of debt financing.

On the other hand, conflicts between shareholders and managers arise because managers hold less than 100 per cent of the residual claim. Consequently, they do not bear the entire cost of these activities. Managers may thus invest less effort in managing the firm's resources, and may be able to transfer firm resources to their own personal benefit, for example through 'empire-building' or by consuming 'perquisites' such as corporate jets, luxurious offices, etc. The manager bears the entire cost of refraining from these activities, but captures only a fraction of the gain. As a result, managers overindulge in these pursuits relative to the level that would maximise firm value. This inefficiency is reduced the larger is the fraction of the firm's equity owned by the manager. Holding constant the manager's absolute investment in the firm, an increase in the debt ratio of the firm increases the manager's share of the equity and mitigates the loss from the conflict between the manager and shareholders. Moreover, as pointed out by Jensen (1986), since debt commits the firm to pay out cash, it reduces the amount of 'free' cash available to managers to engage in the types of pursuits mentioned above. This mitigation of the conflicts between managers and equity-holders constitutes a *benefit* of debt financing.

Jensen and Meckling (1976, p. 117) argue that an optimal capital structure can be obtained by trading off the agency cost of debt against the benefit of debt as shown in Figure 6.2.

The figure shows total agency costs, $A_T(E)$, as a function of the ratio of outside equity to total outside financing, $E = S_o/(B+S_o)$, for a given firm size, V^*, and given total amounts of outside financing $(B + S_o)$, where S_o stands for outside equity finance and B for debt finance. $A_{S_o}(E)$ are the agency costs associated with outside equity, whilst $A_B(E)$ are the agency costs associated with debt. $A_T(E^*)$ are the minimum total agency costs at optimal fraction of outside financing E^*.

A number of implications follow from this analysis. First, one would expect bond contracts to include features that attempt to prevent asset substitution, such

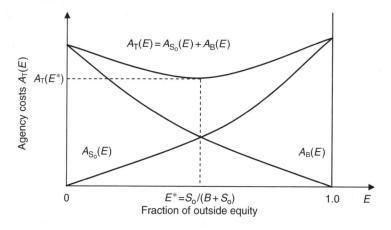

Figure 6.2 The optimal capital structure according to agency theory.

as interest coverage requirements, prohibitions against investments in new unrelated lines of business, etc. Second, industries in which the opportunities for asset substitution are more limited will have higher debt levels *ceteris paribus*. Thus, for example, the theory predicts that regulated public utilities, banks, and firms in mature industries with few growth opportunities will be more highly leveraged. Third, it is optimal for firms with slow or even negative growth, and that have large cash inflows from operations, to have more debt. Large cash flows without good investment prospects create the resources to consume perquisites, build empires, overpay subordinates, etc. Increasing debt reduces the amount of 'free cash' and increases the manager's fractional ownership of the residual claim. According to Jensen (1986) industries with these characteristics today include steel, chemicals, brewing, tobacco, television and radio broadcasting, and wood and paper products. The theory predicts that these industries should be characterised by high leverage ratios. In the Chinese case, one problem with the testing of this hypothesis is the ambiguous classification of industries. Currently there are six broad industry classifications (i.e. manufacturing, retailing, utility, property development, financial services, and conglomerates), and each covers a broad range of business activities. For example, manufacturing industry includes general machinery, chemical engineering, electronics, food processing, and iron and steel. There is no clear classification similar to the International Standard Industry Classification (SITC), or the Standard Industrial Classification (SIC) in North America. Testing of the hypothesis must thus await the Chinese authorities compiling data according to a comprehensive and internationally comparable standard.

Corporate control

One limitation of agency theory is that it assumes the agency problem can be mitigated, or eliminated, by a comprehensive contract which postulates all the future contingencies and states the circumstances in which the manager should take a particular action, as criticised by Hart (1995a,b). But, as discussed in Chapter 2, such a comprehensive contract would be very costly to design and/or execute (Williamson, 1988). It may well be optimal to leave the contract incomplete, and to assign the equity-holders the residual control rights beyond contractual control rights which are assigned to the debt-holders (Aghion and Bolton, 1992). This incomplete contract approach regards equity and debt as 'contingent state' securities. When the firm is financially healthy, it is the equity-holders who have control. But a default of debt repayment will trigger the transfer of control to the debt-holders. Liquidation of the firm and/or managerial sackings are then inevitable. Thus management is constrained by the requirement to ensure a smooth repayment of debt – see Table 6.1.

Two related models share a common concern with conflicts between shareholders and managers, though they differ in the specific ways in which the conflicts arise and in the role of debt. Harris and Raviv (1990) postulate that managers always want to continue the firm's current operations, even if liquidation of the firm would be the preferred option for investors. But debt can force managers

Table 6.1 The key differences in governance structure between debt and equity

	Financial instrument	
	Debt	*Equity*
Contractual constraints	Numerous	Nil
Securities	Pre-emptive	Residual claimant
Intrusion	Nil	Extensive

Source: Williamson (1988).

to liquidate firms, because default may well trigger the managers' job loss. The optimal capital structure is achieved by trading off improved liquidation decisions against higher investigation costs. A different model by Stulz (1990) is based on the assumption that managers always want to invest available funds so as to expand the size of the firm, even though investors might prefer higher dividend payouts. The optimal capital structure in Stulz's model is achieved by trading off the benefits of debt in preventing investment in bad projects with the costs of debt in preventing investment in good projects. Therefore, unlike in the Modigliani–Miller world, changing the capital structure of the firm changes the allocation of power between the insiders and the outside investors, and thus almost surely changes the firm's investment policy (La Porta *et al.*, 2000).

The maturity structure of debt

Not only does the debt ratio exert a discipline on management, but so too does the maturity structure of debt (Diamond, 1991; Berglof and von Thadden, 1994; Barclay and Smith, 1995; Hart, 1995b). In general, a firm will have more than one (class of) investor, and those investors will separate their claims across time and across states of nature, with one investor holding secured short-term claims and another junior long-term claims. If the firm is doing well in the short run, the short-term creditor is repaid, and long-term claim-holders receive all future returns. If the firm is unable to repay in the short term, the short-term creditor forces the firm to transfer or sell part of its assets. The maturity of the remaining claims is extended at the expense of some (not necessarily all) junior long-term claim-holders.

The principal reason for this separation is that the *ex post* bargaining position of an investor with short-term claims is weaker if she/he also has long-term claims because she/he internalises the impact of his/her actions on future revenues. On the other hand separating outside claims over time creates an externality on the side of the short-term investor, which strengthens his/her bargaining power if the firm should attempt to default. The separation of claims across high and low cash-flow states – that is making long-term claims junior to unpaid short-term debt – further discourages strategic default by giving the short-term investor an extra incentive to be tough with the firm.

Lehn and Toft (1996) argue that short-term debt is more likely to provide incentive compatibility between debt-holders and equity-holders, even though short-term debt does not exploit tax benefits as completely as long-term debt. Thus short-term debt must be balanced against bankruptcy and agency costs in determining the optimal maturity of the capital structure. They predict different term structures of credit spreads for different levels of risk.[3]

The model

The dependent variable in the model is the debt ratio. The most appropriate measure of capital structure depends upon the object of the analysis. For instance, the agency problems associated with debt (Jensen and Meckling, 1976; Myers, 1977) largely relate to how the firm has been financed in the past, and thus on the relative claims on firm value held by equity and debt. Here, the relevant measure is probably the amount of debt relative to firm value. Other studies (see, e.g. Aghion and Bolton, 1992) have focused on leverage as a means of transferring control when the firm is economically distressed, from shareholders (or their fiduciaries) to bondholders (or their fiduciaries). Here, the important question is whether the firm can meet its fixed payments, and consequently, a flow measure like the interest coverage ratio is more relevant.

The effects of past financing decisions are probably best captured by the ratio of total debt to capital (defined as total debt plus equity):

$$\text{Leverage 1} \;=\; \frac{\text{Total liabilities}}{\text{Total book value of (debt + equity)}} \tag{6.1}$$

This measure, however, fails to take account of the fact that there are some assets that are offset by specific non-debt liabilities. For example, an increase in the gross amount of trade credit is reflected in a reduction of this measure of leverage. Given that the levels of accounts payable and accounts receivable may jointly be influenced by industry considerations, it seems more appropriate to use a measure of leverage unaffected by the gross level of trade credit. A variant of the above definition is provided by the ratio of total debt to net assets, where net assets are total assets less accounts payable and other liabilities. Although this measure is not influenced by the amount of trade credit, it is affected by factors that may have nothing to do with financing. For example, assets held against pension liabilities may decrease this measure of leverage.

An alternative measure of financial leverage is thus the ratio of total liabilities to the sum of long-term debt and the market value of common stock, as used by Bradley, *et al.* (1984), Titman and Wessels (1988), Opler and Titman (1994), and Gilson (1997).

$$\text{Leverage 2} = (\text{Total liabilities} + \text{ leasing})/[\text{Total liabilities} \\ + \text{ market value of (common stocks + preferred stocks)}] \tag{6.2}$$

Listed companies in China typically do not issue preferred stocks. Moreover, leasing is rarely reported in Annual Reports. So we focus on the roles of short- and long-term debt, and of common stock. We record long-term debt according to a one-year standard, but also include the debt with maturity over one year but which will be returned within one year.[4] To fully capture the determinants of capital structure and look at whether firms are more sensitive to book values or market values when they make financial decisions, we use both measures of leverage in this chapter, following the practice of Rajan and Zingales (1995), Berger *et al.* (1997), and Booth *et al.* (2001).

As regards the explanatory variables, we include the following. The agency costs associated with asset substitution will be lower when the firm has a reputation for the selection of safe projects. The longer the firm's history of repaying debt, the easier it will be to raise debt finance at lower borrowing cost. Diamond (1989) has shown that younger firms typically have less debt than older ones, other things being equal. Thus, we hypothesise that the age of listed companies (AGE), as measured by the years of listing on the stock market, will be an important indicator of corporate credibility, and expect there to be a positive relationship between AGE and the debt ratio.

Jensen (1986) and Stulz (1990) both predict that high leverage can add value by reducing the resources available to managers to finance investments in negative net present value projects. High leverage can also add value by making default more likely, thus increasing the penalty on managers for poor performance (Grossman and Hart, 1982; Gilson, 1989). We therefore hypothesise that the market-to-book value ratio (MBR) should have a negative impact upon the debt ratio.

Several studies have shown that leverage is positively correlated with the extent of managerial equity ownership (Leland and Pyle, 1977; Kim and Sorensen, 1986; Agrawal and Mandelker, 1987; Harris and Raviv, 1988; Stulz, 1988; Amihud *et al.*, 1990; Berger *et al.*, 1997) though they give different explanations. For example, Berger *et al.* (1997, p. 1420) find a positive relation between leverage and management shareholdings and explain it on the grounds that managers whose financial incentives are more closely tied to stockholder wealth will pursue more leveraged capital structures to raise the value of the company. We therefore include the fraction of shares owned by management (MF) as an explanatory variable, and expect it to have a positive effect upon the leverage ratio.

The impact of state ownership on firms' capital structure is rarely studied, either in developed or in developing economies. Yet, as noted in Chapter 3, the amount of debt in the capital structure of SOEs first rose, but later fell, after the onset of reform, particularly after firms were listed. Perhaps the largest shareholder is able to influence the leverage level in line with their interests, irrespective of the wider interests of other shareholders and interested parties. We therefore include the fraction of equity held by the largest shareholder (T1) as an explanatory variable, to capture the effects of this aspect of corporate governance. However, the expected impact upon the debt ratio is unclear. On the one hand, the State may well provide loans on favourable terms to listed companies which are majority-owned by the State. Friend and Lang (1988), and Berger *et al.* (1997,

p. 1421) suggest that managers are forced to take on more debt when an influential monitor is present, and when Board shareholders and debt-holders act as monitoring complements rather than as substitutes. On the other hand, the incumbent management may choose a low level of leverage to avoid the risk of bankruptcy (Berger *et al.*, 1997). Both Amihud *et al.* (1990) and Zeckhauser and Pound (1990) found a negative relationship between the presence of large shareholders and firm leverage.

The combination of the two variables measuring the fraction of shares held by the largest shareholder (T1) and the fraction held by management (MF) provides an insight into the impact of control over the firm's capital structure. Although the Directors of Chinese firms personally hold very small fractions of the shares, they often represent the ownership of State or other institutional shareholders.

The rate of corporate income tax has long been identified as a potential determinant of capital structure. Firms will prefer to have more debt than equity finance because of the tax-shield on interest when the corporate income tax rate is higher, holding the personal income tax rate and the rate on dividend income constant. In China, different corporate income tax rates apply to different types of firms, even though they are all listed companies.[5] Listed companies are normally faced with a 15 per cent tax rate if local tax bureaux permit, but a small number of corporations face a higher rate of 33 per cent.

Companies with foreign investment enjoy a tax holiday during their first two years of establishment, and then only pay 7.5 per cent for the following three years. And companies in high-technology industries also need to pay tax at a rate of only 7.5 per cent. Booth *et al.* (2001) find a negative relationship between the level of leverage and corporate income tax. Following Miller (1977), we expect a positive relationship between the corporate income tax rate (TR) and the debt ratio, in that the higher tax rate will reduce the cost of capital, other things being equal.

The costs associated with the agency relationship are likely to be higher for firms in growing industries, as they have more flexibility in their choice of future investments. More specifically, improvements in a firm's growth opportunities lead to an increase in the agency costs of debt and to a reduction in the agency costs of managerial discretion (Booth *et al.*, 2001). This argument is supported by the empirical findings by Smith and Watts (1992), and Titman and Wessels (1988). We therefore expect the growth of sales (GROWTH) to be negatively related to the debt ratio.

Various studies have shown that a firm's optimal debt level is a decreasing function of the volatility of its earnings (Demsetz and Lehn, 1985; Titman and Wessels, 1988; Booth *et al.*, 2001). We use the standard deviation of the return on equity over the three previous years (1995–97) as a proxy for the volatility of operating conditions (BUSRISK), and expect this to have a negative impact upon the debt ratio. It has also been suggested that the maturity structure of debt has an important role to play in curbing agency costs. Myers (1977), for example, notes that the agency problem is mitigated if the firm issues short-term rather than long-term debt. We therefore include the ratio of long-term to short-term debt (LSR) as an explanatory variable, and expect it to have a positive impact upon the level of leverage.

Theory suggests that large firms are more likely to be debt-financed than their smaller counterparts, for a number of reasons. Large companies are more diversified and thus have more stable cash flows, which helps reduce the risk of the debt. Additionally, large firms may be able to exploit economies of scale in issuing securities. Smaller firms are likely to face higher costs for obtaining external funds, because of information asymmetries. Large firms may also be more mature and hence have a larger fraction of firm value accounted for by assets in place, as opposed to growth opportunities. Diamond (1991) shows that large firms are likely to have established reputations and more firm-specific information publicly available than do small firms, facilitating the issuance of public debt. We thus include firm size as a control variable in our analysis. Firm size can be measured in many different ways. Gilson (1997) uses the natural logarithm of total assets as a proxy of firm size. Anderson and Makhija (1999) measure firm size as the book value of assets, minus the book value of equity plus the market value of outstanding equity. Their research also shows that alternative measures of size, based on annual sales or total asset values, do not materially affect the inferences. Titman and Wessels (1988) use the natural logarithm of sales as their proxy of firm size, and they also report a high correlation (0.98) between the natural logarithm of sales and the natural logarithm of assets. Here we use the natural logarithm of sales (LnSALES) as our proxy of firm size, following Booth *et al.* (2001).

Finally, Chang (1999) argues that there is a negative relationship between the debt ratio and profitability, as more profitable firms can finance higher growth rates internally. Chang's theory is empirically supported by Kester (1986), Friend and Hasbrouck (1988), Titman and Wessels (1988), Rajan and Zingales (1995), Wald (1999), and Booth *et al.* (2001). These findings are robust for both developed economies as well as developing economies. We therefore expect a negative relationship between profitability, as measured by the before-tax return on assets (ROA) and the debt ratio.

Table 6.2 summarises the explanatory variables included in the model and their expected impacts upon the debt ratio. It should be noted that the model does not include all the variables that have been hypothesised in previous studies to have

Table 6.2 The explanatory variables and their expected impacts on the debt ratio

Variable	Description	Predicted sign
Age	Years of the company being listed	+
MBR	Ratio of market value of equity plus total liability to book assets	−
MF (%)	Fraction of outstanding shares held by the management	+
T1 (%)	The fraction of shares held by the largest shareholder	+/−
TR (%)	Corporate income tax	+
GROWTH (%)	Average growth of sales over past three years, 95, 96, 97	−
BUSRISK	Standard deviation of growth of ROE over past three years	−
LSR	Long-term to short-term debt ratio	+
LnSALES	Natural Logarithm of sales	−
ROA (%)	Before tax return on assets	+

an impact upon capital structure. The theory of capital structure, whilst very complex, is still in its infancy (Harris and Raviv, 1991). There is a lack of agreement among different researchers in different economies about which variables are important, what measures are appropriate, and about the correct interpretation of the statistical results.

The data

The sample consisted of 433 manufacturing firms publicly traded on either the SHSE or the SZSE in 1997. Table 6.3 provides descriptive statistics for both the dependent variable(s) and the explanatory variables. The sample exhibits considerable variation in both firm size and capital structure. Firm size is measured by sales denominated in millions of Renminbi, and range from a minimum of 118.5 million yuan to 20.43 billion yuan. The average debt ratios for the sample (43.23 per cent book leverage; 19.38 per cent market leverage) are small by international standards. Rajan and Zingales (1995) report corresponding figures for the United States (52 per cent, 44 per cent), Japan (69 per cent, 49 per cent), Germany (73 per cent, 55 per cent), and the United Kingdom (54 per cent, 40 per cent). The debt levels are also modest (Booth *et al.*, 2001) when compared with Brazil (30.3 per cent, book measure only) and South Korea (73.4 per cent, 64.3 per cent).

A number of observations may be made with regard to the explanatory variables. First, MF is small, being only 0.063 per cent on average. This confirms that the personal stake of top management is still insignificant in the Chinese economy, and is much lower than the average managerial shareholding of 2.7 per cent reported by Berger *et al.* (1997) in their US study. In contrast, the average shareholding of the largest shareholder (T1) is 48 per cent, as has already been the subject of discussion in Chapter 5. The average corporate income tax rate is 12.5 per cent, with a minimum rate of −2.8 per cent (i.e. a tax refund) and a maximum

Table 6.3 Descriptive statistics for the variables in the model

Variable	Mean	Standard deviation	Minimum	Maximum
Leverage 1 (%)	43.2343	17.2357	4.4308	88.9729
Leverage 2 (%)	19.3762	12.9288	0.6121	63.6040
Age	1.8961	1.9331	0.0000	7.0000
MBR	2.9013	1.4878	1.0026	11.8382
MF (%)	0.0630	0.1293	0.0000	2.0804
T1 (%)	48.0011	17.5908	4.1898	88.5819
TR (%)	12.5087	6.8574	−2.7700	33.5200
GROWTH (%)	28.7092	101.7901	−40.9300	1,352.1900
BUSRISK	9.7337	16.0445	0.0500	257.2600
LSR	0.2378	0.3955	0.0000	3.9000
LnSALES	10.4823	1.2046	0.0000	14.2649
ROA (%)	0.0705	0.0686	−0.2616	0.3725

rate of 33.5 per cent. The average growth rate of the companies in the sample was 28.7 per cent, with a minimum rate of −41 per cent and a maximum rate of plus 1,352 per cent! These growth rates reflect the fast expansion of the Chinese economy over the past two decades. Naturally, the high growth rates are accompanied by high business risk, as measured here the standard deviation of the return on equity over three years (BUSRISK): the average figure was 46 per cent.

The empirical results

The model has been estimated using three different regression methods. First we use simple Ordinary Least Squares (OLS). One potential problem with the use of OLS in cross-section models is the presence of heteroscedasticity, with the result that the coefficient estimates are inefficient and the estimates of the standard errors are biased. Thus we also apply the formula below to obtain robust estimates of the coefficients:

$$\hat{v} = \hat{\mathbf{V}} \left(\sum_{j=1}^{N} \mathbf{u}_j' \mathbf{u}_j \right) \hat{\mathbf{V}} \tag{6.3}$$

where $\hat{\mathbf{V}} = (-\partial^2 \ln L / \partial \beta^2)^{-1}$ is the conventional OLS estimator of variance and $\mathbf{u}_j$ (a row vector) is the contribution from the jth observation to the scores $\partial \ln L / \partial \beta$.

The third estimation method tries to eliminate further the influence of outliers. Robust estimates are generated, Cook's D is calculated, and those observations for which $D > 1$ are discarded. Then, following Huber (1964), those observations with small residuals from the robust regression are given weights of unity, whereas those with larger residuals are given gradually smaller weights. Those observations with non-zero residuals are then downweighted according to a smoothly decreasing biweight function. The following econometric models were then estimated using the two alternative measures (Leverage 1 and Leverage 2) for the debt ratio:

$$
\begin{aligned}
\text{Debt ratio} = {}& \alpha + \beta_1 \text{ Age} + \beta_2 \text{ MBR} + \beta_3 \text{ MF} + \beta_4 \text{ T1} + \beta_5 \text{ TR} \\
& + \beta_6 \text{ GROWTH} + \beta_7 \text{ BUSRISK} + \beta_8 \text{ LSR} \\
& + \beta_9 \text{ LnSALES} + \beta_{10} \text{ ROA} + \mu_i
\end{aligned} \tag{6.4}
$$

where debt ratio is Leverage 1 or Leverage 2; α, the intercept; $\beta_1, \ldots, \beta_{10}$, the regression parameters to be estimated; μ_i, the (heteroscedastic) error term.

The regression results are tabulated in Table 6.4 (with Leverage 1 as the dependent variable) and in Table 6.5 (with Leverage 2 as the dependent variable) respectively. Two general observations may be made. The first is that the signs and magnitudes of the regression co-efficients are very stable, whichever regression method is adopted, though the standard errors and hence the t-statistics vary. The second is that the equations with Leverage 2 as the dependent variable give rise to much higher coefficients of determination (approx. 60 per cent, compared to approx. 33 per cent).

Table 6.4 The regression results using Leverage 1 as the dependent variable

Dependent variable	Leverage 1 (book value of debt/book value of total assets)		
Explanatory variables	OLS	Robust regression	Robust Huber regression with biweights
AGE	0.5634	0.5634	0.6465[d]
	(1.38)	(1.40)	(1.53)
MBR	−1.1403[c]	−1.1403[d]	−0.6041
	(−1.72)	(−1.54)	(−0.88)
MF	4.3426	4.3426	5.6914
	(0.81)	(0.99)	(1.02)
T1	−0.0815[c]	−0.0815[b]	−0.0816[c]
	(−1.90)	(−1.97)	(−1.85)
TR	0.0640	0.0640	0.0725
	(0.57)	(0.54)	(0.62)
GROWTH	0.0091	0.0091	0.0090
	(1.33)	(1.31)	(1.27)
BUSRISK	0.1171[a]	0.1171[b]	0.1207[a]
	(2.63)	(2.43)	(2.63)
LSR	2.7773[d]	2.7773[c]	2.7205[d]
	(1.58)	(1.87)	(1.50)
LnSALES	3.5956[a]	3.5956[a]	4.0022[a]
	(5.73)	(5.81)	(6.19)
ROA	−111.9053[a]	−111.9053[a]	−126.6043[a]
	(−7.07)	(−5.12)	(−7.75)
Intercept	16.4460[b]	16.4460[b]	11.7300[c]
	(2.32)	(2.21)	(1.60)
Sample size	433	433	433
R^2	0.35		
Adjusted R^2	0.34	0.35	
F-statistic	22.89	27.20	23.70
P-value	0.00	0.00	0.00

Notes
1 The dependent variable is the debt ratio, as measured by Leverage 1.
2 Three estimation methods are used, as discussed in the text and in Chapter 1.
3 The figures in parentheses are *t*-values.
4 The levels of significance are as follows: 'a' denotes 1 per cent, 'b' denotes 5 per cent, 'c' denotes 10 per cent, and 'd' denotes 15 per cent significance.

We find that firm size, LnSALES, MBR, and profitability (ROA) all have highly significant effects upon the debt ratio as predicted, particularly with the market measure of leverage. The positive coefficient for firm size is as expected, though it is not clear whether this is due to economies of scale, diversification, or the ease of borrowing. All three regression methods show the expected impact of the years of listing (AGE) upon the debt ratio, and the coefficients in the model with the market-valued debt ratio (i.e. Leverage 2) are highly significant. The magnitudes of the coefficients for the two measurements of leverage are roughly

Table 6.5 The regression results using Leverage 2 as the dependent variable

Dependent variable	Leverage 2 (book value of debt/(book value of debt + market value of equity))		
Explanatory variables	OLS	Robust regression	Robust Huber regression with biweights
AGE	0.7008[a]	0.7008[a]	0.5577[a]
	(2.88)	(2.74)	(2.60)
MBR	−3.1337[a]	−3.1337[a]	−2.3709[a]
	(−7.93)	(−4.82)	(−6.89)
MF	2.3105	2.3105	5.0716[c]
	(0.72)	(1.25)	(1.79)
T1	−0.0266	−0.0266	−0.0233
	(−1.05)	(−1.26)	(−1.04)
TR	−0.0626	−0.0626	−0.0420
	(−0.93)	(−0.75)	(−0.71)
GROWTH	0.0038	0.0038	0.0038
	(0.94)	(1.42)	(1.06)
BUSRISK	0.0319	0.0319	0.0209
	(1.20)	(1.35)	(0.89)
LSR	1.6615[d]	1.6615[c]	1.3150
	(1.59)	(1.69)	(1.43)
LnSALES	2.6546[a]	2.6546[a]	2.8354[a]
	(7.11)	(6.04)	(8.61)
ROA	−70.7011[a]	−70.7011[a]	−105.1338[a]
	(−7.50)	(−4.44)	(−12.65)
Intercept	5.3949	5.3949	3.1980
	(1.28)	(1.03)	(0.86)
Sample size	433	433	433
R^2	0.59		
Adjusted R^2	0.58	0.59	
F-statistic	61.12	29.01	92.84
P-value	0.00	0.00	0.00

Notes
1 The dependent variable is the debt ratio, as measured by Leverage 2.
2 Three estimation methods are used, as discussed in the text and in Chapter 1.
3 The figures in parentheses are *t*-values.
4 The levels of significance are as follows: 'a' denotes 1 per cent, 'b' denotes 5 per cent, 'c' denotes 10 per cent, and 'd' denotes 15 per cent significance.

identical at around 0.55–0.70, suggesting that each additional year of history on the stock exchange is associated with, on average, 0.6–0.7 per cent more debt. These findings suggest that corporate credibility may well reduce the cost of borrowing from the banks, and enable firms to establish better lines of credit. An alternative and more fundamental explanation might be that the longer history on the stock market implies greater monitoring from the banks, and thus a reduction of the agency costs of providing debt finance.

The coefficients of MBR are all negative, consistent with our prediction that firms with higher MBR have higher costs of financial distress. This finding may also indicate that the banks' managers make lending decisions comparatively more by reference to the book value of the assets of the borrowing firm. This would agree with the conclusion of Booth *et al.* (2001), in their study of 10 developing countries, that the marginal borrowing power on market value was less than that on book value.

The coefficients of profitability variable (ROA) are negative in all the regressions, as expected. The significance of the coefficients is striking, and indicates that firms with more profitable projects are more inclined to use internally generated funds rather than debt. This may be interpreted, with reference to agency theory following Jensen (1986), as management preferring to use internal funds (less monitoring by banks) than debt (more monitoring from banks). But the confirmation of such an interpretation requires further work when additional data, such as on interest rates, are available.

As regards the corporate governance variables in the model, the estimated coefficients for the fractions of shares owned by management (MF) and the largest shareholder (T1) are consistent with our predictions, though the MF variable is insignificant in all regressions but one. The variable T1 has a significant negative effect upon the book value measure of leverage, but an insignificant effect upon the market value measure. One possible explanation is that the agency costs may be reduced when there is a large shareholder, due to the greater willingness of large shareholders to monitor the performance of the managers. An alternative explanation, related to the finding in Chapter 5 that corporate performance is negatively related to the size of the State shareholding, is that the largest shareholders prefer lower levels of debt so as to avoid financial distress, regardless of the value of the companies.

It is also important to consider the direction of causality between the capital structure and the ownership structure. Friend and Hasbrouck (1988) suggest the possibility of reverse causality: a high level of debt may increase the risk attached to the firm stock, and drive out outside shareholders. However, it should be noted that the ownership structure of many Chinese firms is rather inflexible in comparison to other economies, in that large shareholders don't have the freedom to alter their shareholdings according to the financial position of the firm. Their scope for financial decision-making is limited to the choice of debt level, and not to adjusting the ownership structure.

The corporate tax (TR) and the expected growth rate (GROWTH) both have coefficients that are significant at the 10 per cent level. However, the negative coefficients for the tax rate were unexpected, though significant in only one regression. Perhaps this is because those firms in China, which pay the higher rates of tax, are usually those in which the State has a greater stake. And the State-controlled banks are either more willing, or obliged, to lend to such firms, hence a positive link is observed between the tax rate and the level of debt. Also unexpected is the positive coefficient of growth, which appears to be against the argument that equity-controlled firms have a tendency to invest sub-optimally. The volatility in operating conditions (BUSRISK) is significant at the 5 per cent level in the regression on the book measure of leverage, and insignificant in the regression on the market measure of debt. The 'surprising' positive sign agrees with the findings by Booth *et al.* (2001), who detected a positive relationship between business risk and the debt level in four of the ten countries under study. Booth *et al.* (2001) offered no explanation. Perhaps the interpretation is that firms have more chances to finance their activities through debt in a more volatile business environment, or maybe that more risky firms find it harder to repay debts (cf. the situation with Enron in the United States).

Finally, LSR has a marginally significant effect upon the debt ratio, and the coefficient is positive as expected. This result is consistent with the findings by Booth *et al.* (2001). It shows that those Chinese firms with higher proportions of long-term debt tend to have more total debt. In other words, firms prefer to take on more debt only when they have access to long-term debt, rather than to short-term debt. Since long-term debt is usually used to finance tangible assets, and short-term debt is used for intangible assets, the results could also imply that firms may have better access to debt servicing when the debt is for long-term investment. Alternatively, we can draw upon the theoretical discussion of the effects of the maturity structure upon the agency problem (Barclay and Smith, 1995), and suggest that the financial decision-makers in the firm prefer long-term debt to short-term debt to avoid more frequent monitoring from the debt providers.

Concluding remarks

In this study, we have examined the determinants of capital structure in a sample of 433 Chinese listed companies in the manufacturing sector. It has been the first ever such study for China. We have found that older firms, and those with higher mar-ket-to-book value ratios, are likely to have more debt. And larger, faster-growing and more profitable firms are likely to have less debt. The extent of the share-holding held by management does not have a significant impact upon the debt level, whereas that by the largest shareholder has a negative impact. For the most part, our findings have been consistent both with our theoretical predictions and with the conclusions of the studies carried out by Booth *et al.* (2001) for emerg-ing markets, and Rajan and Zingales (1995) for developed countries. According to Booth *et al.* (2001, pp. 31–2):

> In general, debt ratios in developing countries seem to be affected in the same way and by the same types of variables that are significant in developed countries. However, there are systematic differences in the way these ratios are affected by country factors, such as GDP growth rates, inflation rates, and the development of capital markets.

However, it is still important to be aware of the legal and institutional differences between China and the Western economies. Here we want to stress two points that are particularly relevant to China. First, Baer and Gray (1996) argue that debt is often considered to be a 'soft' rather than a 'hard' constraint in many transitional economies, and this has certainly been true for the SOEs in China. But the debt constraint is undoubtedly hardening for Chinese listed companies in which the Government acts as a shareholder, rather than as the sole owner.[6] The Annual Reports of the listed companies show that the majority of legal cases between them and other parties are related to debt repayment. And the decisions of the Courts are being implemented sooner. Second, the markets for corporate control are still not mature in China. Listed companies in the West have the freedom to issue equity even when performance is poor. The shares of the majority of listed companies in China are under the control of the State authorities or other institutional shareholders, and may not be traded on stock markets, though this is currently under review by the policy-makers. There are occasional cases where the shares held by the State or by the institutional shareholders have been traded to other parties, but the transference was only effected with the permission of the State authority and/or other shareholders. Furthermore, Chinese companies are not allowed to make SEOs, and debt may be the only channel for raising additional finance.

What are the implications of these findings in the context of China? The average debt level of Chinese listed companies is low compared to their counterparts in Western economies. Managers will typically employ more debt finance, the more confident they are about the outcome of projects. But, in China's business environment as in other emerging and transitional economies where the economic and legal systems to protect foreign investors' interests are weak, agency costs are likely to be high. As Kogut (1996) has pointed out, foreign investors may sometimes require an equity stake as high as 75 per cent in order to ensure effective control of a firm, whereas a local investor may only need a 25 per cent shareholding. Furthermore, foreign investors have a variety of options for providing capital to China. Debt finance may be the safest option: the investor receives a steady return when the business is doing well, and can assume control if/when the business runs into difficulties. Equity investment may however be the more attractive option because of the potentially higher returns, as long as there is a sound governance system. The positive link between the level, and the term structure, of debt confirms this point. Management will choose a higher level of debt only when it has access to long-term debt finance, but long-term debt comes with potentially higher agency costs compared to short-term debt due to the less frequent screening.

Finally, it is important to realise that foreign investors are rarely completely passive adherents to the corporate governance systems of their host countries. They shape and mould those systems, either wittingly or unwittingly, through their presence. Hopefully, they promote sounder governance mechanisms by introducing good codes of behaviour and, to the extent that this is the case, China is more fortunate in being the recipient of a much greater inflow of FDI than the countries of Central and Eastern Europe and of the former Soviet Union.

7 Chinese corporate groups

A perspective from governance structure[1]

Introduction

The previous chapters have focused on various issues related to corporate governance in Chinese listed companies. However, the listed companies, which have been transformed into 'modern enterprise systems' in the light of 'market economy' principles, only constitute a part of the whole Chinese economy. More importantly, they occupy a lower level in the hierarchy of governance structure under the corporate groups. The task of this chapter is a critical investigation of the behaviour of corporate groups.

We begin the investigation of Chinese corporate groups with two quotes that focus on the management and the internal architecture of modern business organisations – one from Francis Fukuyama (1995), and the other from Alfred Chandler (1980):

> The Chinese constitute the world's largest racial, linguistic and cultural group. They are spread across a vast geographical area and live in variety of states, from the still communist People's Republic of China to overseas Chinese settlements in Southeast Asia to industrial democracies like the United States, Canada and Great Britain. Despite this variation in political environment, it is nonetheless possible to speak of a relatively homogenous Chinese economic culture (Fukuyama, 1995, p. 70). The hallmark of this Chinese economic culture is 'small scale enterprises' and the cause is the 'very great difficulty Chinese family businesses seem to have in making the transition from family to professional management'.
>
> (Fukuyama, 1995, p. 74)

> The modern business enterprise is defined by its two major characteristics. First, it contains many distinct operating units, each with its own administrative offices, its own full-time salaried manager, and its own sets of books and accounts that can be audited separately from those of the larger enterprise. Theoretically, each could operate as an independent business enterprise. The second salient characteristic of the modern business enterprise is therefore that it employs a hierarchy of middle- and top-salaried managers who supervise the work of the units under its control and who form an entirely new class of businessmen.
>
> (Chandler, 1980, pp. 10–11)

We quote Fukuyama not to refute his facile generalisation, but to focus on the crucial importance of salaried managers in the emergence of the 'modern enterprise' which, in organisational architecture, is akin to the large enterprise or corporate group. The two attributes of the modern enterprise that Chandler singles out refer exclusively to its managerial organisation, and neglect its financial architecture. We would argue that financial factors play a central role in shaping large enterprises and corporate groups in China, so we would add a third attribute. This attribute is that the modern enterprise derives its capital from a diversified mix of debt instruments and equity, usually traded on the stock market.

The fine details aside, there is an abundance of modern enterprises in China with the characteristics identified by Chandler. As yet, not all such enterprises possess the third characteristic, though many of them have been converted into shareholding corporations. The plan is eventually to transform all large enterprises into joint stock corporations with their shares listed on the stock market. This would facilitate a diversification of the sources of capital, but the degree of diversification will depend crucially on attitudes towards State ownership, which are changing, and on the development of the financial sector.

The State-led industrialisation in the People's Republic of China (PRC) skipped the historical stage that each capitalist economy went through in its own way, of a transition from family businesses to managerial businesses. What is called the 'managerial revolution' in business histories of capitalism (Chandler, 1977) was simply a by-product of this process. This is not only true of China or of post-Communist economies, but also of capitalist economies where public enterprises have played a lead role in industrialisation. Starting in 1952, when the socialist command economy officially began, China spawned a huge economic bureaucracy, which is not fundamentally different from bureaucracies found in large enterprises in market economies. As pointed out by Wilson (1989, p. 114), 'business firms are also bureaucracies, and McDonalds is a bureaucracy that regulates virtually every detail of its employees' behaviour by a complex and all-encompassing set of rules'. The principal problem in China is not one of the transition from family management, as it still is in Korean *chaebols*, but of re-orienting the enterprise management from just organising production to seeking higher returns on assets and investment.

Multi-divisional units have also been a prominent feature of the Chinese economy. Such units include not only large enterprises but, more importantly, industrial Ministries and bureaux (at the sub-central levels), especially after the extension of financial and managerial autonomy to enterprises. In fact, the latter group fits particularly well with Chandler's qualification that each constituent unit should have its own administrative office, its own full-time salaried manager, and its own sets of books and accounts that can be audited separately from those of the larger enterprise. This latter group is of special importance in the Chinese context because many of the recent additions to the list of Chinese corporate groups are commercial reincarnations of industrial Ministries, or provincial or municipal industrial bureaux. This trend will continue for some time given that many provincial or municipal bureaux have yet to be transformed into companies.

Here it is also important to point out that multi-divisional organisation and conglomerates are not alien to planned economies. Well before the downfall of Communism, a number of East-European economies undertook groupings of independent enterprises to improve their industrial performance (Granick, 1976). In the 1950s, following the example of the then Soviet Union and the command economies of East Europe, China organised industrial trusts (enterprise groups). Some of them still survive, albeit in a modified form.

Our purpose in pointing to the homology between the economic organisations of a command economy and the present-day Chinese enterprises is not to deny the importance of the institutional change in China that is underway, but to establish an evolutionary link between the two. This link matters because, in structure and personnel, many Chinese enterprises continue to bear the deep imprints of their genealogy. On a general note, genealogy is important in gaining an understanding not only of large enterprises in China, but also in market economies. Were it not so, we would observe a far greater uniformity in the structures of firms across economies than we actually do. The transactions cost approach to industrial organisation, pioneered by Coase and currently popular in economics, has contributed valuable insights but it cannot explain why differences in the institutional and financial structure of firms continue to persist.[2]

Related to this, we would also argue that the influence of Korean *chaebols* or Japanese conglomerates have had on Chinese industrial policy is due as much to the fact that China already has in place large and multi-divisional economic organisations as to their central role in the meteoric rise of their parent economies. There are structural similarities between large Chinese corporate groups and their East Asian counterparts but, as we point out later, also major differences. The particular features of Chinese enterprises (large or small) arise from the fact that they emerge and operate in an economic environment permeated with government decision-making with the following two features:

- The distribution of economic decision-making between the central and territorial governments and intra-government relations – later referred to as the 'territorial division of the government'.
- The division of economic activities into branches running through the 'economic administration' consisting of the central industrial ministries and their territorial counterparts (industrial bureaux), which is currently undergoing a radical change – later referred to as the 'industrial division of economic administration'.

The main theme of this chapter is that the division of the government into territorial jurisdictions, and of the division of economic administration by industrial branches, imposes a two-way grid on economic decision-making that has had wide ramifications for the structure of large enterprises/corporate groups in China and their evolution. This grid is currently undergoing a radical change because of the abolition of many of the central industrial Ministries and also of industrial bureaux in territorial governments, that may in time have a profound influence on the organisational structure of corporate groups. But the territorial division of the government has been, and will continue to be, of special importance in China because of its geographical expanse and regional diversity. There are no developed market economies, apart perhaps from the United States and Canada, which compare with China in this regard. In contrast to China, the territorial dimension seems to have had only a marginal, if any, influence on the industrial structure in South Korea and Japan.

In China the corporate group (*jituan*) does not seem to be an *appellation controlée*: that is, there is no particular organisational and financial structure as, for example, there is in developed market economies. A varied range of Chinese enterprises now carry the label 'corporate group', and the term seems to be treated as synonymous with 'modern enterprise'. For example, four (the Panda Group, the Hualu Group, the Rainbow group and the Changjiang Group) of the eleven 'group corporations' in the electronics industry consist of just one enterprise each, whilst another three (the Zhongshan Group, the Shenzhen Saige Group and the Zhenghua Corporation) consist of more than ten enterprises each. Here we treat the term 'corporate group' as synonymous with large enterprise, and use the terms interchangeably. The adjective 'large' should be interpreted relative to the Chinese, rather than the international standard.

The chapter is organised as follows. The next section draws up a list of the salient features of corporate groups and large enterprises, to serve as a background for the subsequent discussion. The section 'Ownership structure' discusses the ownership pattern of Chinese industrial enterprises. The section 'The structure of Chinese industry' analyses the relative importance of large enterprises/corporate groups in the wider context of industrial structure. The section 'Industrial restructuring' discusses the current trends in industrial restructuring, and the final section concludes.

The salient features of corporate groups

This section focuses on the principal activities and historical origins of a representative sample of large enterprises/corporate groups. Most of these are 'National Corporations', which currently number around 147. Their establishment represents a shift of the focus of enterprise reform towards organisational restructuring and internal management, and away from the re-allocation of control rights between the enterprise management and government agencies which culminated in the '14 Rights of Enterprise Managers'.[3]

Arguably, the National Corporations are underpinned by an industrial strategy that draws its inspiration from East Asian experiences, and the expectation is that these would be the driving forces in the modernisation of Chinese industry. These Corporations report to the State Council and compared with other Chinese enterprises their managers have more discretion in decision-making, and preferential access to bank credit. Many of them have also been granted the keenly sought-after privilege of listing on the domestic and also on foreign stock markets. In principle, the status 'National Corporation' is conditional, and subject to withdrawal in the case of poor performance. However, no withdrawal has yet to be enforced.

The representative sample of large enterprises/corporate groups exhibits the following ten salient features, though this list is not exhaustive and the features are not mutually exclusive:

1   Although the 'National Corporation' is a recently invented status, many of these enterprises have a long history dating back to the pre-reform period or even before, and were large State enterprises even at the start of the reform period. Several of these 'old' enterprises are the offspring of the 156 projects aided by the then Soviet Union during the first-five year plan (1952–56). Most of the National Corporations with a pre-1979 history are in the metallurgy, chemicals and machine building industries, reflecting the heavy industry bias of the period. Examples include the giant Anshan Iron and Steel Group (*Angang*), which were founded by the Japanese in the 1930s during their occupation of the Northeast, as was the Benxi Iron and Steel Corporation (*Bengang*). All steel enterprises with the status of a National Corporation date back to the pre-1979 period, with the exception of the Baoshan Iron and Steel Group (*Baogang*) which was established in the early 1980s. Other examples are the First and Second Heavy Machinery Groups. These corporations still retain many of their old features, though they have undergone mutations over the reform period.

2   There are as yet not many large enterprises/corporate groups that have resulted from the mergers of previously independent enterprises. Among the few exceptions are the Dongfeng Automobile Group, the China Jialing Group (motor bicycles), and the China Petrochemical Corporation (SINOPEC) after its re-configuration in 1998. This may change in the near future as the restructuring of large and medium enterprises and industries proceeds and, as will be discussed in the section 'Industrial restructuring', mergers have risen in frequency.

3   Among the list of National Corporations, there are a notable number of natural resource-based enterprises or public utilities, with varying degrees of monopoly power arising from a mixture of industry characteristics, such as natural monopoly and network externalities, and entry control by the Central Government. Aside from some enterprises in the electricity industry, most of these owe their large size to the rapid growth of their respective markets over the reform period. Examples include:

   • in the telecommunications industry, China Telecom (which in 1999 was split into four components) and its supposed competitor, China Unicom;
   • in the electricity industry, various regional power groups which date back to the pre-1979 period, and post-1978 establishments such as the Huaneng Power group and the State Power Corporation;
   • in the air transport industry, Air China, and the regional airlines such as East China Airlines and South China Airlines;

- in natural resource-based industries, the China Minerals and Metals Import and Export Group (Minmetal) and the recently established China National Petroleum Corporation (CNPC), a transformation of the former Ministry of Oil and Gas.

Reflecting the central government control of their industries, many of these enterprises have been formed from the central cores or offshoots of now-abolished industrial Ministries or government Departments. Likely additions to their ranks include the Post Office and perhaps, in time, the railways. In many ways, they resemble State-owned enterprises in developed market economies. As a result of the rapid expansion of their respective domestic markets since 1979, several of these enterprises already rank as large firms by international standards. The CNPC ranks among the Fortune top 500 and, in terms of the number of fixed lines (though not in turnover), China Telecom is already the second largest telephone company in the world. It is important to emphasise the close link between the rapid growth of the Chinese economy, and the emergence of these large Chinese enterprises/corporate groups on the international stage. Given that these enterprises are expected to be profit seeking, their monopolistic position raises the as yet unresolved issue of their regulation.

4   There are a number of large enterprises in industries that are either new in China or have only become sizeable in recent years. Examples include:

- In the electronic and computer industries, the Legend (*Lianxiang*) Group, the Stone (*Sitong*) Group, and the Great Wall Computer Group.
- In the passenger vehicles industry, the First, the Second, and the Shanghai Automobile Group, each of which has a controlling share in an associated Sino-foreign production venture.
- In the consumer durables industry, the Sichuan Changhong and Qingdao Hisense and Haier Groups.

The enterprises in this category are in industries producing internationally traded goods, are already competitive, and will become even more so when China is finally able to enjoy the full benefits of WTO membership. One result of intense competition in the consumer durables industry is the widening differentiation between the market leaders and the laggards, and a growing importance of brand names. Take-overs and mergers are already common in these industries, and a likely outcome is the elimination of most of the small and medium-sized enterprises. Given the size of the Chinese market, those surviving the process of natural selection should be large enterprises by world standards.

5   The sample also includes enterprises from China's huge military industrial complex covering both military hardware and associated civilian products. In fact, some of the leading Chinese corporate groups of today started off as military enterprises. For example, the Changhong Group, the largest enterprise in

the electronics industry, was initially a producer of radars. There are ten large enterprises/corporate groups under the control of the 'Commission for Science and Industry for National Defence', including the following:

- The North China Industries Group Corporation (Norinco) and the South China Industries Group Corporation: both are conventional weapons producers, which have diversified into a wide range of other activities.
- Two corporations in the nuclear industry.
- Four corporations in aerospace and aviation, covering both civilian and military products.
- Two shipbuilding corporations, one military and another civilian.

Given China's position as a major world power, these military-cum-civilian enterprises should always constitute a significant proportion of Chinese corporate groups. However, China's military industry is undergoing radical change because of two trends: the technical upgrading of the armed forces, and the recent policy to divest the military of its economic activities. A significant proportion of the Chinese State enterprises in severe financial difficulties are enterprises specialising in military hardware.

6 There are two geographical features of the Chinese corporate groups that stand out. First, rather than being confined to the developed coastal provinces only, they are fairly widely distributed. This is due partly to various policies to disperse industry geographically, which date back to the Third Front policy of the late 1960s and the 1970s (Naughton, 1988). But it is also partly due to the keen competition among territorial governments to develop local industry, and to obtain centrally funded projects. As a result, a number of corporate groups are based in the relatively under-developed southwestern and northwestern provinces. The second characteristic is that many of the Chinese corporate groups are confined to just a city or a province. This is linked closely with the dispersion of enterprise ownership rights among the territorial governments, which we discuss later. There are two main exceptions to this general rule: the off-shoots of central industrial Ministries which supervised 'centrally-controlled' enterprises all over China (e.g. the CNPC, the China National Power Corporation, and the Huaneng Power Group), and some groups in newly developed industries such as consumer durables (e.g. the Sichuan Changhong, Qingdao Hisense and Shenzhen Konka (kanjia) groups).

7 Notwithstanding their size and multi-unit structure, most of the Chinese corporate groups are specialised along the industrial classification that runs through the economic administration. As yet, there are no Chinese counterparts of multi-industry conglomerates such as Mitsubishi, Mitsui, Samsung or Hyundai (Ungson *et al.*, 1997). Related to this, there is a relative absence of vertically integrated groups cutting across the administrative division of industries. For example, there is no heavy machinery enterprise that is prominent in metallurgy. The usual observation that command economies tended

to encourage a greater degree of vertical integration than in market economies does not seem to apply to large Chinese enterprises. By international standards, they tend to be less diversified and vertically integrated. The reason is that the industrial divisions running through the economic administration creates vested interests that act as barriers to the expansion of enterprises across industries.

8   The list of Chinese corporate groups includes a number of international trading and shipping enterprises, reflecting the control of international trade by the Central Government. These include the China Chemical Industry Import and Export Group (SINOCHEM), the China Food and Oil Import and Export Corporation, and the China Shipping Company (COSCO) – all of which are divided along the industrial classifications used for economic administration. These enterprises owe their large size to the rapid growth since 1978 of China's GDP, and the even more rapid growth of China's foreign trade.[4] The Chinese trading groups tend to be more specialised than the Japanese and Korean trading companies. Their monopolistic positions are under strong threat from two sources: first, the extension of direct international trading rights to more enterprises including those in the non-State sector and, second, China's membership of the WTO.

9   Some industries are notably absent from the list of large enterprises/corporate groups. There are none in the retail trade. Moreover, despite its huge construction market, China does not yet have construction groups that stand out at the national level, let alone at the international level. The reason is that Ministries, large enterprises, and territorial governments have tended to run their own in-house construction companies. Construction is the one major activity in China that tends to be integrated with other activities. Financial institutions are also absent from the list, not because there are no large finance companies in China but because they still have the hybrid status of enterprises and Government Departments. All four of the main State-owned commercial banks are large enough to figure in the Fortune 500 list.

10   Finally, the relations between the financial institutions and large enterprises/corporate groups in China are distant compared to those in market economies. Though large State enterprises have been heavily reliant on bank loans since the mid-1980s, the four main commercial banks have little control over the use of the loaned funds and no say in enterprise governance. This is changing, albeit slowly, with the decision to convert a part of the non-performing debt of selected State enterprises into equity held by 'Asset Management Companies' (AMCs) controlled by the creditor banks. Besides, though many corporate groups are share holding companies, equity-holders other than government agencies play little role, if any, in enterprise governance. This may also change in the near future as Chinese corporate groups tap the domestic and foreign stock markets for investment funds, and also with the establishment of the AMCs controlled by the four State-owned commercial banks. The relationship between the enterprises and the financial institutions and markets is discussed further in the next section.

There is thus a considerable diversity of large enterprises/corporate groups. Their ownership structure, and their relative importance in the Chinese economy are discussed in the next two sections.

Ownership structure

In this section, we consider two sets of issues drawing on the discussion in Hansmann (1996):

- Enterprise governance, in particular the appointment and monitoring of managers, and of performance and control over enterprise activities and boundaries.
- The relationship between the enterprise and the suppliers of its capital, including those without a formal ownership stake.

The discussion is not confined to the large enterprises/corporate groups, but covers all enterprises in the industrial sector for which data are readily available. We thus exclude 7.5 million small and micro industrial enterprises, and focus on the 162,033 'independent accounting' industrial enterprises at and above the township level. Table 7.1 provides an analysis of these enterprises classified by their formal ownership status.

The first two ownership forms, SOEs and COEs, are pre-reform categories, but have since undergone various changes both in governance structure and in the sources of their capital. The next two categories, shareholding enterprises and foreign-funded enterprises, are post-1978 categories, and most of these enterprises are mutations of SOEs or COEs. The 'others' category includes enterprises

Table 7.1 The ownership status of industrial enterprises with independent accounting systems, 1999

Type of enterprise	Number (% of total)	Gross output (%)	Net output (%)	Fixed assets (%)	Employment (%)
SOEs and State controlled enterprises	61,301 (37.8)	48.9	56.3	61.6	54.5
COEs	42,585 (26.3)	17.1	14.7	8.5	15.2
Shareholding enterprises	4,480 (2.8)	7.2	7.5	7.6	
Foreign-funded enterprises	26,837 (16.6)	26.1	22.5	28.2	30.3
Others	26,830 (16.6)	0.7	N/A	N/A	

Source: State Statistical Bureau (2000).

with the status of Government Departments, and private enterprises which, as distinct from household enterprises (*geti hu*), have become significant only recently.

A salient feature of the four categories is that government ownership permeates all of them. COEs are a close, but lesser, kin of the SOEs in that they are controlled by lower government tiers, at the county-level or below, or their urban counterparts. Of the 4,480 share holding enterprises, around 1,000 of the largest are listed on the domestic stock markets, and a small percentage of them are also listed on foreign stock markets. Eighty per cent of them are at least majority government owned, and only slightly more than 10 per cent of them are COEs. And a substantial percentage of foreign-funded enterprises (around 70 per cent) are joint or co-operative ventures with, in most cases, a SOE or a COE. Thus the diversification of ownership forms since 1979 has, for the most part, involved a mutation in government ownership, along the following four lines.

- The assignment of ownership claims in proportion to capital contributions (usually by territorial governments). This is a common principle in market economies, and was first used in the second half of the 1980s to finance large projects in the electricity industry.
- The proliferation of multi-level ownership, whereby a government-owned company fully or partly owns enterprises with different ownership forms (including SOEs, COEs, and joint ventures).
- Mixed government-private ownership as in Sino-foreign joint ventures.
- The introduction of tradable equity, but mostly with majority government ownership as in the corporations listed on the domestic and foreign stock markets.

The common element in the above four mutations is a diversification in the sources of investment funds which, as we argue later, has been and is likely to be a principal driving force in the transformation of the ownership pattern especially of large enterprises/corporate groups. In the case of Sino-foreign joint ventures, additional motives have been the acquisition of advanced technology and raising exports.

The data in Table 7.1 also highlight something of the current plight of the SOEs. The SOEs remain the bedrock of Chinese industry, accounting for 56.3 per cent of net output and 61.6 per cent of fixed assets. This gap between their shares of fixed capital and of net output reflects their domination of the capital-intensive and high technology industries. However, their share of industrial employment (54.5 per cent) is only slightly lower than their share of net output, whereas the usual pattern in market economies is that the employment share should be substantially less than the output share. One reason for this anomaly is the employment of surplus labour; another is the extensive social and welfare responsibilities which occupy a substantial part of their labour force. As a group, the SOEs are weighed down by comparatively high endowments of capital and labour, and their future survival depends crucially on reducing their employment share relative to their output share. This is now clearly recognised in China. Over the last few years, the SOEs have shed a substantial percentage of their labour force and the aim of the current social security reforms is to transfer social and welfare responsibilities from enterprises to the Ministry of Labour and Social Security, and its provincial counterparts. Furthermore, the current round of enterprise reforms envisages 'conglomeration' in the case of large and medium-size SOEs, and 'flexibility' in the case of small SOEs. Flexibility covers a wide range of possible mutations, including take-overs by large SOEs, outright sales, and conversion into employee partnerships. The SOE, as currently constituted, is an endangered species.

The large enterprises and corporate groups do not fit exclusively within any one ownership category. Some are SOEs, but most are either former SOEs or government departments now converted into shareholding enterprises, but with majority or full government ownership. Comparatively few large units are shareholding corporations with only a minority public stake, or are foreign-funded enterprises. Foreign-funded enterprises tend to be small, though the category includes some of the best-known brand names in China. Furthermore, a large SOE or a shareholding enterprise with majority government ownership (e.g. a National Corporation) can have subsidiaries with differing forms of ownership (termed earlier as 'multi-level ownership'): COEs, Sino-foreign joint ventures, or private enterprises.

Under its initiative to modernise enterprises, the Chinese Government plans to convert all large and medium SOEs into shareholding corporations. But the significance of this proposal for enterprise governance will depend crucially on whether such corporations are 'open', or 'closed' with all equity held by government organizations. A substantial majority (around 60 per cent) of the existing shareholding corporations fall into the 'closed' category, which means that their ownership is not markedly different from the SOEs. However, there are two current initiatives that are crucial to the future evolution of the large enterprises: the transformation of the closed shareholding corporations into open corporations, and the creation of a governance structure for diversified ownership, including multi-level ownership. The transformation of closed into open shareholding enterprises, with their equity traded on the domestic and foreign stock markets, is motivated by the pressing need to raise investment funds for modernisation. One recent example of this was the sale, in April 2000, of a substantial percentage of equity in the CNPC on the Hong Kong and New York stock markets.

What are the implications of the dominance of government ownership in many large enterprises? As noted by many observers, government ownership in China is not a unified, but an internally divided phenomenon reflecting the division of the government into territorial jurisdictions and their hierarchy. The ownership rights in government-owned enterprises (supervisory oversight and claim on profits) are dispersed across many government tiers, from the centre down to the township (or its urban equivalent), and even further down to the level of 'mass' (quasi-governmental) organisations such as villages or urban neighbourhoods. Moreover, government-owned enterprises are not all on par with one another; they are ordered according to the government hierarchy. Corporate groups and large enterprises tend to be under the ownership of the central or provincial governments, whilst those enterprises owned by lower government tiers tend to be smaller. However, this has begun to change with the growth of successful (or market-selected) enterprises owned by lower government tiers. For example, Changhong – the largest enterprise in the electronics sector and now a share-holding corporation – started off as an enterprise owned by a medium-size city (i.e. Mianyang). A number of TVEs are now counted among the corporate groups: for example, the Kelon (Guangdong) and Chunlan (Jiangsu) groups both are well known in the consumer durables sector. Furthermore, the central government has exclusive jurisdiction over certain industries, such as the oil and gas industry and many of the public utilities. All government tiers can establish enterprises subject to this central jurisdiction over industries and, as we shall see in the next section, this has played a central role in shaping China's industrial structure. A large Chinese city would normally have enterprises owned by all government tiers, from the centre down to the urban district.

The dispersion of ownership rights across government tiers has had wide ramifications for both the functions of the government tiers and for relations between them. All government tiers (down to the lowest level) have departments devoted to the supervision of enterprises in their respective domains. Over the reform period, these departments have developed into hybrid organizations with two distinct roles, which are being separated by the government reorganisation currently under way. First, these organisations performed the functions of co-ordination and supervision in relation to enterprises in their domain, similar to that of head offices of multi-divisional firms or conglomerates. From this standpoint, an industrial ministry or bureau, together with its subordinate enterprises, resembled an M-form conglomerate (to use a term coined by Williamson, 1991) specialising in a particular product range. This analogy has begun to take a concrete organisational form over the past few years with the conversion of industrial ministries at the central level, and bureaux at the sub-central levels, into limited-liability companies (or corporations) encompassing enterprises they had previously supervised. The establishment of these corporations marks an important departure from the enterprise reforms, undertaken from 1979 to the early 1990s, that focused almost exclusively on the transformation of enterprises, but not of industrial departments. This shift of focus was prompted by the realisation that the reform of enterprises requires not only their restructuring, but also the granting of operational autonomy to the enterprise management. We explore the implications of this for industrial restructuring in the section 'Industrial restructuring'. Second, the industrial departments also performed regulatory functions covering all enterprises in the industry regardless of their ownership status, a role which in a market economy would be performed by a government agency or a non-commercial public body. These regulatory functions are being transferred to the State Economic and Trade Commission (SETC) at the central level, and to its territorial subsidiaries. The separation of the two functions is an important step towards a disengagement of the role of the government as owner, from its regulatory role.

What are the ramifications of the dispersion of ownership rights for horizontal and vertical relations between government tiers? In developed market economies, inter-tier relations are dominated by fiscal issues, such as the distribution of taxation power and expenditure responsibilities, and enterprise ownership is of marginal significance. The reverse is the case in China. Fiscal issues, although important, take second place to enterprise ownership in inter-tier relations, as the revenue (both from taxation and other sources) that a government tier has at its disposal depends crucially on the enterprises under its control. This gives government tiers a powerful incentive to protect and enlarge the portfolio of enterprises under their control, which engenders a rivalrous relationship between them. The establishment of National Corporations with special privileges, and the transformation of the components of industrial ministries, have significantly extended the role of the central government in the governance of large enterprises. Provincial and lower-tier governments have responded to this potential, if not actual, threat to their span of economic control by encouraging the formation of their own corporate groups. Thus the proliferation of such groups in recent years is in part underpinned by intra-government rivalry.

In the broader context of enterprise governance, a large Chinese enterprise is a nexus of (economic, social and political) practices, not just of contracts – as market-economy firms are usually characterised. Enterprises are important political organizations, and function as nodes of the Party organisation. All large enterprises have a Party Committee, headed by a Secretary equal in rank to the chief executive officer (CEO). Furthermore, the appointment of the CEOs of large public enterprises is subject to approval by the Party organisation at the relevant level. The implication is that political considerations cast a long shadow on the management of large enterprises and the selection of their chief executives.

How much impact does this have on the functioning of large enterprises and their evolution? The impact has to be judged with reference to the likely state of affairs without the Party having any say in enterprise governance. Views within the Party about ownership transformation and industrial restructuring are as diverse as those outside the Party. Even if the Party had no say, the CEOs would be drawn from largely the same pool as at present. There does not seem to be any strong evidence that the current system of appointment excludes significant numbers of potentially capable managers. Here it is instructive to point out that, in East-European economies that have undergone enterprise privatisation on a large scale, most of the CEOs of privatised enterprises have managerial experience dating from the pre-transition period. Similarly, the top management of privatised UK companies are largely drawn from those who occupied senior managerial positions in the same companies before privatisation. This is not surprising given the informational advantage of incumbent managers over outsiders. In the Chinese context, political reliability and managerial capability do not seem to be mutually exclusive. But there is a problem of alignment between the ownership status and the political role of the enterprise which, although minor at present, is likely to grow. In principle, the problem does not arise in enterprises with majority government ownership. But it does arise in enterprises in which the government holds no more than a minority stake. The problem exists in Sino-foreign joint ventures, and is currently resolved through makeshift arrangements. The numbers of such enterprises will increase with the growth not only of private ownership and majority foreign ownership, but also of open shareholding corporations. The implication is that the current political role of enterprises acts as an impediment to a transformation in the ownership structure, especially the large enterprises and corporate groups which are seen as the bulwark of the one-party State. The likely pattern of evolution is a loosening political control in small and medium-sized enterprises, but not in the key large enterprises and corporate groups.

Turning to the relationship between enterprises and the sources of their capital, the external investment funds for the SOEs and COEs took the form of grants from the Government, or quasi-government organisations such as rural communes, in the pre-reform period. These grants were akin to capital subscription by the owners, and the sources of capital were fully aligned with the allocation of ownership and control over the enterprises. Over the course of the reform period, however, there has been a progressive divergence between, on the one hand, the ownership and control pattern of enterprises and, on the other hand, their sources of capital. From the early 1980s onwards, loans have progressively replaced investment grants and, in 1999 for example, budgetary appropriations accounted for a mere 9.7 per cent of investment funds in all State-units (in industry and other sectors). Domestic banks and financial markets accounted for 23.4 and 14 per cent of funds, respectively. One result of the heavy dependence for investment funds on bank loans for almost twenty years is the relatively high ratio (by international standards) of long-term debt to assets. In the large SOEs, which have been the principal recipients of bank loans, the average ratio was 62 per cent in 1999 (SSB, 2000, p. 439) and in some it was as high as 90 per cent. If short-term bank debt is also included, the amount of debt exceeds their total assets.

In contrast to their market-economy counterparts, the Chinese commercial banks, although nominally financially independent, have neither the rights of debtholders nor equity in the indebted enterprises. Even in the event of debt default (which is widespread), they have neither a pre-emptive claim on enterprise assets, nor play any role in enterprise governance as banks do even in economies, such as the United States, where they do not hold equities. The implication is that the current assignment of ownership rights in enterprises rests crucially on a faulty enforcement of debt claims, the counterpart of which is a non-solvent commercial banking sector. There is a widening incompatibility between making the four main commercial banks solvent, which is essential for an overhaul of the financial sector, and maintaining the current pattern of ownership of large enterprises and of investment financing. This has to change, as is increasingly realised in China. A significant step towards reducing this incompatibility is the decision to swap non-performing debt for equity in large enterprises. The potential implications of this swap for the ownership pattern and the governance structure of large enterprises run wide and deep, even though it is no more than an exchange of assets within the State sector. First, this will within a few years create sizeable blocks of shares in large enterprises held by non-governmental organisations, albeit by Asset

Management Companies (AMCs) under the umbrella of the four State-owned commercial banks. The proposed AMCs are likely to behave differently from government organisations holding enterprise equities, because they are expected to be profit seeking. Second, the creation of concentrated equity ownership will in time have a knock-on effect on the monitoring of managers and on enterprise performance. Third, as the equity acquired by AMCs is potentially saleable not only to domestic but also to foreign investors, the swap opens up scope for a large-scale transfer of equities, and thus for mergers and take-overs and eventually a market in corporate control. An example of this is the sale to a US corporation by Cinda (the AMC attached to the Construction Bank) of its majority stake in the Bengbu Thermal Electricity Station in April 2001.

The structure of Chinese industry

In this section, we seek to answer two related questions:

- How important are large enterprises and corporate groups in Chinese industry, and has their relative importance changed over the reform period?
- What are the salient features of China's industrial structure, given the particular nature of government decision-making?

As in the previous section, the analysis is limited to industrial enterprises with independent accounting systems at the township level and above. Table 7.2 provides a statistical picture of the relative importance of large, medium, and small enterprises according to their numbers, gross output, and net output.[5]

Table 7.2 The size distribution of industrial enterprises with independent accounting systems, 1999

Size	Numbers (% of total)		Gross output (% of total)		Net output (% of total)		Relative size[b]	
	1981	*1999*	*1981*	*1999*	*1981*[a]	*1999*	*1981*	*1999*
Large	1,500 (0.4)	7,864 (4.9)	25.4	43.4	29.0	48.7	112	17.8
Medium	3,500 (0.9)	14,371 (8.9)	17.7	13.6	16.8	12.9	33	3.1
Small	376,500 (98.7)	139,798 (86.3)	56.9	43.0	54.3	38.4	1	1

Source: State Statistical Bureau (2000).

Notes

a The 1981 figures for net output are estimates calculated by using the ratio of net to gross output in 1999 for the corresponding category.

b The figures for 'relative size' are derived by dividing each category's share of gross output by the number of firms, and the normalising of the results by setting the ratio for small enterprises equal to unity.

One striking feature of China's industrial structure to emerge from this table is the polarisation between a comparatively few large enterprises (mostly SOEs or shareholding enterprises with majority government ownership) and numerous small enterprises. Each group accounts for similar shares of net output (48.7 and 38.4 per cent respectively in 1999), whilst medium-sized enterprises are relatively unimportant, only accounting for 12.9 per cent of net output. If the figures for 1981 and 1999 are compared, it is evident that large enterprises have raised their gross output share by around 18 percentage points largely at the expense of small enterprises. It is likely that their share of net output will have risen even more, though the data for 1981 are estimated. It thus appears that, over the reform period, large enterprises have risen in importance in the industrial sector, and this sector accounts for almost half of GDP in China.

However, caution is necessary when interpreting these statistics so this conclusion needs to be qualified in two respects. First, the apparent rise in market concentration may well be a statistical artefact, and concentration may actually have fallen. Second, by international standards, the Chinese industrial structure is marked out by the relative importance of small not large enterprises. We discuss these in turn.

The change in output shares between 1981 and 1999 has been accompanied by substantial increases in the numbers of large and medium enterprises. The numbers of large and medium-sized enterprises have multiplied almost four-fold, whereas the numbers of small enterprises have fallen. However, the reduction in the numbers of small enterprises is due largely to the re-classification of many as 'too small to be counted as sizeable enterprises'. As the increase in the numbers of large enterprises far exceeds the rise in their share of gross output (4.4 compared to 1.7 times), the 'average' large enterprise of 1999 was far smaller than the 'average' large enterprise of 1981. The same also holds for medium-sized enterprises. The final column of Table 7.2 highlights these changes by comparing the average gross outputs of large- and medium-sized enterprises with that of the average small enterprise. The change between 1981 and 1999 is dramatic. An average large enterprise in 1999 accounted for 17.8 times the gross output of an average small enterprise, compared to 113 times in 1981. And an average medium-sized enterprise had only 3.1 times the gross output of the average small enterprise in 1999, compared to 33 times in 1981. The relative differences between large, medium, and small enterprises were far smaller in 1999 than in 1981, especially between medium and small enterprises. Furthermore, the apparent rising importance of large enterprises is due to the increase in their numbers, and not to the faster growth of extant large enterprises compared to other enterprises.

When assessing the rising importance of large enterprises and their economic power in the Chinese economy, it is thus important to keep in mind the fact that their numbers have risen sharply over the reform period, as have the numbers of medium-sized enterprises. To the extent that market competition depends on numbers and on relative differences between large, medium, and small enterprises, Chinese industry is far more competitive in 1999 than it was in 1981. Here it is instructive to compare China with other economies. In South Korea, the top

30 *chaebols* accounted for around 30 per cent of GDP at the end of 1997 (on the eve of the financial crisis). By international standards, the Chinese economy is characterised by the relative importance of small enterprises rather than by the dominance of large enterprises. Although large enterprises are ubiquitous in developed market economies, the relative importance of small enterprises varies widely amongst them.

What explains the proliferation of large and medium-size industrial enterprises? This can be explained in terms of the role of government in the establishment and disappearance of enterprises, through closures or mergers.[6] A paradox is that government control over enterprise establishment (or entry) is usually associated with a restriction in enterprise numbers, rather than a proliferation that we observe in the Chinese context. The explanation lies in the structure of government decision-making with the two-way division, between territorial jurisdiction and economic administration by industrial branches, as mentioned in the introduction. As a result, the relations between government tiers and departments in China are both hierarchical and rivalrous (or competitive). They are hierarchical in the sense that the discretion at the disposal of each government tier depends on the tier above, though this hierarchy leaves ample room for lower government tiers to pursue their interests, but within limits. The intra-governmental relations are also rivalrous in that each government tier and industrial department differentiates between enterprises under and outside its control, and aims to promote those under its control through the growth of existing enterprises, the establishment of new enterprises, and the sustainment of non-viable enterprises. Such rivalry also existed in the pre-reform period, but the latitude open to territorial governments for promoting enterprises was restricted for two reasons. First, there was centralised control over the distribution of key materials and inputs, and limited international trade. Second, there was an almost complete absence of credit facilities. Together, these two factors constituted a substantial barrier to the establishment of new enterprises, especially medium and large ones.

Both factors began to erode in importance from the early 1980s, and had largely disappeared by the early 1990s. The market-oriented reforms led to a huge increase in the establishment of new enterprises, aided and abetted by government tiers and industrial departments all keen to enlarge the local industrial base. Given the rarity of closures and mergers until recently, each newly established unit has been a net addition to the enterprise population. The proliferation of enterprises has been particularly pronounced in those segments of industry where the set-up investment is low (such as assembly), and in industries that are not within the exclusive jurisdiction of the Central Government (such as oil and gas, and telecommunications). Two examples illustrate the result of the combination of a high entry rate, and an exceptionally low exit rate, of enterprises that has been a central feature of Chinese industry until recently. First, the vehicles industry consists of 112 assembly factories with a total output of around 1.8 million vehicles, and all but a few with an installed capacity well short of the minimum for technical efficiency. Second, the number of enterprises producing television sets is around eighty, and of these the top ten account for 80 per cent of sales. There is both a positive and negative side to the enterprise proliferation. The positive side is the emergence of a competitive industrial structure, without any anti-monopoly policy on the part of the government. The intense market competition evident over the last few years is a cumulative result of the competitive investment by territorial governments in old and new industries since the early 1980s. The negative side is that, in many industries, the numbers of enterprises exceed the sustainable level. Thus, unlike in some other transitional economies, the principal problem in China is not the dominant position of a few large industrial enterprises, but a surfeit of enterprises producing similar products with many too small to exploit economies of scale or scope. Thus the major issue for industrial restructuring in China is more the consolidation of fragmented productive capacity, and less the break-up of large enterprises.

Industrial restructuring

'Restructuring and consolidation' have been forced on to the top of the reform policy agenda by the mixture of intense market competition and a concomitant deterioration in the financial position of enterprises. Our discussion of industrial restructuring in this section revolves around two sets of issues:

- How effective are the evolving procedures for the exit of non-viable enterprises, assuming that the present industrial structure is non-sustainable?
- What is the role of holding companies or corporate groups in industrial restructuring?

Though enterprise closures[7] are still rare, a wave of enterprise groupings or mergers is sweeping Chinese industry. As an instrument of enterprise rationalisation, mergers are not new in China. The first regulation to facilitate vertical and horizontal mergers was issued in 1980, and then put into practice a few years later to set up the Dong Feng motor group, now a National Corporation (Chen, 1997). This first major exercise in industrial restructuring took a number of years to complete and, despite the general recognition that many Chinese industries were too fragmented for efficiency, enterprise mergers remained rare occurrences until the mid 1990s.

Since then, restructuring has become the centrepiece of enterprise reform. Mergers are regarded as the preferred method for dealing with insolvent enterprises, which have grown in numbers as the combined result of deterioration in the financial position of enterprises and an increase in enterprise numbers over the reform period. For example, around 1,500 (23 per cent) of the 6,599 large and medium-size SOEs making a loss at the end of 1997 had disappeared within a year, mostly as a result of mergers or groupings with other enterprises but with some closures. Furthermore, mergers also extend to small SOEs and COEs (including TVEs), rather than being confined to large and medium SOEs. Finally, a notable feature of the current situation is that the impetus for mergers not only comes from the Central Government as it did in the 1980s, but also from provinces and cities. Mergers are now also initiated by enterprise managers, whereas previously they were arranged only by government agencies. There is now an emerging market in enterprises, which may in time develop into a market in corporate control. To complement the moves to secure the exit of non-viable enterprises, the Central Government is trying to stem future additions to the ranks of non-viable enterprises by banning the establishment of new enterprises in over two hundred industrial branches with substantial excess capacity.

In comparison to market economies, mergers and take-overs in China are distinguished by two related features:

• They do not involve any financial transactions in property titles, but only an administrative fiat.
• The government (taken as a tiered network) is always a central party.

Given that government has an ownership stake in most enterprises, mergers and consolidations in China are administrative measures and do not involve any financial transactions. A notable example was provided by the creation in 1998 of the China National Petroleum Corporation (CNPC) and the China Petrochemical Corporation (SINOPEC),[8] both large enough to rank in the Fortune 500. Previously both corporations were hybrids – government organisations-cum-enterprise groups – with CNPC specialising in the upstream end, and SINOPEC in the downstream end, of the oil industry. In 1998, as part of the abolition of the Ministry of Chemicals Industry (which controlled SINOPEC) and the Ministry of Oil and Gas, both were transformed into diversified oil corporations through an administrative re-apportionment of the upstream and downstream facilities between them. The operation, although huge in terms of assets, involved no financial transactions as all the enterprises were SOEs, but it did involve considerable pressure by the government on CNPC to part with some of its upstream enterprises.

Although mergers and the re-arrangement of enterprises in China do not involve financial transactions, there are still transactions costs when they cut across departmental or territorial jurisdictions, especially the latter. The most important of these costs concerns devising a formula for the exercise of ownership rights in the entities resulting from mergers and consolidations. Arguably these transactions costs were high enough in the past to have precluded mergers and restructuring which might have made economic sense then, but which have only taken place recently.

Given that they are intermediated by the government, mergers and consolidations in China are deeply affected by intra-government relations and government priorities. A pressing concern for government departments or tiers is to reduce the number of loss-making enterprises under their respective jurisdictions, and much of government policy towards mergers is driven by this imperative. With closures regarded as too extreme for general use, government tiers and departments employ a mixture of pressure and incentives to induce profitable enterprises to take over loss-making or non-viable enterprises. A common form is to make the grant of a privilege or preferential treatment conditional upon taking over one or more loss-making enterprises. This is illustrated in the selection of enterprises for listing on the stock market (domestic or foreign) that is keenly sought by large enterprises. New listings are rationed, as are further primary issues of shares by already-listed companies. Provincial governments are each allowed to put forward a specified number of enterprises for listing. A tacit condition for an enterprise to be selected for listing is that it takes over one or more loss-making enterprises in the province.

At a general level, there are two aspects to mergers and conglomerations with implications for the future evolution of the industrial structure in China. First, their scope is usually limited to enterprises in the jurisdiction of the government tier or department arranging the merger. Thus one arranged by the Central Government would normally be confined to enterprises controlled by the Central Government, and similarly for mergers arranged by provincial governments. There have been in recent years instances of take-overs cutting across territorial government boundaries, such as the take-over of loss-making TV firms by the Shenzhen Konka (Kanjia) and the Sichuan Changhong groups. But such mergers and take-overs are severely restricted by the transactions costs of negotiating agreements on the future status of the acquired enterprises and on the distribution of ownership rights. The second aspect is that an enterprise may agree to take over a loss-making enterprise only because of the associated side benefits, such as the acquisition of land, tax concessions, debt write-offs, or the promise of investment funds from the government. In many cases, these side benefits, rather than industrial rationalisation, may well be the primary motive of the enterprise agreeing to a take-over. The implication is that the current wave of mergers and consolidations is not a simple process of industrial rationalisation, but a process overlaid with a variety of motives including cross-subsidisation and the protection of the local industrial base against erosion from market competition. It is creating corporate groups with both high and low chances of survival as viable entities.

A salient feature of the current wave of industrial restructuring is that it is combined with a radical reorganisation of the industrial administration. Most of the industrial Ministries have been abolished. The enterprises in their jurisdictions have been regrouped, and turned into National Corporations or limited-liability companies, and their policy role has been taken over by the SETC. Similar changes are taking place further down the territorial ladder, at the provincial and municipal levels. A number of provinces and municipalities, following the initial examples of Shanghai and Shenzhen, have converted their industrial bureaux into holding companies (or Asset Management Companies) and others are due to follow suit. The National Corporations, or companies arising out of the overhaul of the industrial administration, comprise the group of enterprises supervised by their respective parent industrial Ministries or bureaux. But they are more akin to corporate groups or holding companies in market economies, than were the abolished Ministries and bureaux. Their establishment, though initially no more than a change in formal status combined with a regrouping of enterprises, introduces two elements that hold important implications for the future evolution of large enterprises and corporate groups. First, they have greater managerial control over subordinate enterprises, compared to the parent Ministries or bureaux. Second, being financially independent, these holding companies have a much greater economic incentive to aim for a profit enhancing restructuring or merger of enterprises under their control. Some of them (such as CNPC) are pressing ahead with a radical overhaul of their subsidiaries. Thus the likely impact of the current round of administrative reorganisation will be to facilitate a conglomeration of previously independent enterprises into corporate groups. But mirroring the configuration of National Corporations or holding companies, much of this regrouping will involve enterprises within an industry, and between enterprises in the same territorial jurisdiction. Examples of the regrouping of enterprises across territorial jurisdictions and industries, especially the former, will be few and far between until the development of a market in corporate control which, at present, is no more than a distant possibility.

Concluding remarks

We conclude this chapter by reiterating the principal themes:

- Large enterprises/corporate groups have risen in importance over the reform period, especially in the industrial sector. The increase in their share of gross industrial output is due to a growth in the number of such enterprises, not to the faster growth of the large enterprises inherited from the planning period. As a result, the average large industrial enterprise/corporate group in 1999 was smaller than at the outset of economic reforms in 1981. An implication is that the rise in the relative importance of large enterprises has not been associated with a concentration of economic power in the hands of a few enterprises. By international standards, the Chinese industrial structure is marked by the relative importance of small, not large enterprises.
- The rise in the importance of large enterprises/corporate groups is due to the exceptionally rapid growth of per capita income since 1979, the huge size of the Chinese population, and the sharp growth in China's international trade. A substantial percentage of the Chinese enterprises that are large by international standards are public utilities, banks, trading companies, or natural resource-based industries. Nine Chinese enterprises were listed in the 1999 Fortune top 500, of which two were public utilities, four were banks, two were international trading companies, and one was an oil company. The export market is a minor contributor to the size of the large Chinese enterprises/corporate groups, unlike with the Korean *chaebol*s.
- The structure of the large Chinese enterprises/corporate groups, and their pattern of specialisation, bear the deep imprint of both the division of the government into territorial jurisdictions, each jealously controlling a group of enterprises, and the division of economic administration on industrial lines. The latter is becoming blurred because of the reorganisation of the government. But, given China's geographical expanse and regional diversity, the

territorial division of the government, and the hierarchy and rivalry that go with it, will continue to play a central role in shaping China's industrial structure. Here it is important to note that the territorial dimension has played no significant role in the evolution of Korean and Japanese corporate groups.

- The large Chinese enterprises/corporate groups do not fit one format, but are diverse in their genealogy and structure. Some date back to the planning period, whilst others are post-1979 developments. The large Chinese enterprises/corporate groups tend to be less diversified and vertically integrated, compared to those in Japan and Korea. Most are focused on one industry, and there are no Chinese counterparts of multi-industry conglomerates such as Mitsubishi, Mitsui, Samsung or Hyundai.

- The large Chinese enterprises/corporate are diverse in terms of formal ownership status. A large majority of them are either SOEs, or former SOEs or government departments now converted into shareholding enterprises predominantly with full government ownership. Comparatively few large units are shareholding corporations with only a minority public ownership stake, or foreign-funded enterprises. Most large enterprises/corporate groups embrace a variety of ownership forms in that their subsidiaries may be COEs, or joint ventures with foreign firms or, recently, with private enterprises. All large SOEs are due to be converted into shareholding corporations. But the exact significance of the proposed conversion for enterprise governance will depend crucially on whether such corporations are 'open', or 'closed' with all equity held by government organisations. The latter are not much different from SOEs. There is evidence of a trend towards the conversion of all closed shareholding enterprises into open enterprises, motivated by the pressing need to raise investment funds for modernisation.

- The driving force behind the mutation of the pattern of ownership of large Chinese enterprises/corporate groups is the need to diversify the sources of finance. A crucial factor in this regard is the widening incompatibility between, on the one hand, maintaining the present ownership pattern of enterprises and, on the other hand, a further reform of the commercial banking sector. It is the former that has to give, given the urgent necessity of the latter. The decision to swap non-performing debt for equity held by profit-seeking AMCs is an initiative with far-reaching ramifications for the enterprise ownership structure.

- The large Chinese enterprises/corporate groups are important nodes of political organisation and control, and are regarded as the bulwarks of the one-party State. The diversification of the ownership pattern of large enterprises/corporate groups will sooner or later bring to the fore the issue of the role of the Party in enterprises. This is an issue that has been occasionally raised, only to be glossed over, and it does not lend itself to a straightforward solution.

- The transformation of the entrepreneurial operations of the industrial Ministries and bureaux into companies with their own budgets is likely to accelerate the process of regrouping and enterprise restructuring. The change has already set in motion a process of the consolidation of enterprises into corporate groups. However, given the structure of government decision-making in China, much of this consolidation will be confined to enterprises in the same industry, and owned by the same government tier. Such a consolidation, though limited in scope, should enhance efficiency by reducing fragmentation and should also avoid the dangers of a rise in monopoly power, except in industries that are exclusively controlled by the Central Government.

8 General conclusions and future work

The findings and the implications of the study

The specific subject of enquiry in this book is corporate governance in the context of the Chinese economy, with particular reference to the companies listed on the two official stock exchanges. This is the first systematic and comprehensive study of these issues in China from a positive perspective and using econometric methods to analyse rich datasets, some of which were obtained directly from the SZSE. The main theories underpinning the book are the theory of incomplete contracts and agency theory. It is argued that the separation of ownership and control in modern corporations, and the impossibility of foreseeing, writing, and enforcing a comprehensive contract lead to agency problems. The basic argument is thus that corporate governance matters, and that it has an impact upon corporate performance.

The specific findings of the individual chapters will now be summarised. The institutional background of the Chinese financial system reform was reviewed and analysed in Chapter 3, and the main findings were:

1 Financial reform in China, and the corporatisation of the SOEs, has been motivated by the expansion of the Chinese economy, and the need for capital beyond the capacity of public fiscal revenues. As local government has taken a greater and greater share of fiscal income, Central Government has found it increasingly difficult to finance projects through the State budget. Given the high levels of personal savings in the State Bank, the Chinese Government first decided to reform the financing of the SOEs by funding new State projects (except some key projects) with debt instead of equity. The underlying motive was to make the project managers accountable for the repayment of debt, that is to make the capital invested by the government a 'hard constraint'.

2 But the corporatisation of the SOEs is not just about the search for new sources of capital, and can only be properly understood in the context of the reallocation of resources. This is also true for the formation of the new governance structures, where there has been a shift from monopoly State control to shared control, even though control is still dominated by various State authorities.

3   In choosing a model of corporate governance, the policymakers have favoured a stylised Anglo-American model in principle, but the reality has been a mixture of the Anglo-American and German–Japanese models. Furthermore, although the stated objective is an open, fair, multiple, and competitive shareholding system, and the policy-makers have been trying to reduce over-concentrated State shareholdings, progress in moving from the current situation of insider-dominated shareholdings and a main bank system has been a gradual process and the end is not yet in sight.

The implications of Chapter 3 are that, notwithstanding the fact that there is no perfect corporate governance mechanism, and that the development of an appropriate mechanism for China is a gradual and path-dependent process, there is still an imperative to move forward as quickly as possible in order to minimise the associated costs. However, the maturity of a sound corporate governance system that sustains longer-term development is inextricably linked to the success of economic, legal and cultural development in Chinese society as a whole.

The underpricing of IPOs was investigated in Chapter 4 in the context of corporate control and its private benefits, in the particular case of China. We found evidence of high IPO premiums in a sample of 467 listed companies that had publicly issued equity to outside investors. We then linked the IPO underpricing to the corporate control mechanism, and found that the underpricing was negatively related to the proportion of shares held by the largest single shareholder, after controlling for other well-known factors. This finding confirms our argument that, when the regulatory environment is poor, the controlling shareholders are able to pursue their private benefits more easily and without penalty. The outside investors perceive this, and take a more cautious strategy to IPOs, leading to lower IPO pricing. This study further examined the impact of the ownership of the largest single shareholders on IPO underpricing. We found lower IPO returns in firms where the largest shareholders are State-owned, and higher returns in firms with larger domestic shareholdings. This implies the potential for a good corporate governance mechanism.

These findings support the predictions of the extant literature, but add to it by highlighting the importance of corporate control in providing private benefits. Whilst the asymmetric information theory provides a powerful explanation of why IPOs should be underpriced, the theory cannot explain why there are different returns across the IPOs. But this can be explained by a consideration of the corporate control mechanism.

The findings in Chapter 5 suggest that the influence of ownership structure upon corporate performance is considerably more complicated than had been previously understood. Not only does ownership concentration have an impact upon firms' performance, but the nature of the large shareholders is also an important determinant. A State shareholding, either through a State agency or through a State solely-owned institution, leads to inefficient capital allocation. In contrast, the presence of domestic shareholders can improve firm performance. A management shareholding, as a mechanism for providing top management with a proper incentive scheme, needs more attention, both in theory and in practice.

A negative effect upon corporate performance of the proportion of tradable shares signals the absence, or immaturity, of the markets for corporate control. The tradable shares, mainly held by the public, do not have a sufficient influence, either through vote or by the 'Wall Street rule', to monitor management. This raises a number of issues related to the legal aspects of corporate governance, which require urgent attention both in China and in other transition economies (e.g. Russia) and also some developed countries such as Italy. This research also suggests that the formation of an optimal ownership structure, which maximises firm value, is retarded by the stipulation that all shares held by institutional entities at the IPO should not be freely traded.

A conclusion that emerges from the analysis of Chapters 4 and 5 is that the ownership structure matters. More specifically, State ownership leads to poor market performance either during the IPO stage or the after-market stage. This points to the need for a retreat of State ownership in public corporations, as suggested by Qian (2001), though perhaps not at the speed experienced in Russia.

The focus of attention was extended in Chapter 6 to the determinants of capital structure in a sample of 433 Chinese listed companies in the manufacturing sector. It was the first ever such study for China. We found that older firms, and those with higher market-to-book value ratios, are likely to have more debt. And larger, faster-growing and more profitable firms are likely to have less debt. The extent of the shareholding held by management does not have a significant impact upon the debt level, whereas that by the largest shareholder has a negative impact. For the most part, our findings have been consistent both with our theoretical predictions and with the conclusions of the studies carried out by Booth *et al.* (2001) for emerging markets, and Rajan and Zingales (1995) for developed countries.

However, it is still important to be aware of the legal and institutional differences between China and the Western economies. Here we want to stress two points that are particularly relevant to China. First, Baer and Gray (1996) argue that debt is often considered to be a 'soft' rather than a 'hard' constraint in many transitional economies, and this has certainly been true for the State-owned enterprises in China. But the debt constraint is undoubtedly hardening for Chinese listed companies in which the Government acts as a shareholder, rather than as the sole owner.[1] The Annual Reports of the listed companies show that the majority of legal cases between them and other parties are related to debt repayment. And the decisions of the Courts are being implemented sooner. Second, the markets for corporate control are still not mature in China. Listed companies in the West have the freedom to issue equity even when performance is poor. The shares of the majority of listed companies in China are under the control of the State authorities or other institutional shareholders, and may not be traded on stock markets, though this is currently under review by the policy-makers. There are occasional cases where the shares held by the State or by the institutional shareholders have been traded to other parties, but the transference was only effected with the permission of the State authority and/or other shareholders. Furthermore, Chinese companies are not allowed to make seasonal equity offerings, and debt may be the only channel for raising additional finance.

A political perspective into the governance structure of the Chinese corporate groups was taken in Chapter 7. The principal findings were listed in the final section of that chapter, and will not be repeated here.

The findings from this book not only enrich our knowledge about the functioning of the Chinese corporate governance system, but also provide a guide for future policy-making at both the government level and the corporate level. Thus corporate governance matters, though it is not a panacea for all the problems faced by the SOEs. There is a need to point out that corporate governance is a dynamic issue not only in the sense that it interacts with its surrounding environment, but also in that it is a framework within which the constituent parts must support each other to achieve a smooth functioning. In the Anglo-American model, for example, the existence of the market for corporate control is essential to correct managerial failures, yet such a market is missing in China due to the concentrated and illiquid system of shareholding. The smooth functioning of a corporate governance system relies upon, and complements, the existence of competitive markets, properly implemented commercial and contract legal systems, and independent professional legal and accounting services. As Kester (1994) pointed out, the existence of product market competition, and mutual monitoring and selective intervention by large, equity-owning stakeholders, can be highly effective means of controlling agency and transaction costs. Kester also suggests that extensive reliance on implicit, relational contracting in the context of long-term commercial relationships may yield other substantial operating and transactional efficiencies. Thus a corporate governance system should be implemented in a way that is complementary with other systems that have evolved in history, and may only be understood in this context.

The limitations of the study

This study of corporate governance in China, as the first of its kind, is limited in both depth and scope. In particular, we would like to draw attention to the following limitations:

- A perfect stock market, which can accurately reflect all the information related to the firm and its environment, is required if Tobin's Q is to be a useful measure of corporate performance. This would be a strong assumption, even in many well-developed economies, and is certainly an optimistic portrayal of China. There is also substantial anomalous behaviour by individual firms, though the systematic effects of this can be minimised by analysing a large sample.
- The data used in this study relate to the listed companies, the majority of which are large, key SOEs. These companies were selected for listing by the appropriate ministries and/or local governments, receive priority access to the stock markets to raise finance for their projects, and are provided with loans at favourable rates by banks that are instructed to do so. The sample is thus not representative of all firms in the Chinese economy. The findings and

conclusions of this study are thus limited to the listed companies, and should not be extrapolated to the economy as a whole. Furthermore, the conclusions should be considered in the light of the overall process of SOE reform.

- One possible criticism of all such studies in emerging or transitional economies is that the underpinning theories, which have generally been formulated on the basis of the experience in developed countries, may be invalid. In this study, there are two tiers of theories. The first tier relates to the theory of incomplete contracts and agency theory, and is concerned with the existence of corporate governance issues. Here, it is reasonable to assume that the forecasting of the future, the writing of contracts, and the enforcement of those contracts are even more difficult in transitional economies, and that the contracts are likely to be even more incomplete than in developed economies. As to the applicability of agency theory, there is a huge literature reporting serious agency problems in transition economies, and these problems are probably more complex than those in the western economies. The second tier of theories includes those that focus more on the specific issues of corporate governance (i.e. IPO underpricing, ownership structure and corporate performance, and capital structure). In these chapters, we have proceeded cautiously and pointed out both the assumptions and the institutional background required by the standard theory. For example, the theory of capital structure requires debt to be a hard constraint on management, but this assumption arguably does not hold in the Chinese context. Nevertheless, it is interesting to note that the findings of Chapter 6 confirm that the determinants of capital structure in China are qualitatively consistent with those in other emerging markets (Booth *et al.*, 2001) and those in developed economies.

- The fast growth of the Chinese Economy since the adoption of economic reform has been impressive. This has not only provided numerous subjects for researchers to study, but also difficulties in presenting a 'true' picture of the Chinese economy. The data used in this book relate to the period 1995–99 in Chapter 4 (IPOs), to 1997 in Chapters 5 and 6 (ownership structure and capital structure), and 1999 for Chapter 7 (corporate groups). There is thus a slight mismatch in the data used in the various empirical chapters, but it is our belief that the fundamental institutional background did not change markedly over this period in a way that might radically amend our findings.

The need for further research

Research on corporate governance is in its infancy, and there is considerable scope for future work. First, the theories themselves are in development, even though tremendous advances have been made in recent years. Second, a major part of the literature is based upon conditions in the developed economies, and the assumptions and preconditions of the various theories should be carefully examined before applying these theories to transitional economies. Third, the scope of corporate governance stretches far beyond economics, into the legal and

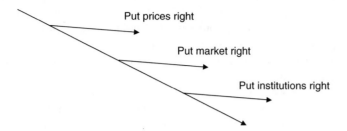

Figure 8.1 The development of economics.
Source: Williamson (1996).

institutional arrangements that have evolved from the history of each individual economy. The schematic diagram given in Figure 8.1 from Williamson (1996) illustrates the evolution of the study of corporate governance.

More specifically, the collection of additional data could generate additional understanding of the corporate governance system in China. The data used in the studies of both ownership structure and capital structure relate only to the year 1997. Further years of data would enable these issues to be investigated not only in a cross-sectional manner, but also in time-series analysis. Additional data on the long-term returns after IPOs would enable us to extend our research into the long-term performance associated with various ownership structures. This would not only provide more interesting conclusions than a study of short-term returns, but would also be a topic that has yet to be investigated either in developed or developing economies (Ritter, 1991; Loughran and Ritter, 1995). This work will be started after the completion of this research.

As regards ownership structure, there are two obvious avenues in which the current work could be extended. First, it would be sensible to consider more fully situations where the largest single shareholder is holding only a few more shares than the second largest shareholder. The current model ignores the second largest shareholder, yet it might be relatively easy for the second largest shareholder to become the largest by simply purchasing a small proportion of the outstanding shares. In short, a more comprehensive analysis should take account of the relative sizes of the large shareholders. Second, it would be interesting to investigate the role of foreign capital in listed companies. There are more than a 100 listed companies with foreign-owned shares, some of them with controlling positions. The availability of information on these companies provides an excellent opportunity to study whether the foreign investors are passive profit-takers or active managers.

The Chinese stock markets are ranked third in Asia in terms of market capitalisation. Should the future development of these markets be based upon the Anglo-Saxon model, where the stock market provides both a major source of finance and a mechanism for corporate control, or the German–Japanese model, where the banks play a stronger role in finance and governance? Or should development be based upon a distinctive mixture of the two? The Chinese evidence reveals the co-existence of a free-rider problem, which is a typical concern in the Anglo-Saxon model, and poor protection of minority shareholders, which is commonly seen in other economies – see La Porta *et al.* (1998, 2000, 2002).

This is a positive (what is happening) rather than a normative (what should be) study of corporate governance. Nevertheless, the findings are important as a governance system should not only provide monitoring and incentives for performance, but should also encourage experimentation, adoption, and the diffusion of better practices (Kogut, 1996). However, given the path-dependence of institutional evolution (North, 1992), it is perhaps unwise to adopt wholesale the corporate governance system of another country. A more realistic approach may be to allow the emergence and development of a Chinese model of corporate governance to take place within a well-designed legal and regulatory environment.

Notes

1 Introduction

1 The term 'capital structure' has been used in the literature to refer both to the relative composition of different types of contracts (e.g. of debt and equity), and to the relative composition of these contracts between different groups of investors (e.g. between an entrepreneur and any external investors). In this book, we adopt the definitions provided by Jenson and Meckling (1976) who define 'capital structure' as 'the relative quantities of bonds, equity, warrants, trade credit etc.', and 'ownership structure' as 'the relative amounts of ownership claims held by insiders (management) and outsiders (investors) with no direct role in the management of the firm'.

2 In this book, we refer to 'management' as all people and institutions who directly undertake strategic decision-making in the corporation, including senior managers as employees as well as the Directors of the Board as delegates of the general shareholders.

3 Such accounting measures are still used, where appropriate, in the study.

4 We intend to replicate these studies with more recent data once the new data becomes available.

5 Much of this information will be useful in future studies such as the relationship between Board structure and corporate performance.

6 More detailed descriptions can be seen in STATA Reference Manual Release 5 volume 3, pp. 46–57, 171–2.

7 As Wallace and Silver (1988, p. 265) point out, 'Generally speaking, it is probably a good idea to use the White option routinely, perhaps comparing the output with regular OLS output as a check to see whether heteroskedasticity is a serious problem in a particular set of data.' Cited in Gujarati (2003, p. 418).

8 More discussion on the methods used in the study of corporate governance can be found in Demsetz and Villalonga (2001).

2 Theoretical approaches to corporate governance

1 According to Williamson (1975), the transactions costs consist of the costs of searching for products, negotiation costs, the costs of writing contracts, and the costs of implementing the contracts.

2 Coase (1937) defined the boundaries of the firm as that range of exchanges over which the market system was suppressed, and resource allocation was accomplished instead by authority and direction.

3 See Hart (1995b) for more discussion of these arguments.

4 A more recent study on the ownership structures of Western European countries is reported in Faccio and Lang (2002).

5 The nine economies included Hong Kong, Indonesia, Japan, South Korea, Malaysia, the Philippines, Singapore, Taiwan, and Thailand.
6 For a more detailed analysis of the theory of incomplete contracts, see the special issue (volume 66, 1999) of the *Review of Economic Studies*.
7 An alternative term for the 'complete' contract is the 'comprehensive' contract, which is one that will never need to be revised or complemented (Williamson, 1985).
8 Holstrom and Tirole (1989) list four similar factors making a contract incomplete: (i) contingencies not foreseen; (ii) too many contingencies to write into a contract; (iii) monitoring costs; and (iv) legal costs.
9 Physical, or non-human, assets include machines, buildings, inventories, lists of clients, patents, copyrights, etc. Human capital is excluded since, in the absence of slavery, the (ultimate) right to decide how human capital is used always resides with the possessor of the human capital.
10 A more detailed comparison of corporate governance systems around the world can be found in the appendix at the end of this chapter.
11 See La Porta *et al.* (1997, 1998, 2000, 2002) and Berndt (2000) for a detailed discussion with emphasis on the differences in the historical and legal environments.
12 If there were a known best way to organise an economy, then the influence of politics and social values might be seen as a constraint. But capitalism is not limited to one single type, nor can an as yet untried but superior form of capitalist organisation be ruled out. A desirable feature of any reform package is thus an allowance for an evolutionary path of trial, effort and adaptation (Murrel, 1992; Frydman and Rapacynzshi, 1994). Political and social institutions play an important role in guiding the process of evolution and transformation.
13 A legal person is defined in China as an institution, or a legal entity that is not a natural person, but with the rights to own assets, sign contracts and sue or be sued.

3 The evolution of corporate governance in China

1 See the website (www.csrc.gov.cn) of the CSRC.
2 The data are taken from the CSRC daily market report on 31 October 2001. This is available at the website www.csrc.gov.cn
3 In May 2001, the financial authorities relaxed the restriction on the sale of B shares so that they could be bought not just by foreign investors, but by anyone with foreign currencies (particularly US$). This was designed to help the recovery of the nearly dead B-shares market.
4 The nature of debt and equity in SOEs will be discussed further below.
5 In China, the CEOs are more often called the General Managers.
6 See CSRC (1995), at the website www.csrc.gov.cn
7 See CSRC (1999) 'A Guideline on the Offer Price Settings in IPO'.
8 The highest P/E ratio was 84 (SHSE, 2001).
9 In some countries (e.g. the United States), the IPO will be cancelled if the proportion of shares successfully sold to the public does not reach a certain level.
10 See *Zhongguo Zhengquan Bao (Chinese Securities News)*, 16 August 2000 at http://www.chinaonline.com/features/m_guide/media/Publications/china_securities/china_securities.html
11 See the CSRC daily market report on 2 November 2001 at www.csrc.gov.cn
12 Issued by the People's Bank of China in 1996 – see Tam (1999) for more details.
13 See various issues of the *Securities Times* (China) in July 2001 at www.securitiestimes.com.cn
14 La Porta *et al.* (1998) point out that the extent of legal protection of outside investors differs enormously across countries.

4 The effect of ownership structure on the underpricing of Initial Public Offerings

1 The term 'winner's curse' comes from the auction literature. In a sealed bid auction with bidders who have some independent private information on the blue of the item being auctioned, the highest bidder at the auction finds out *ex post* that their valuation was probably too high. Thus, the person who wins the auction may be cursed by learning that s/he overpaid.
2 For example, the shares of Ford are issued in two classes: those with voting rights, and those without. The shares with voting rights are held by the Ford family, and are never traded on the Stock Exchange.
3 See also Barclay *et al.* (1993) on the private benefits of control in closed-end mutual funds, and DeAngelo and DeAngelo (1985) for a study of the concentration of managerial ownership and control in dual-class share corporations in the United States.
4 The focus of the Jones *et al.* paper was on governmental behaviour in privatisation programmes around the world, and was thus more macro-oriented than the current study.
5 Defined as the difference between the first-day market closing price minus the IPO price divided by the IPO price.
6 Published in Chinese by *Securities Times* (China), one of the leading financial newspapers in China.
7 In comparison, Krigman *et al.* (1999) report that 25 per cent of a sample of 1,232 US IPOs during 1988–95 were overpriced and suffered first-day trading losses.
8 We tested the relationship between the P/E ratio and industry dummies, and found that it was not significant.
9 Both studies report a negative relation between IPO return and firm size. Similar results are also reported by Su and Fleisher (1999) for China.
10 The World Bank (1995) argued that the non-discretionary allocation of shares, by mechanisms such as a lottery, exacerbated the underpricing tendency. The participants at the 12th Annual Conference of the CEA (UK) also pointed out the potential multicollinearity between the explanatory variables, Lottery and Methods. We checked this by (1) running an ANOVA on the two variables and found only small r^2 between the two, and (2) dropping Methods from the list of explanatory variables in later regressions and found that R^2 decreased markedly. These results suggest there is not a serious multicollinearity problem, especially given the large sample size. See Maddala (1977) for further details.
11 TOPOWNER is significant, at least at the 15 per cent level, in all four regressions.
12 See the *China Securities Times* (17 April 2000).

5 Ownership structure as a corporate governance mechanism

1 This is a later version of the paper published on the *Economics of Planning* 34: 53–72, 2001 with the same title.
2 The State agencies are the BSAM at its various hierarchic levels, as discussed in Chapter 3.
3 Demsetz and Villalonga (2001) report an average management shareholding of 1.54 per cent in the United States.
4 There is also concern about corporate governance in the United States, following the scandals at many high profile corporations.

6 The determinants of capital structure

1 This chapter is an updated version of the paper presented at the Annual Conference of the Academy of International Business (UK) at the University of Strathclyde, Glasgow in April 2000.

2 See the detailed survey by Harris and Raviv (1991).
3 Sarig and Warga (1989) find similar term structures empirically.
4 Long-term debts are recorded as reported if they are positive, and as zero otherwise.
5 In some cases, listed companies can face tax rates that are different from their subsidiaries. Consolidated tax figures are recorded when companies exert a controlling interest in other firms.
6 Both the requirement upon, and the expectation of, the Government to provide other benefits such as housing and full employment to the listed companies, have also been reduced though not eliminated.

7 Chinese corporate groups: a perspective from governance structure

1 An earlier version of this paper was co-authored with Athar Hussain and presented as 'Political Economy of Chinese Corporate Groups' at the International Conference on the 'Emergence and the Structuring of Corporate Groups in P R China: an International Perspective' at the University of Hong Kong in November 1999.
2 See Winter (1991) for a critique of the transactions cost approach.
3 The '14 Rights' were enunciated by the State Council in 1992. In various ways they have been surpassed by changes in recent years, especially the reorganisation of industrial ministries and bureaux.
4 The ratio of exports and imports to GDP rose almost four-fold from 9.7 per cent in 1978 to 36.5 per cent in 1999.
5 The classification, set by the State Economic and Trade Commission in 1988 and still in use at present, is based on production capacity and the size of fixed assets. Different criteria have been set in accordance with the characteristics of different sectors, where as there is no strict requirement regarding the employment and sales volume of each enterprise. Those criteria are mainly targeted at state-owned industrial enterprises and there are no clear and unified criteria for enterprises of other types.
6 To a degree the government also plays a central role in the birth of private or fully foreign-owned enterprises, though not in their closure.
7 We use the term 'closure' in preference to 'bankruptcy', because the latter covers a wide range of outcomes including closure, merger and take-over.
8 SINOPEC was not created in 1998, but was transformed from a petrochemical to a diversified corporate group through a transfer of upstream enterprises.

8 General conclusions and future work

1 Both the requirement upon, and the expectation of, the Government to provide other benefits such as housing and full employment to the listed companies, have also been reduced though not eliminated.

References

Aghion, Philippe and Patrick Bolton (1992), 'An "Incomplete Contracts" Approach to Financial Contracting', *Review of Economic Studies* 59, 473–94.

Agrawal, Anup and Gershon Mandelker (1987), 'Managerial Incentives and Corporate Investment and Financing Decision', *Journal of Finance* 42, 823–37.

Alchian, Armen and Harold Demsetz (1972), 'Production, Information Costs, and Economic Organisation', *American Economic Review* 62, 777–95.

Allen, Franklin (2001), 'Do Financial Institutions Matter?', *Journal of Finance* 56, 1165–75.

Amihud, Yakov, Baruch Lev, and Nickolaos Travlos (1990), 'Corporate Control and the Choice of Investment Financing: the Case of Corporate Acquisitions', *Journal of Finance* 45, 603–16.

Anderson, Christopher and Anil Makhija (1999), 'Deregulation, Disintermediation, and Agency Costs of Debt: Evidence from Japan', *Journal of Financial Economics* 55, 309–39.

Ang, James, Rebel Cole, and James Wuh Lin (1999), 'Agency Costs and Ownership Structure', *Journal of Finance* 55, 80–106.

Aoki, Masahiko (1995), 'Controlling Insider Control: Issues of Corporate Governance in Transition Economies', in Masahiko Aoki and Hyuan-Ki Kim (eds), *Corporate Governance in Transition Economies – Insider Control and the Role of Banks*, Washington DC: The World Bank, 3–29.

Asquith, Daniel, Jonathan Jones, and Robert Kieschnick (1998), 'Evidence on Price Stabilisation and Underpricing in Early IPO Returns', *Journal of Finance* 53, 1759–73.

Baer, Herbert and Cheryl Gray (1996), 'Debt as a Control Device in Transitional Economies: the Experiences of Hungary and Poland', in Roman Frydman, Cheryl Gray, and Andrzej Rapaczynski (eds), *Corporate Governance in Central Europe and Russia*, Volume I, Budapest: Central European University Press, 68–110.

Banz, Rolf (1981), 'The Relationship between Return and Market Value of Common Stocks', *Journal of Financial Economics* 9, 3–18.

Barca, Fabrizio, Magda Bioda, Luigi Cannari, Riccardo Cesari, Carlo Gola, Giuseppe Manitta, Giorgio Salvo, and Luigi Signorini (1994), *Proprieta, Modelli di Controllo e Riallocazione Nelle Imprese Industriali Italiane*, Bologna, II Mulino.

Barclay, Michael and Clifford Holderness (1989), 'Private Benefit from Control of Public Corporations', *Journal of Financial Economics* 25, 371–95.

Barclay, Michael and Clifford Smith (1995), 'The Maturity Structure of Debt', *Journal of Finance* 50, 603–31.

158 *References*

Barclay, Michael, Clifford Holderness, and Jeffrey Pontiff (1993), 'Private Benefits from Block Ownership and Discounts on Closed-end Funds', *Journal of Financial Economics* 33, 263–91.

Beatty, Randolph and Jay Ritter (1986), 'Investment Banking, Reputation, and the Underpricing of Initial Public Offering', *Journal of Financial Economics* 15, 3–29.

Berger, Philip, Eli Ofek, and David Yermack (1997), 'Managerial Entrenchment and Capital Structure Decision', *Journal of Finance* 52, 1411–38.

Berglof, Eric (1990), *Corporate Control and Capital Structure: Essays on Property Rights and Financial Contracts*. Unpublished PhD Thesis, Stockholm School of Economics, Stockholm.

Berglof, Erik and Ernst-Ludwig von Thadden (1994), 'Short-Term versus Long-Term Interests: Capital Structure with Multiple Investors', *Quarterly Journal of Economics* 109, 1055–84.

Bergstrom, Clas and Kristian Rydqvist (1992), 'Differentiated Bids for Voting and Restricted Voting Shares in Public Tender Offers', *Journal of Banking and Finance* 16, 97–114.

Berle, Adolf and Gardiner Means (1932), *The Modern Corporation and Private Property*, New York, Macmillan.

Berndt, Markus (2000), *Global Differences in Corporate Governance System Theory and Implications for Reforms*. Discussion Paper No. 303, Harvard Law School, Cambridge MA.

Blair, Margaret (1995), *Ownership and Control: Rethinking Corporate Governance for the Twenty-First Century*, Washington DC: The Brookings Institution.

Bolton, Patrick and David Scharfstein (1990), 'A Theory of Predation based on Agency Problems in Financial Contracting', *American Economic Review* 90, 94–106.

Bolton, Patrick and David Scharfstein (1998), 'Corporate Finance, the Theory of the Firm, and Organisations', *Journal of Economic Perspectives* 12, 95–114.

Bolton, Patrick and Ernst-Ludwig von Thadden (1998), 'Blocks, Liquidity, and Corporate Control', *Journal of Finance* 53, 1–26.

Booth, James and Lena Chua (1996), 'Ownership Dispersion, Costly Information, and IPO Underpricing', *Journal of Financial Economics* 41, 291–310.

Booth, Laurence, Varouj Aivazian, Asli Demirguc-Kunt and Vojislav Maksimovic (2001), 'Capital Structures in Developing Countries', *Journal of Finance* 56, 87–113.

Boycko, Maxim, Andrei Shleifer and Robert Vishny (1995), *Privatizing Russia*, Cambridge MA: M.I.T. Press.

Bradley, Michael, Greg Jarrell, and Han Kim (1984), 'On the Existence of an Optimal Capital Structure: Theory and Evidence', *Journal of Finance* 39, 857–78.

Brennan, Michael and Julian Franks (1997), 'Underpricing, Ownership and Control in Initial Public Offerings of Equity Securities in the UK', *Journal of Financial Economics* 45, 391–413.

Brook, Yarib, Robert Hendershott, and Darrell Lee (2000), 'Corporate Governance and Recent Consolidation in the Banking Industry', *Journal of Corporate Finance* 6, 141–64.

Burkart, Mike, Denis Growb, and Fausto Panunzi (1997), 'Large Shareholders, Monitoring, and the Value of the Firm', *Quarterly Journal of Economics* 112, 693–728.

Cadbury, Adrian (1992), *The Final Report of the Committee on the Financial Aspects of Corporate Governance – the Code of Best Practice*, London: Gee and Co. Ltd.

Campbell, Tim (1979), 'Optimal Investment Financing Decisions and the Value of Confidentiality', *Journal of Financial and Quantitative Analysis* 14, 913–24.

Campbell, John, Andrew Lo, and Craig Mackinlay (1997), *The Econometrics of Financial Markets*, Princeton: Princeton University Press.

Carleton, Willard, James Nelson, and Michael Weisbach (1998), 'The Influence of Institutions on Corporate Governance through Private Negotiations: Evidence from TIAA-CREF', *Journal of Finance* 53, 1335–62.

Chan, Kalok and Wai-Ming Fong (2000), 'Trade Size, Order Imbalance, and the Volatility-Volume Relation', *Journal of Financial Economics* 57, 247–73.

Chandler, Alfred (1977), *The Visible Hand*, Cambridge MA: Harvard University Press.

Chandler, Alfred (1980), 'The United States – The Seedbed of Managerial Capitalism', in Temin, Peter (ed.) (1994), *Industrialisation in North America*, Oxford: Blackwell Press.

Chandler, Alfred (1990), *Scale and Scope: The Dynamics of Industrial Capitalism*, Cambridge MA: Harvard University Press.

Chang, Chun (1999), 'Capital Structure as Optimal Contracts', *North American Journal of Economics and Finance* 10, 363–85.

Charkham, Jonathan (1994), *Keeping Good Company: A Study of Corporate Governance in Five Countries*, Oxford: Clarendon Press.

Che, Jiahua and Yingyi Qian (1998), 'Insecure Property Rights and Government Ownership of Firms', *Quarterly Journal of Economics* 113, 467–96.

Chemmanur, Thomas (1993), 'The Pricing of Initial Offerings: A Dynamic Model with Information Production', *Journal of Finance* 48, 285–304.

Chemmanur, Thomas and Paolo Fulghieri (1995), *Information Production, Private Equity Financing, and the Going Public Decision*. Working paper, New York: Columbia University.

Chen, Qiaosheng (1997) 'On the Adjustment of China's Industrial Structure', in Fumio Itoh (ed.), *China in the Twenty-First Century: Politics, Economy and Society*, Tokyo: United Nations University Press.

China Securities Regulatory Commission (CSRC) (1996), *The Provisional Regulations on Stock Issuance*, Beijing: CSRC.

China Securities Regulatory Commission (CSRC) (1997), *The Circular of the Decision that Places the Shanghai Stock Exchange and the Shenzhen Stock Exchange under the Direct Management of CSRC*, Beijing: CSRC.

China Securities Regulatory Commission (CSRC) (1999), *A Guideline on the Offer Price Settings in IPO*, Beijing: CSRC.

China Securities Regulatory Commission (CSRC) (2000), *China Securities Market Yearbook 2000*, Beijing: CSRC.

Chung, Kee and Stephen Pruitt (1994), 'A Simple Approximation of Tobin's Q', *Financial Management* 23, 70–74.

Child, John (1994), *Management in China During the Age of Reform*, Cambridge: Cambridge University Press.

Cho, Myeong-Hyeon (1998), 'Ownership Structure, Investment, and the Corporate Value: an Empirical Analysis', *Journal of Financial Economics* 47, 103–21.

Chowdhry, Bhagwan and Ann Sherman (1996), 'International Differences in Oversubscription and Underpricing of IPOs', *Journal of Corporate Finance* 2, 359–81.

Claessens, Stijn, Simeon Djankov, and Liang Lang (2000), 'The Separation of Ownership and Control in East Asian Corporations', *Journal of Financial Economics* 58, 81–112.

Coase, Ronald (1937), 'The Nature of the Firm', *Economica* 4, 386–405.

Coffee, John (1991), 'Liquidity versus Control: the Institutional Investor Voice', *Columbia Law Review* 91, 1277–338.

Coffee, John (1996), 'Institutional Investors in Transitional Economies: Lessons from the Czech Experience', in Roman Frydman, Cheryl Gray and Andrzej Rapaczynski (eds),

Corporate Governance in Central Europe and Russia, volume I, Budapest: Central European University Press, 111–86.

Cole, Rebel and Hamid Mehran (1998), 'The Effect of Changes in Ownership Structure on Performance: Evidence from the Thrift Industry', *Journal of Financial Economics* 50, 291–317.

Copeland, Thomas and Fred Weston (1992), *Theory of Finance and Corporate Policy*, 3rd edition, Wokingham, England: Addison Wesley.

Daigler, Robert and Marilyn Wiley (1999), 'The Impact of Trader Type on the Futures Volatility–Volume Relation', *Journal of Finance* 54, 2297–316.

De Angelo, Harry and Ronald Masulis (1980), 'Optimal Capital Structure under Corporate and Personal Taxation', *Journal of Financial Economics* 8, 3–27.

De Angelo, Harry and Linda De Angelo (1985), 'Managerial Ownership of Voting Rights: a Study of Public Corporations with Dual Classes of Common Stock', *Journal of Financial Economics* 14, 33–70.

Degeorge, Francois and Richard Zeckhauser (1993), 'The Reverse LBO Decision and Firm Performance: Theory and Evidence', *Journal of Finance* 48, 1323–574.

Demirguc-Kunt, Asli and Ross Levine (1996), 'Stock Markets, Corporate Finance, and Economic Growth: an Overview', *World Bank Economic Review* 10, 221–39.

Demsetz, Harold (1983), 'The Structure of Ownership and the Theory of the Firm', *Journal of Law and Economics* 26, 375–90.

Demsetz, Harold and Kenneth Lehn (1985), 'The Structure of Corporate Ownership: Causes and Consequences', *Journal of Political Economy* 14, 1155–77.

Demsetz, Harold and Belen Villalonga (2001), 'Ownership Structure and Corporate Performance', *Journal of Corporate Finance* 7, 209–33.

Denis, David and Atulya Sarin (1999), 'Ownership and Board Structures in Publicly Traded Corporations', *Journal of Financial Economics* 52, 187–223.

Dewenter, Kathryn and Paul Malatesta (1997), 'Public Offerings of State-Owned and Privately-Owned Enterprises: an International Comparison', *Journal of Finance* 52, 1659–79.

Diamond, Douglas (1989), 'Reputation Acquisition in Debt Markets', *Journal of Political Economy* 97, 828–62.

Diamond, Douglas (1991), 'Debt Maturity Structure and Liquidity Risk', *Quarterly Journal of Economics* 106, 709–37.

Dittus, Peter and Stephen Prowse (1996), 'Corporate Control in Central Europe and Russia: Should Banks Own Shares?' in Roman Frydman, Cheryl Gray, and Andrzej Rapaczynski (eds), *Corporate Governance in Central Europe and Russia*, volume I, Budapest: Central European University Press, 20–67.

Easterbrook, Frank and Daniel Fischel (1991), *The Economic Structure of Corporate Law*, Cambridge MA: Harvard University Press.

Faccio, Mara and Larry Lang (2002), 'The Ultimate Ownership of Western European Corporations', *Journal of Financial Economics* 65, 365–95.

Fama, Eugene and Michael Jensen (1983), 'Separation of Ownership and Control', *Journal of Law and Economics* 26, 301–25.

Fama, Eugene and Kenneth French (1992), 'The Cross-section of Expected Stock Returns', *Journal of Finance* 47, 427–65.

Franks, Julian and Colin Mayer (1994), *Ownership and Control*, mimeo, London Business School.

Franks, Julian and Colin Mayer (1995), *Ownership, Control and Performance of German Corporations*, mimeo, London Business School.

Friend, Irwin and Joel Hasbrouck (1988), 'Determinants of Capital Structure', in Andy Chen (ed.), *Research in Finance*, volume 7, New York: JAI Press.

Friend, Irwin and Larry Lang (1988), 'An Empirical Test of the Impact of Managerial Self-interest on Corporate Capital Structure', *Journal of Finance* 43, 271–81.

Frydman, Roman, and Andrzej Rapaczynski (1994), *Privatisation in Eastern Europe: is the State Withering Away?* Budapest: Central European University Press.

Fukuyama, Francis (1995), *Trust – The Social Values and the Creation of Prosperity*, London, Hamish Hamilton.

Gallant, Ronald, Peter Rossi, and Gorge Tauchen (1992), 'Stock Prices and Volume', *Review of Financial Studies* 5, 199–242.

Gilson, Stuart (1989), 'Management Turnover and Financial Distress', *Journal of Financial Economics* 25, 241–62.

Gilson, Stuart (1997), 'Transaction Costs and Capital Structure Choice: Evidence from Financial Distressed Firms', *Journal of Finance* 52, 161–95.

Granick, David (1976), *Enterprise Guidance in Eastern Europe*, Princeton: Princeton University Press.

Greenbury, Richard (1995), *Report of the Committee on Executive Remuneration*, London: Gee and Co. Ltd.

Greene, William (1993), *Econometric Analysis*, New York: Macmillan.

Grinblatt, Mark and Chuan Yang Hwang (1989), 'Signalling and the Pricing of New Issues', *Journal of Finance* 44, 393–420.

Grossman, Sanford and Oliver Hart (1980), 'Takeover Bids, the Free Rider Problem, and the Theory of the Corporation', *Bell Journal of Economics* 11, 42–64.

Grossman, Sanford and Oliver Hart (1982), 'Corporate Financial Structure and Managerial Incentives', in John McCall (ed.), *The Economics of Information and Uncertainty*, Chicago IL: University of Chicago Press, 107–40.

Grossman, Sanford and Oliver Hart (1986), 'The Cost and Benefits of Ownership: a Theory of Vertical and Lateral Integration', *Journal of Political Economy* 94, 691–719.

Grossman, Sanford and Oliver Hart (1988), 'One Share-one Vote and the Market for Corporate Control', *Journal of Financial Economics* 20, 175–202.

Gujarati, Damodar (2003), *Basic Econometrics*, 4th Edition, New York: McGraw-Hill.

Hansmann, Henry (1996), *The Ownership of Enterprise*, Cambridge MA: Harvard University Press.

Harris, Milton and Arthur Raviv (1988), 'Corporate Governance: Voting Rights and Majority Rules', *Journal of Financial Economics* 20, 203–35.

Harris, Milton and Arthur Raviv (1990), 'Capital Structure and the Information Role of Debt', *Journal of Finance* 45, 321–45.

Harris, Milton and Arthur Raviv (1991), 'The Theory of Capital Structure', *Journal of Finance* 46, 297–355.

Hart, Oliver (1988), 'Incomplete Contracts and the Theory of the Firm', *Journal of Law, Economics and Organization* 4, 119–39.

Hart, Oliver (1995a), 'Corporate Governance: Some Theory and Implications', *Economic Journal* 105, 678–89.

Hart, Oliver (1995b), *Firms, Contracts and Financial Structure*, Oxford: Clarendon Press.

Hart, Oliver and Bengt Holmstrom (1987), 'The Theory of Contracts', in Truman Bewley (ed.), *Advances in Economic Theory*, Cambridge: Cambridge University Press.

Hart, Oliver and John Moore (1990), 'Property Rights and the Nature of the Firm', *Journal of Political Economy* 98, 1119–58.

Hart, Oliver and John Moore (1995), 'Debt and Seniority: an Analysis of the Role of Hard Claims in Constraining Management', *American Economic Review* 85, 567–85.

Hart, Oliver and John Moore (1999), 'Foundation of Incomplete Contracts', *Review of Economic Studies* 66, 115–38.

Hart, Oliver, Andrei Shleifer and Roberts Vishny (1997), 'The Proper Scope of Government: Theory and an Application to Prisons', *Quarterly Journal of Economics* 112, 1127–61.

Hay, Donald, Derek Morris, Guy Liu, and Shujie Yao (1994), *Economic Reform and State-Owned Enterprises in China, 1979–1987*, Oxford: Clarendon Press.

Helwege, Jean and Nellie Liang (1996), 'Is there a Pecking Order? Evidence from a Panel of IPO Firms', *Journal of Financial Economics* 40, 429–58.

Hertzel, Michael and Richard Smith (1993), 'Market Discounts and Shareholder Gains for Placing Equity Privately', *Journal of Finance* 48, 459–89.

Holderness, Clifford, Randall Kroszner, and Dennis Sheehan (1999), 'Were the Good Old Days That Good?: Changes in Managerial Stock Ownership Since the Great Depression', *Journal of Finance* 54, 435–69.

Holmstrom, Bengt (1979), 'Moral Hazard and Observability', *Bell Journal of Economics* 10, 4–29.

Holmstrom, Bengt and John Roberts (1998), 'The Boundaries of the Firm Revisited', *Journal of Economic Perspectives* 12, 73–94.

Holmstrom, Bengt and Jean Tirole (1989), 'The Theory of the Firm', in Richard Schmalensee and Robert Willig (eds) *Handbook of Industrial Organisation*, volume I, Amsterdam, North-Holland, 51–133.

Holmstrom, Bengt and Jean Tirole (1993), 'Market Liquidity and Performance Monitoring', *Journal of Political Economy* 101, 678–709.

Horner, Melchior (1988), 'The Value of the Corporate Voting Right: Evidence from Switzerland', *Journal of Banking and Finance* 12, 69–83.

Houston, Joel and James, Christopher (1996), 'Banking Information Monopolies and the Mix of Private and Public Debt Claims', *Journal of Finance* 51, 1863–89.

Huber, P. J. (1964), 'Robust Estimation of a Location Parameter', *Annals of Mathematical Statistics* 35, 73–101.

Hussain, Athar and Jian Chen (1999), 'Changes in China's Industrial Landscape and their Implications', *International Studies of Management & Organisation* 29, 5–20.

Ibbotson, Roger (1975), 'Price Performance of Common Stock New Issues', *Journal of Financial Economics* 2, 235–72.

Ibbotson, Roger, and Jay Ritter (1995), 'Initial Public Offerings', in Robert Jarrow, Vojislav Maksimovic, and William Ziemba (eds), *Handbook in Operations Research and Management Science – Finance*, New York: Elsevier, 993–1016.

Ibboston, Roger, Jody Sindelar, and Jay Ritter (1988), 'Initial Public Offering', *Journal of Applied Corporate Finance* 1, 37–45.

Jain, Bharat and Omesh Kini (1994), 'The Post-Issue Operating Performance of IPO Firms', *Journal of Finance* 49, 1699–726.

Jensen, Michael (1986), 'Agency Costs of Free Cash Flow, Corporate Finance, Takeovers', *American Economic Review* 76, 323–29.

Jensen, Michael (1989), 'Eclipse of the Public Corporations', *Harvard Business Review*, 61–74.

Jensen, Michael (1993), 'The Modern Industrial Revolution, Exit, and the Failure of Internal Control System', *Journal of Finance* 48, 831–80.

Jensen, Michael and William Meckling (1976), 'Theory of the Firm: Managerial Behaviours, Agency Cost and Ownership Structure', *Journal of Financial Economics* 3, 305–60.

Jensen, Michael and Richard Ruback (1983), 'The Market for Corporate Control: the Scientific Evidence', *Journal of Financial Economics* 11, 5–50.

Jones, Steven, William Megginson, Robert Nash, and Jeffry Netter (1999), 'Share Issue Privatisation as Financial Means to Political and Economic Ends', *Journal of Financial Economics* 53, 217–53.

Joskow, Paul (1985), 'Vertical Integration and Long Term Contracts: the Case of Coal Burning, Electric Generating Plants', *Journal of Law, Economics and Organization* 2, 33–80.

Kahn, Charles and Andrew Winton (1998), 'Ownership Structure, Speculation, and Shareholder Intervention', *Journal of Finance* 53, 99–130.

Kang, Jun-Koo and Anil Shivdasani (1995), 'Firm Performance, Corporate Governance, and Top Executive Turnover in Japan', *Journal of Financial Economics* 38, 29–58.

Karpoff, J. (1987), 'The Relation between Price Changes and Trading Volume: a Survey', *Journal of Financial and Quantitative Analysis* 22, 109–26.

Kay, John and Aubrey Silberston (1995), 'Corporate Governance', *National Institute Economic Review* 84, 84–97.

Kester, Carl (1986), 'Capital and Ownership Structure: a Comparison of United States and Japanese Manufacturing Corporation', *Financial Management*, 5–16.

Kester, Carl (1994), 'Industrial Groups as Systems of Contractual Governance', *Oxford Review of Economic Policy* 8, 24–44.

Kim, Moonchul and Jay, Ritter (1999), 'Valuing IPOs', *Journal of Financial Economics* 53, 409–37.

Kim, Wi Saeng and Eric Sorensen (1986), 'Evidence on the Impact of the Agency Costs of Debt in Corporate Debt Policy', *Journal of Financial and Quantitative Analysis* 21, 131–44.

Kogut, Bruce (1996), 'Direct investment, Experimentation, Corporate Governance', in Roman Frydman, Cheryl Gray, and Andrzej Rapaczynski (eds), *Corporate Governance in Central Europe and Russia*, volume I, Oxford: Oxford University Press, 293–332.

Koh, Francis and Terry Walter (1989), 'A Direct test of Rock's Model of the Pricing of Unseasoned Issues', *Journal of Financial Economics* 23, 251–72.

Kole, Stacey (1994), *Management Ownership and Firm Performance: Incentives or Rewards?* Working paper 93-10, Rochester NY: University of Rochester.

Kornai, János (1980), *Economics of Shortage*, Amsterdam and Oxford, North-Holland.

Krigman, Laurie, Wayne Shaw, and Kent Womack, Amos (1999), 'The Persistence of IPO Mispricing and the Predictive Power of Flipping', *Journal of Finance* 54, 1015–44.

Lang, Larry and Rene Stulz (1994), 'Tobin's Q, Corporate Diversification, and Firm Performance', *Journal of Political Economy* 102, 1248–80.

La Porta, Rafael, Florencio Lopez-de-Silanes, and Robert Vishny (1998), 'Law and Finance', *Journal of Political Economy* 106, 1113–55.

La Porta, Rafael, Florencio Lopez-de-Silanes, and Andrei Shleifer (1999), 'Corporate Ownership Around the World', *Journal of Finance* 54, 471–517.

La Porta, Rafael, Florencio Lopez-de-Silanes, Andrei Shleifer, and Robert Vishny (1997), 'Legal Determinants of External Finance', *Journal of Finance* 52, 1131–50.

La Porta, Rafael, Florencio Lopez-de-Silanes, Andrei Shleifer, and Robert Vishny (2000), 'Investor Protection and Corporate Governance', *Journal of Financial Economics* 58, 3–28.

La Porta, Rafael, Florencio Lopez-de-Silanes, Andrei Shleifer, and Robert Vishny (2002), 'Investor Protection and Corporate Valuation', *Journal of Finance* 57, 1147–70.

Lease, Ronald, John McConnell, and Wayne Mikkelson (1983), 'The Market Value of Publicly-Traded Corporations', *Journal of Financial Economics* 11, 439–71.

Lease, Ronald, John McConnell, and Wayne Mikkelson (1984), 'The Market Value of Different Voting Rights in Closely Held Corporations', *Journal of Business* 57, 443–67.

Lehn, Kenneth and Klaus Toft (1996), 'Optimal Capital Structure, Endogenous Bankruptcy, and the Term Structure of Credit Spreads', *Journal of Finance* 51, 987–1019.

Leland, Hayne (1994), 'Debt Value, Bond Covenants, and Optimal Capital Structure', *Journal of Finance* 49, 1213–52.

Leland, Hayne and David Pyle (1977), 'Information Asymmetries, Financial Structure, and Financial Intermediation', *Journal of Finance* 32, 371–88.

Levy, Haim (1983), 'Economic Valuation of Voting Power of Common Stock', *Journal of Finance* 38, 79–93.

Lin, Cyril (2000), *Corporatisation and Corporate Governance in China's Economic Transition*, mimeo, Department of Economics, University of Oxford.

Lipton, David and Jeffrey Sachs (1990), *Privatisation in Eastern Europe: the Case of Poland*, Brookings Papers on Economic Activity, Washington DC: The Brookings Institution.

Logue, Dennis (1973), 'On the Pricing of Unseasoned Equity Issues: 1965–1969', *Journal of Financial and Quantitative Analysis* 8, 91–103.

Loughran, Tim and Jay Ritter (1995), 'The New Issues Puzzle', *Journal of Finance* 50, 23–52.

Loughran, Tim, Jay Ritter, and Kristian Rydqvist (1994), 'Initial Public Offerings: International Insights', *Pacific Basin Finance Journal* 2, 165–99.

McDonald, J. G. and A. K. Fisher (1972), 'New Issue Stock Price Behaviour', *Journal of Finance* 27, 97–102.

Mace, Myles (1971), *Directors, Myth and Reality*, Boston MA: Harvard Business School Press.

Maddala, G.S. (1977), *Econometrics*, London, England: McGraw-Hill.

Mauer, David and Lemma Senbet (1992), 'The Effect of the Secondary Market on the Pricing of Initial Public Offerings: Theory and Evidence', *Journal of Financial and Quantitative Analysis* 27, 55–79.

Maug, Ernst (1998), 'Large Shareholders as Monitors: Is There a Trade-off between Liquidity and Control?' *Journal of Finance* 53, 65–97.

Mayer, Colin (1990), 'Financial Systems, Corporate Finance and Economic Development', in Glenn Hubbard (ed.), *Asymmetric Information, Corporate Finance and Investment*, Chicago IL: University of Chicago Press, 307–32.

Mayer, Colin (1994), 'Stock Markets, Financial Institutions and Corporate Performance', in Nicholas Dimsdale and Martha Prevezer (eds), *Capital Markets and Corporate Control*, Oxford: Clarendon Press, 179–94.

Megginson, William (1990), 'Restricted Voting Stock, Acquisition Premiums, and the Market for Corporate Control', *Financial Review* 25, 175–98.

Merton, Robert (1987), 'Presidential Address: a Simple Model of Capital Market Equilibrium', *Journal of Finance* 42, 483–510.

Michaely, Roni and Wayne Shaw (1994), 'The Pricing of Initial Public Offerings: Tests of Adverse Selection and Signalling Theories', *Review of Financial Studies* 7, 279–319.

Mikkelson, Wayne, Megan Partch, and Ken Shah (1997), 'Ownership and Operating Performance of Companies that Go Public', *Journal of Financial Economics* 44, 281–308.

Milgrom, Paul and John Roberts (1992), *Economics, Management and Organisation*, Englewood Cliffs NJ: Prentice Hall.

Miller, Merton (1977), 'Debt and Taxes', *Journal of Finance* 32, 261–75.

Miller, Merton (1997), 'Alternative Strategies for Corporate Governance in China', in Merton Miller (ed.), *Merton Miller on Derivatives*, New York: John Wiley & Sons.

Miller, Merton (1998), 'Financial Markets and Economic Growth', *Journal of Applied Corporate Finance* 11, 8–15.

Modigliani, Franco and Merton Miller (1958), 'The Cost of Capital, Corporation Finance, and The Theory of Investment', *American Economic Review* 48, 261–97.

Modigliani, Franco and Merton Miller (1963), 'Corporate Income Taxes and the Cost of Capital: a Correction', *American Economic Review* 53, 433–43.

Mok, Henry and Y. V. Hui (1998), 'Underpricing and Aftermarket Performance of IPOs in Shanghai, China', *Pacific-Basin Finance Journal* 6, 453–74.

Morck, Randall, Andrei Shleifer, and Robert Vishny (1988), 'Management Ownership and Market Valuation: an Empirical Analysis', *Journal of Financial Economics* 20, 293–513.

Murphy, Kevin (1985), 'Corporate Performance and Managerial Remuneration', *Journal of Accounting and Economics* 7, 11–42.

Murrell, Peter (1992), 'Evolution in Economics and in the Economic Reform of Centrally Planned Economics', in Christopher Clague and Gordon Rausser (eds), *The Emergence of Market Economies in Eastern Europe*, Cambridge MA: Blackwell Press, 35–53.

Myers, Stewart (1977), 'Determinants of Corporate Borrowing', *Journal of Financial Economics* 5, 147–75.

Myers, Stewart (1984), 'The Capital Structure Puzzle', *Journal of Finance* 39, 575–92.

Myers, Stewart and Nicholas Majluf (1984), 'Corporate Financing and Investment Decisions when Firms have Information that Investors Do Not Have', *Journal of Financial Economics* 13, 187–221.

Naughton, Barry (1988), 'Third Front Defence Industrialization in the Chinese Interior', *China Quarterly* 115, 351–86.

North, Douglas (1992), *Institutions, Institutional Changes and Economic Performance*, New York: Free Press.

Opler, Tim and Sheridan Titman (1994), 'Financial Distress and Corporate Performance', *Journal of Finance* 49, 1015–40.

Organisation for Economic Co-operation and Development (OECD) (1999), *OECD Principles of Corporate Governance*, Paris: OECD.

Pagano, Marco (1993), 'The Flotation of Companies on the Stock Market: a Coordination Failure Model', *European Economic Review* 37, 1101–25.

Pagano, Marco and Ailsa Roell (1998), 'The Choice of Stock Ownership Structure: Agency Costs, Monitoring and the Decision to Go Public', *Quarterly Journal of Economics* 113, 187–225.

Pagano, Margo, Fabio Panetta, and Luigi Zingales (1998), 'Why Do Companies Go Public? An Empirical Analysis', *Journal of Finance* 53, 27–64.

Perotti, Enrico (1995), 'Credible Privatisation', *American Economic Review* 85, 847–59.

Prowse, Stephen (1994*), Corporate Governance in an International Perspective: A Survey of Corporate Governance Mechanisms among Large Firms in the United States, the United Kingdom, Japan and Germany*. Economic Papers No. 41, Bank of International Settlements, Basle.

Qian, Yingyi (1995), 'Reforming Corporate Governance and Finance in China', in Masahiko Aoki and Hyung-Ki Kim (eds), *Corporate Governance in Transition*

Economies: Insider Control and the Role of Banks, Washington DC: The World Bank, 215–52.

Qian, Yingyi (2001), 'Government Control in Corporate Governance as a Transitional Institution: Lessons from China', in Joseph Stiglitz and Shahid Yusuf (eds), *Rethinking the East Asian Miracle*, New York: Oxford University Press, 295–321.

Rajan, Raghuram (1992), 'Insiders and Outsiders: the Choice Between Informed and Arms'-length Debt', *Journal of Finance* 52, 1367–400.

Rajan, Raghuram and Luigi Zingales (1995), 'What do We Know about Capital Structure Choice? Some Evidence from International Data', *Journal of Finance* 50, 1421–60.

Reinganum, Marc (1981), 'Misspecification of Capital Asset Pricing: Empirical Anomalies based on Earnings' Yields and Market Values', *Journal of Financial Economics* 9, 19–46.

Ritter, Jay (1987), 'The Costs of Going Public', *Journal of Financial Economics* 19, 269–81.

Ritter, Jay (1991), 'The Long-run Performance of Initial Public Offerings', *Journal of Finance* 46, 3–27.

Robinson, Michael and Robert White (1990), *The Value of a Vote in the Market for Corporate Control*, Working paper, York University.

Rock, Kevin (1986), 'Why New Issues Are Underpriced', *Journal of Financial Economics* 15, 187–212.

Roe, Mark (1993), 'Some Differences in Corporate Structure in Germany, Japan, and the United States', *Yale Law Journal* 102, 1927–2003.

Roe, Mark (2000), *Political Foundations for Separating Ownership from Corporate Control*, Paper presented at the London School of Economics.

Roll, Richard (1988), 'R^2', *Journal of Finance* 43, 541–66.

Ross, Stephen (1977), 'The Determination of Financial Structures: an Incentive Signalling Approach', *Bell Journal of Economics* 8, 23–40.

Ross, Stephen (1985), 'Debt and Taxes and Uncertainty', *Journal of Finance* 40, 637–57.

Rouwenhorst, Geert (1999), 'Local Return Factors and Turnover in Emerging Stock Markets', *Journal of Finance* 54, 1439–64.

Ruud, Judith (1993), 'Underwriter Price Support and the IPO Underpricing Puzzle', *Journal of Financial Economics* 34, 135–51.

Sarig, Oded and Arthur Warga (1989), 'Some Empirical Estimates of the Risk Structure of Interest Rates', *Journal of Finance* 44, 1351–60.

Schiavo-Campo, Salvatore and Dominique Pannier (1996), *Corporate Governance of Public Enterprises: The Comparative Experience*, World Bank Technical Paper No. 323, Washington DC, World Bank.

Schmidt, Klaus (1996), 'The Costs and Benefits of Privatization: An Incomplete Contracts Approach', *Journal of Law, Economics, and Organization* 12, 1–24.

Schmidt-Hebbel, Steven Webb, and Giancarlo Corsetti (1992), 'Household Savings in Developing Countries: First Cross-country Evidence', *World Bank Economic Review* 6, 529–74.

Schwert, William (1989), 'Why does Stock Volatility Change over Time?' *Journal of Finance* 44, 1115–54.

Securities Times (1998), *A Guide for Investment in Shanghai and Shenzhen Securities Exchanges* (1997), Shenzhen, China: Haitian Press.

Shanghai Stock Exchange (SHSE) (2000), 'An Analysis of Survey Questionnaires on Corporate Governance in Listed Companies', *Listed Company* 6, 24–37.

Shanghai Stock Exchange (SHSE) (2001), 'The IPO Process in China: a Retrospective over the Past Ten Years', *Listed Company* 5, 7–11.

Shavell, Steven (1979), 'Risk Sharing and Incentives in the Principal and Agent Relationship', *Bell Journal of Economics* 10, 55–73.

Shleifer, Andrei (1998), 'State versus Private Ownership', *Journal of Economic Perspectives* 12, 133–50.

Shleifer, Andrei and Robert Vishny (1986), 'Large Shareholders and Corporate Control', *Journal of Political Economy* 94, 461–88.

Shleifer, Andrei and Maxim Boycko (1993), 'The Politics of Russian Privatization', in Olivier Blanchard *et al.* (eds), *Post Communist Reform: Pain and Progress*, Boston MA: MIT Press, 53–80.

Shleifer, Andrei, and Robert Vishny (1994), 'Politicians and Firms', *Quarterly Journal of Economics* 109, 995–1025.

Shleifer, Andrei and Robert Vishny (1997), 'A Survey of Corporate Governance', *Journal of Finance* 52, 737–83.

Shyam-Sunder, Lakshmi and Stewart Myers (1999), 'Testing Static Tradeoff against Pecking Order Models of Capital Structure', *Journal of Financial Economics* 51, 219–44.

Slovin, Myron and Marie Sushka (1993), 'Ownership Concentration, Corporate Control Activity, and Firm Value: Evidence from the Death of Inside Blockholders', *Journal of Finance* 48, 1293–321.

Smith, Cliff and Ron Watts (1992), 'The Investment Opportunity Set and Corporate Financing, Dividend, and Compensation Policies', *Journal of Financial Economics* 32, 263–92.

State Economic Reform Commission (1994), *On Selection of a Batch of Large and Medium-size State-Owned Enterprises to Experiment with Modern Enterprise Systems* (in Chinese), Beijing: SERC.

State Statistical Bureau (China) (1981), *Statistical Yearbook of China 1981*, Beijing: Zhongguo Tongji She (State Statistics Publishing House).

State Statistical Bureau (China) (1995), *Statistical Yearbook of China 1995*, Beijing: Zhongguo Tongji She (State Statistics Publishing House).

State Statistical Bureau (China) (2000), *Statistical Yearbook of China 2000*, Beijing: Zhongguo Tongji She (State Statistics Publishing House).

Stoughton, Neal and Josef Zechner (1998), 'IPO-Mechanisms, Monitoring and Ownership Structure', *Journal of Financial Economics* 49, 45–77.

Stulz, Rene (1988), 'Managerial Control of Voting Rights: Financial Policies and the Market for Corporate Control', *Journal of Financial Economics* 20, 25–54.

Stulz, Rene (1990), 'Management Discretion and Optimal Financing Policies', *Journal of Financial Economics* 26, 3–27.

Su, Dongwei and Belton Fleisher (1999), 'An Empirical Investigation of Underpricing in Chinese IPOs', *Pacific-Basin Finance Journal* 7, 173–202.

Tam, On Kit (1999), *The Development of Corporate Governance in China*, London: Edward Elgar.

Tam, On Kit (2000), 'Models of Corporate Governance for Chinese Companies', *Corporate Governance* 8, 52–64.

Tenev, Stoyan and Chunlin Zhang (2002), *Corporate Governance and Enterprise Reform in China: Building the Institutions and Modern Markets*, Washington DC: World Bank and the International Finance Corporation.

Titman, Sheridan and Roberto Wessels (1988), 'The Determinants of Capital Structure Choice', *Journal of Finance* 43, 1–19.

Tobin, James (1969), 'A General Equilibrium Approach to Monetary Theory', *Journal of Money, Credit, and Banking* 1, 15–29.

Tobin, James and William Brainard (1968), 'Pitfalls in Financial Model Building', *American Economic Review*, 59, 99–102.

Ungson, Gerardo, Richard Steers, and Seung-Ho Park (1997), *Korean Enterprise – The Quest for Globalisation*, Cambridge MA: Harvard Business School Press.

Wald, John (1999), 'How Firm Characteristics Affect Capital Structure: an International Comparison', *Journal of Financial Research* 22, 161–87.

Wallace, Dudley and Lew Silver (1988), *Econometrics, An Introduction*, Reading, Massachusetts: Addison-Wesley Publishing Co., Inc.

Weimer, Jeroen and Joost Pape (1999), 'A Taxonomy of System of Corporate Governance', *Corporate Governance* 7, 152–66.

Welch, Ivo (1989), 'Seasoned Offerings, Imitation Costs and the Underwriting of IPOs', *Journal of Finance* 44, 421–9.

Williamson, Oliver (1975), *Markets and Hierarchies: Analysis and Antitrust Implications*, New York: Free Press.

Williamson, Oliver (1985), *The Economic Institutions of Capitalism*, New York: Free Press.

Williamson, Oliver (1988), 'Corporate Finance and Corporate Governance', *Journal of Finance* 43, 567–91.

Williamson, Oliver (1991), 'The Logic of Economic Organisation', in Williamson, Oliver and Sidney Winter (eds), *The Nature of the Firms: Origins, Evolution, and Development*, New York and Oxford: Oxford University Press, 90–116.

Williamson, Oliver (1996), *The Mechanisms of Governance*: New York: Oxford University Press.

Wilson, James (1989), *Bureaucracy – What Government Agencies Do and Why They Do It*, New York: Basic Books.

Winter, Sidney (1991), 'On Coase, Competence and Corporation', in Oliver Williamson and Sidney Winter (eds), *The Nature of the Firm – Origins, Evolution and Development*, New York and Oxford: Oxford University Press.

World Bank (1995), *China: The Emerging Capital Markets*, Washington DC: The World Bank.

Wruck, Karen (1989), 'Equity Ownership Concentration and Firm Value', *Journal of Financial Economics* 23, 3–28.

Wu, Jinglian (1994), *Xiandai Gongsi Yu Qiye Gaige* (Modern Companies and Enterprise Reform), Tianjin: Tianjin People's Publishing House.

Xu, Chenggang and Juzhong Zhuang (1996), 'Profit-Sharing and Financial Performance in the Chinese State Enterprises: Evidence from Panel Data', *Economics of Planning* 29, 205–22.

Xu, Xiaonian and Yan Wang (1997), *Ownership Structure, Corporate Governance, and Corporate Performance: the Case of Chinese Stock Companies*. Policy Research Working Paper 1794, Economic Development Institute, The World Bank.

Yafeh, Yashay and Oved Yosha (1995), *Large Shareholders and Banks: Who Monitors and How*, CEPR Discussion paper No. 1178, London.

Yosha, Oved (1995), 'Information Disclosure Costs and the Choice of Financing Source', *Journal of Financial Intermediation* 4, 3–20.

Zeckhauser, R. J., and J. Pound (1990), 'Are Large Shareholders Effective Monitors? an Investigation of Share Ownership and Corporate Performance', in Glenn Hubbard (ed.), *Asymmetric Information, Corporate Finance and Investment*, Chicago IL: University of Chicago Press, 149–80.

Zhou, Xianming (2001), 'Understanding the Determinants of Managerial Ownership and the Link between Ownership and Performance: Comment', *Journal of Financial Economics* 62, 559–71.

Zingales, Luigi (1994), 'The Value of the Voting Rights: a Study of the Milan Stock Exchange Experience', *Review of Financial Studies* 7, 125–48.

Zingales, Luigi (1995), 'Insider Ownership and the Decision to Go Public', *Review of Economic Studies* 62, 425–48.

Zingales, Luigi (1998), 'Corporate Governance', in Peter Newman (ed.), *The New Palgrave Dictionary of Economics and the Law*, London: Stockton Press, 497–503.

Zingales, Luigi (2000), 'In Search of New Foundations', *Journal of Finance* 55, 1623–53.

Zwiebel, Jeffrey (1995), 'Block Investment and Partial Benefits of Corporate Control', *Review of Economic Studies* 62, 161–85.

Index

The letter n following a page number indicates a reference in the footnotes.